Sustainability for Healthcare Management

Sustainability is not unique to health, but is a unique vehicle for promoting healthy values. This book challenges healthcare leaders to think through the implications of our decisions from fiscal, societal and environmental perspectives. It links health values with sustainability drivers in order to enlighten leadership about the value of sustainability as we move toward a new paradigm of health. The authors explore leadership priorities and link them to sustainability, through an imaginary health leader, Fred, the Chief Executive Officer (CEO) of Memorial Hospital, a community hospital based in the United States. Each chapter frames a leadership priority and accompanying sustainability driver through a storyline that involves the main character, Fred, and his colleagues.

Every chapter includes leadership tools, illustrations and tables with tips and data to make an evidence-based case in support of health sustainability. Practical applications enhance each chapter by providing real examples of sustainability accomplishments and reflections from healthcare leaders bring such examples to life. The book includes a healthcare sustainability syllabus as well as suggested reading and teaching resources.

By bringing together the key concepts of leadership and environmentally sustainable healthcare operations, this book is a unique resource to researchers, students and professionals working in health and healthcare management. Readers will also gain an appreciation for translating leadership priorities into sustainability tactics with beneficial operational outcomes.

Carrie R. Rich serves as the Senior Director of Vision Translation at Inova Health System. She developed and teaches a Healthcare Sustainability curriculum for higher education, piloted as an adjunct faculty member at Georgetown University. She is also CEO of The Global Good Fund, a foundation dedicated to developing young high potential leaders.

J. Knox Singleton is CEO of Inova Health System, one of the nation's most integrated and most wired healthcare delivery systems and one of the largest in the metropolitan Washington region. He is a director and officer of a variety of community organizations that address issues such as affordable housing and human services.

Seema S. Wadhwa created and oversees the Sustainability Department at Urban Ltd. where she leads the healthcare industry in pursuing enhanced environmental practices that align with business imperatives. Current projects include Director of Sustainability for Inova Health System and Director of the Healthier Hospitals Initiative, a national initiative of more than 500 hospitals with more than $20 billion in purchasing power working to align with a more sustainable business model.

'This book addresses the responsibilities and opportunities for health services administrators to move institutions beyond "going green." Healthcare consumers will increasingly look to healthcare organizations to lead the sustainability mandate. The sustainability transformation begins with this conceptual and practical guide.' – *Kenneth White, Department of Health Administration, Virginia Commonwealth University, USA*

'For hospitals, sustainability of the environment is a priority on several fronts, including the clear connections with population and individual health, as well as the significant physical and energy resources required by hospitals to provide care 24/7. This book frames the leadership challenges and imperatives in a compelling way, calling on all healthcare leaders – executives, clinicians and trustees – to make the environment and sustainability a top priority in an expanded vision of health.' – *Richard J. Umbdenstock, President and CEO of the American Hospital Association (AHA), USA*

'This book is essential reading for all future healthcare leaders. It is time for healthcare managers and policy decision-makers to pay greater attention to the larger environment. We must educate our students, both national and international, that health systems whether large or small, exist in communities. Sometimes these environments appear robust but sometimes they need greater attention and protection. We must make healthcare sustainability an integral part of our curricula for leaders and managers.' – *Peggy Leatt, Professor and Chair, Department of Health Policy and Management, University of North Carolina, USA*

'This groundbreaking book makes a powerful case that sustainability in healthcare is a strategic priority for the 21st century. The authors demonstrate in friendly and accessible language the critical role of leadership in driving sustainability throughout their organizations. Sustainable healthcare is the best path to lower costs, improved environmental performance, better patient and worker safety and healthier communities.' – *Gary Cohen, President, Health Care Without Harm, USA*

Sustainability for Healthcare Management
A leadership imperative

Carrie R. Rich, J. Knox Singleton and Seema S. Wadhwa

Routledge
Taylor & Francis Group
LONDON AND NEW YORK

earthscan
from Routledge

First published 2013
by Routledge
2 Park Square, Milton Park, Abingdon, Oxon, OX14 4RN

Simultaneously published in the USA and Canada
by Routledge
711 Third Avenue, New York, NY 10017

*Routledge is an imprint of the Taylor & Francis Group, an
informa business*

British Library Cataloguing in Publication Data
A catalogue record for this book is available from the British
Library

Library of Congress Cataloging-in-Publication Data
Rich, Carrie R.
Sustainability for healthcare management : a leadership imperative
/ Carrie R. Rich, J. Knox Singleton, Seema S. Wadhwa.
p. ; cm.
Includes bibliographical references and index.
I. Singleton, J. Knox. II. Wadhwa, Seema S. III. Title.
[DNLM: 1. Conservation of Natural Resources--economics--
United States. 2. Delivery of Health Care--organization &
administration--United States. 3. Decision Making,
Organizational--United States. 4. Environmental Health--United
States. W 84 AA1]
362.1--dc23
2012026708

ISBN13: 978-0-415-53035-4 (hbk)
ISBN13: 978-0-415-53036-1 (pbk)
ISBN13: 978-0-203-07489-3 (ebk)

Typeset in Sabon by Saxon Graphics Ltd, Derby

Printed and bound in the United States of America
by Edwards Brothers, Inc.

Contents

Acknowledgements

Projects that resonate deeply as purposeful and personally challenging tend to be a lot harder to accomplish than they initially appear. Somewhere between the enthusiasm and promise of getting started and tying up the myriad final details lie two significant vales of trial that must be overcome.

One chasm to be crossed is the tedium and fatigue that comes from lengthy, sustained creative effort. The only antidote for the fatigue factor is the periodic application of encouragement and coaching that sustains the authors both intellectually and emotionally. For such encouragement, we need to acknowledge the support of our families, friends and colleagues who reminded us that we could do this and that, in fact, the project was worth doing.

The second challenge is supplementing missing skills and perspectives in the collective personage of the three authors. For providing the missing understanding of how to create compelling, well reasoned writing, we must thank Gary Filerman. For filling our gaps in grammatical and literary construction, we thank Marilyn Lasky. For supplementing our ability to keep the literary "trains running on time," we must credit Carole Guerard, Carolyn Billetdeaux, Jamie Huffcut and Amjaad Al-Hussain.

For coaching us through our first book project and their unfailing patience with our rookie mistakes, we must thank our publishing team, Khanam Virjee and Helena Hurd

Finally, the authors acknowledge that it must be illegal to have the amount of fun we shared in writing this book. Where some collaborators have been traumatized enough by shared writing experience to say "never again," the authors are already plotting their next project with a mixture of expectation and glee.

We hope the collective alchemy of great Indian food, creative red hair and offbeat Southern literacy will combine again to serve the world by helping leaders create a more sustainable and healthful society.

Carrie's personal acknowledgement

It is inevitable that I gave part of myself when writing this book. I am forever grateful for the way so many people have poured so much of their lives into me. Pup and Nan, Mom and Dad, Bo-Bo and Paula, thank you for being irreplaceable contributing editors of my life.

Knox's personal acknowledgement

I want to acknowledge the sacrifices made by my family as I have taken time away from sharing life with them to do this work. To my children, I want to express my appreciation for their inspiration to think about their future and the planet and health system that we bequeath to them in the coming years.

I wish to thank my co-authors, Seema and Carrie, for educating me in the basic principles of sustainability and its application to both the field of healthcare administration and the mission of improving community health. While they have not succeeded in making me into an expert, their dogged educational ministrations have raised my awareness and knowledge base of the subject and its application to an exponential degree.

I also wish to thank the Inova family for its continual reminder of what things are most important in our lives—our families, our colleagues and our privilege of serving our patients and the health of the communities we serve. It is those values and the steadfast commitment among the Inova family that provide the foundation upon which rests any contribution our writing may bring to the healthcare field or its leaders. For that I am truly grateful.

Seema's personal acknowledgement

To my dear parents who have loved me, supported me and yet always challenged me to be more and do more. I have been inspired by your hard work and dedication over the years. I am in awe at all that you have accomplished. I am moved by your open hearts and your willingness to give to all. Your unrelenting faith and your commitment to family has been a foundation for me to grow from. It is from you that I have learned that when you dream big, it is possible to get there with hard work. To my sister Bava, thank you for trail-blazing a path for me to follow and having the confidence to pursue your desire to change the world with a career in environmental sustainability when it was not a common path. You have shown me that passion is success. To Jyoti and Dillan, for nurturing me from the basics of a roof over my head to the warmth of hugs, I am grateful to you for guiding me to a path that helped me get where I am today without knowing what I was getting into. To Mini, Sunny, Anjali and Rohan, for providing an aspiration of the balance between personal growth, professional growth and personal relationships. It is from this high bar that I have built my standard.

To my many friends (you know who you are) who have seen me through so much, in many phases of my life. To my mentors for believing in me, teaching me and helping me be the best me I can be because I want to be just like you. To those who have touched my heart and shaped the path of my life, I thank you for helping me grow.

Foreword—sustainability drives healthcare values

sustainability
Pronunciation: /səˌstānəˈbilitē/
noun

Hospitals are reaching for a new definition of their role in community health that goes beyond traditional measures. Hospitals are one of the few types of institution that have the mission, intellectual resources, reach into centers of influence, ability to command attention and leadership potential to help guide the community toward improved sustainability. Sustainability is about long-term maintenance of economic, social and ecological well-being. Inevitably, healthcare influences the balance of this triple bottom line. This concept is at once philosophical and operational, moral and practical. The threat caused by the current patterns of resource utilization will assure the diminution of human health if we do not achieve a balance of sustainability. Today's landscape is grim. Globally, we are failing by measures of economic prosperity, social equality and ecological stewardship. There is no alternative to investing in a sustainable future; healthcare and the communities we serve are damaged by the failure to achieve sustainability objectives. There is no doubt about the threat to fiscal, environmental and human health if we maintain the *status quo*. Healthcare is part of the problem.

But in every community, healthcare can be part of the solution. Healthcare's stake is unique. Although unable to independently battle the forces that contribute to the problem, healthcare can be a model of response at the local and societal levels, a source of expertise and a catalyst of action for a sustainable future.

Are the full implications of healthcare sustainability well known? Certainly, not by all. Many healthcare organizations will be content with traditional roles of community benefit. Traditional community benefit is an immensely important contribution, but at a level of engagement that falls short of potential contribution and community responsibility. The achievement of sustainability requires a broader engagement by healthcare.

The role of the hospital is evolving as medicine advances both scientifically and organizationally from being the curative center to being the center of health. The new reality is that the hospital institution has a unique responsibility to address the challenges of sustainability to the extent that the hospital is responsible for community health. Hospitals must reach for a new definition of the health of the community, one that goes beyond the traditional measures of community benefit. The hospital is the only institution that has the mission, intellectual resources, reach into centers of influence, ability to command attention, and leadership potential to help guide the community toward sustainability. That is the full implication of sustainability for the hospital and the basis of a new social compact.

The mission of this book is to catalyze transformational change in the healthcare industry through sustainability. This book is not about tree hugging, nor is it about affection for Mother Nature, though there is a time and place for that. There is more to sustainability than environmentalism. The environmental movement does, however, provide a platform for the emergence of sustainability as the new mantra that integrates economic, political and moral forces to address the threats to the environmental dimensions of well-being. The essence of the new compact is clear. Through sustainability, healthcare renews its commitments to prevention and wellness, strengthening its compact between provider and community. Converting this compact into explicit, achievable objectives that address sustainability implications for a given community is a long, complicated process. It requires informed, thoughtful and committed professional healthcare administrators to focus institutional attention and energy on the consequences for the hospital and the health of the community.

The challenge of sustainability mandates an expansion of the scope of health administration professionalism

What value does the healthcare organization add to the community? It is in the answer to this question that the role of healthcare sustainability is addressed. If the value of the healthcare organization to its community is restricted to curative care and serving as a "doctors' workshop," then the hospital has what can be defined as a limited value framework (the hospital performs quality medical care). The administrator with a limited value framework says, "We are not in the business of healing the environment. We take care of sick people." The weakness of this limited value framework is that it does not align with the community's health needs. Making people whole again is an important part of healthcare needs, but it is only one dimension of a community's broader health needs.

How does the broader value framework get built into the DNA of the hospital? There is at least one set of people with the perspective to look across resources and into the community, to envision a broader value impact on the community, which we call a healthy community. Not every hospital or healthcare leader will be prepared for this challenge, but most hospital administrators are positioned to aggregate skills and resources as valuable contributors to achieving the community's healthcare sustainability goals. Executive leadership sets the tone.

If you go into an average town of 30,000 people and look around, you will find that a hospital is an indispensable community resource, woven into the fabric of community life. Every community depends on access to a hospital. The person who runs the hospital is probably ideally positioned (due to status, access to resources and place in the community) to improve the quality of life in terms of health and well-being, to create sustainable conditions in which people are most likely to flourish. Healthcare leadership has an opportunity to be the first citizen of sustainability because it is a dimension of healthcare. It can be a calling but above all it is a mandate—to be the person who raises the issue, facilitates the conversation and brings together the players. The hospital becomes a model, a demo for the sustainable citizen from which the entire community benefits. That role requires visionary leadership to bring a set of values and a sense of values not only to, but for, the community. Sustainability is central to the concept and definition of healthcare, and therefore is the business of healthcare and healthcare leadership.

The journey

This book is about the first steps in the journey of one hospital and its leadership team to lay the foundation of the new compact known as healthcare sustainability. The fabled Memorial Hospital is an important model of an organization in transition. The hospital integrates the full spectrum of services as the primary health resource for a large suburban and rural population. It has the respect of the citizenry, the support of community leadership, and well established relationships with educational institutions, government and public health agencies. It is, by most measures, a successful healthcare institution, and its actions and activities are highly visible. The hospital is an adopter of environmentally friendly processes and procedures, but not without roadblocks and hiccups along the way.

This sustainability story follows the journey of Fred, Chief Executive Officer of Memorial Hospital, whose first executive role is as the newly minted hospital administrator. In the unrefined text of a narrated story, Fred provides vision and leadership for Memorial Hospital to leap beyond society's primary healthcare expectations to become a locally celebrated and nationally recognized healthcare sustainability leader. The organizational and leadership components of each chapter bring Fred one step closer to achieving the new provider–community compact, one that internalizes healthcare sustainability for community benefit. Achieving this mission requires informed and thoughtful commitment from Fred to focus institutional attention and energy on the consequences for the hospital and the health of the community. This book tells the story of the first steps in the journey of Fred and Memorial Hospital to describe how engaged, empowered teams advance healthcare sustainability objectives.

This book is a healthcare leadership resource for translating healthcare sustainability from governance to operations. It provides healthcare decision-makers with the information needed to navigate an ever-changing landscape, without being a dogmatic manual. The value-based principles exposed in this book are timeless.

Preface

The *eureka* moment for any leader is that moment in which we identify the right question to ask. Like any great journey, this book will guide you to ask meaningful questions rather than take you to an answer. The book is about the thought process of sustainability. It's less about the details of a sustainability program and more about the big picture: sustainability as a vehicle for achieving leadership priorities.

Sustainability will open doors if you, the leader, ask the right questions. The first step on this journey is to have an open mind to embrace a future that is about health, not just healthcare. Sustainability is about the triple bottom line: not just cost, not just the community, not just the environment, but a combination of all three component parts. A healthy hospital strives to create a healing environment for patients and a healthy workplace for staff and the community it serves. Sustainability is about physician and employee engagement, cost-effectiveness and risk management, not just "going green." It is about wasting less, which inherently means saving more. Sustainability is about managing existing goals and transforming the way we think about the future of health.

The healthcare sector increasingly recognizes the critical link between human health and environmental health. Notable health systems such as Kaiser Permanente and Catholic Healthcare West, among others, paved brave inroads at a time when sustainability was not yet valued as the cover story. It's not just the large systems that are influencing sustainability in healthcare. Gundersen Lutheran, for instance, is one of the most forward thinking sustainable healthcare organizations in the industry. Today, hospitals across the country and around the world, in diverse settings serving diverse populations, are developing organizational sustainability programs. Such programs build positive reputations by reducing the environmental impact of facilities and operations while concurrently saving money and minimizing liability and compliance risks.

As we are too well aware, healthcare costs are spiraling out of control. Healthcare spending comprises roughly 17.6 per cent of the United States economy at a cost of $2.5 trillion in 2009, projected to reach 19.3 per cent by 2019, and management of chronic disease is costing the country more than $1 trillion annually[1]. Meanwhile, there is mounting scientific evidence that environmental exposures are having a negative impact on public health[2]. During this time of reform and transition, healthcare leaders are under pressure to exercise the ethical imperative to "First, do no harm" (US National Library of Medicine, 2010). This oath creates an obligation to address operations that could have a negative impact on the health of patients, staff and the community.

Sustainability programs have the potential to reduce costs while protecting patient, staff and public health and well-being. Hospitals are the epicenter of the healthcare world as it exists today and concentration points of care delivery. This concentration of care in one location also concentrates the environmental footprint of hospitals. Hospitals in the United States generate more than 5.9 million tons of waste each year,[3] are the second largest commercial users of energy (behind commercial food service),[4] and use toxic chemicals in the process of treating patients, processing lab results and cleaning floors. Emerging science documents the growing effects of low-level chemical exposures on infants, children and fertility. A study in *The Lancet* reveals that nurses have the highest incidence of work-related asthma of any occupation studied, followed closely by cleaning staff.[5] This book demonstrates that all of these challenges and others can be addressed and reversed through sustainability efforts.

Sustainability is no longer an emerging trend—it has partnered handily with mainstream business frameworks of increased efficiency and process improvement to demonstrate ongoing value to companies and organizations that build sustainability into standard operating procedures. Siemens is one example of a company that champions sustainability as a core business differentiator. While sustainability programs are being integrated across the business spectrum, perhaps nowhere is the focus more appropriate than in our nation's challenged health system.

One dimension of this changing perspective means recognizing why and how sustainability permeates throughout every aspect of hospital operations. Leadership around healthcare sustainability began slowly. In the mid-2000s, however, as the drumbeat for sustainability grew stronger in the corporate world and the early pioneers in the healthcare space demonstrated that they could reduce environmental footprints while—surprise—saving money, the number of hospitals engaging in sustainability work began to climb. Today, healthcare facilities leading the way in environmental excellence range from rural, critical-access hospitals in Montana to sprawling metropolitan hospitals in the medical mecca of Boston. Facilities across the spectrum share an important common thread that is integral to their successes: senior-level buy-in and engagement, ongoing support and leadership. Healthcare executives play a critical role in helping healthcare sustainability programs grow to fruition.

The healthcare community is no stranger to change. Hospitals are constantly faced with the challenge of how to communicate effectively and sustain change within the multitude of systems involved in delivering excellent patient care. When a healthcare organization commits to the concept of environmental sustainability, it is embarking on change within its culture. To be effective, cultural change requires executive champions, and is most successful when the rationale for change resonates with staff at all levels. Creating a culture that embraces and integrates sustainability is driven by leadership, coordination, education and accountability.

This book provides indispensable resources to demonstrate why hospitals should consider prioritizing an early and aggressive sustainability strategy with clear, measurable and realistic goals and objectives. We developed this book to assist senior management in recognizing the value added by sustainable activities. Most of all, this book will provide the necessary tools to enable healthcare leaders to weave sustainability into the cultural fabric of your organization.

Characters

Character	Role
Amalie DuBois	Sustainability Director
Denise O'Hare	Chief Financial Officer
Dr Grisha Vladimir	Physician—orthopod
Dr Jenny Bea	Physician—pediatrician
Dr Mordechai Goldberg	Primary Care Physician
Dr Shmuel Cohen	Physician—hospitalist
Felipe Gonzalez	Vice President of Materials Management
Fiona O'Malley	Director of Marketing and Communication
Fred	Chief Executive Officer
Kadine Johnson	Chief Nursing Executive
Lorenzo Lopez	Director of Environmental Services
Mr Singh	Director of Engineering
Ms Crumpmuffet	Executive Assistant
Melvin Monroe	Vice President of Design and Construction
Dr Arundati Rupee	Clinical Department Chair
Dr Leah Gehry	Internist
Dr John Kusek	Chair of Obstetrics and Gynaecology
Mrs Penelope Lobatnic	Patient

Character	Role
Dr Benji Renata	Women's Health Primary Care Physician
Lucient Uguayo	Chief Technology Officer
Dr Humphrey Hedge	Chief Medical Officer
Georgia Trohv	Surgical Services Nurse
Franco Popellero	Surgical Services Unit Director
Gregor Verug	Director of Safety and Security
Lori Prince	Vice President of Human Resources
Sandy Smith	Director of Facilities
Julie Schmooly	Patient
Liam Ludwig	Director of Food Services

1   Hippocrates was right

Figure 1.1 What is sustainability?

A told story

FRED: I think, probably, the most painful moment of my life was when I
had to go in front of the Chairman of the Board at my first big-time
job as the newly minted Chief Executive Officer (CEO) of Memorial
Hospital. I followed a seasoned CEO who served thirty-five years,
since the hospital was founded. I mistakenly thought that a change in
leadership and fresh perspective would be a welcomed, easy
undertaking. And there I found myself, confessing that I didn't have
all the answers to concerns the Board expressed. Little did I know
that the prior CEO had actually retired ten years before his
announcement was made. In fact, just about every major stakeholder
of the institution had lost faith in the organization. Today, the
Chairman of the Board asked that we have a discussion about his idea
that the hospital "go green" as a top priority. As the CEO, "going
green" was not exactly at the top of my priority list. I just couldn't
imagine how going green would impact any of the dozen problems
that I thought were in the way of the institution going forward.

The Chairman didn't seem to understand that we were in a life-or-
death situation. We were an institution that couldn't borrow money.
We had lost the confidence of our admitting physicians, had the

highest employee turnover rate of any hospital in the county, and we were generally thought of—by both elected officials and local business leaders—as somewhere around the World War I era in terms of our corporate responsibility. Ignoring all that, the Chairman wanted me to focus on "going green." Give me a break! I was doing all I could just to survive. Forget the sustainability stuff.

Where did sustainability come from anyway?

The current sustainability movement originated with the World Commission on Environment and Development (more commonly known as the Brundtland Commission), which was convened by the United Nations in 1983. In its report, *Our Common Future*, the Commission defined sustainable development as "development that meets the needs of the present without compromising the ability of future generations to meet their own needs" (1987, p. 43)[6]. The Commission established the point that what is often regarded simply as an environmental crisis is really a complex system of interconnected problems, and that these are caused primarily by human activities that overburden the Earth's natural carrying capacity. It is now a commonly known fact that localized problems concerning air quality, water quality, soil depletion, species loss, habitat loss, food production and energy supply are often related to one another in falling-dominoes fashion. We have increasingly come to understand how physical environmental problems such as these are almost always linked, to a greater or lesser degree, in a vicious spiral with specific social conditions. Economic, political and cultural factors drive changes to the physical environment and affect the Earth's natural systems; changes to those systems in turn force changes—often dramatic and sudden—in the realm of human society. Global climate change, which was still largely a speculative hypothesis at the time of the Brundtland Commission's meetings, has emerged as perhaps the most dramatic and emblematic case of this kind.

(Bartels and Parker, 2011, p.43)

What are the drivers of sustainability?

Understanding what drives sustainability is an important subject to be mastered by today's healthcare leaders, whether at the board, executive, middle-management, or trainee/educational level. Regrettably, there is often a paucity of understanding of sustainability and the variables that drive or influence its adoption in many, if not most, of these groups.

FRED: I'm hearing more and more of my peers say, "I think we need a sustainability program. We need to be involved." What's driving this sustainability movement? The truth is, I don't have the answers yet. So I phoned my friend and colleague Knox Singleton, Chief Executive Officer of Inova[7] in Northern Virginia. Inova hosted its first sustainability conference in 1992, long before sustainability in healthcare was commonly part of leader conversations. So Knox, why did you champion sustainability at Inova back in the day?

KNOX SINGLETON: As CEO of Inova, the drive to adopt sustainability as an organizational priority was largely a result of our employees; our employees then and now think about sustainability and really care about it. I've found that young people, especially, are increasingly educated or fired up about everything related to sustainability. Of course, the people who were young in 1992 are middle-aged today!

FRED: Knox, I notice the same thing. The younger employees behave as though sustainability is a given, or should be. And that may very well be. It's us "seasoned" and experienced folks, we're the ones who need to be educated about sustainability, it seems, not the other way around.

KNOX: I think that's a fair assessment, Fred. Generally speaking, young leaders believe the notion that environmental responsibility is a core value that they should practice in their personal and professional lives. To some degree, it's sort of a "secular faith" that all of us have a duty to address the environmental problems of the world. Just like service to others, at some level, sustainability appears to be a universally held value to generation Y.

FRED: I think I'm starting to get it, or at least be more open-minded to the idea of sustainability as a leadership priority.

KNOX: I'm sure you'd agree that part of the challenge in leading an organization is defining the higher-order values that guide the purpose of why employees engage in the work we do.

FRED: Sure, of course. We've adopted the Studer model (Studer, 2004) of patient service for that very reason.

KNOX: Then your employees are familiar with Quint Studer talking about the two key attributes people want from their employment experiences. First, people want the ability to have an impact on their work environment and team. Second, people want to feel like their work has purpose as part of a larger community.[8] They want their work to contribute to some purpose greater than their own self-interest. Some people find purpose in faith or a specific religion. Some people seek purpose by being a positive, good person, helping others and sustaining the world. Whether the affiliation is religious or not, these values transcend human differences; they are core, high-level values common to most everyone.

FRED: (*Gazing out the window, rapping his pen on the desk*) I sure have a lot to think about.

KNOX: Me too. I'm still learning about sustainability. The challenge remains how to meld health improvement with engagement around sustainability into a holistic leadership style.

FRED: Well that's good to hear, to be honest. This sustainability stuff is still a bit disconnected for me.

KNOX: I think that if you look at the core of healthcare, beyond making people better, it's rooted in the Hippocratic Oath to "First, do no harm." Today, many healthcare employees feel that purpose in responsibility for care of the planet. They believe in equity through shared use of natural resources. Remember, the principal reason why I embraced sustainability as a leader was that I felt it was one of the core values of many, many people who work within our healthcare family. Many employees understand that failure to use resources responsibly can have unintended, negative consequences on the environment and community. Sustainability is in line with what Hippocrates had in mind.

The Studer model

Two aspects of work that employees value about their employer:

- People want the ability to have an impact on their work environment and team.
- People want to feel like their work has purpose as part of a larger community. They want their work to contribute to a purpose greater than themselves.[9]

What in the world is a table of tables?

A table of tables is a decision-making tool used to prioritize the values and drivers of a given industry and/or market sector. This leadership tool can be used to evaluate the case for healthcare sustainability. The sustainability-leadership table of tables is one such tool that resulted in clear patterns, ultimately creating vision alignment for this book. Vision alignment achieved through the tables of tables frames sustainability concerns in the context of a framework that resonates with healthcare leadership.

The sustainability-leadership table of tables

Sustainability can be used as a tool to frame leadership priorities, and ultimately can be used to enhance alignment among stakeholders around the promotion of health. The following lists outline key healthcare priorities from a leadership perspective as well as key sustainability drivers from the perspective of a healthcare Sustainability Director.[10] A holistic view of leadership requires an integration of these two sets of values/ drivers. That alignment is the premise upon which this book is based. In short, *sustainability is a vehicle for driving leadership priorities*.

Table 1.1 Leadership priorities related to sustainability drivers

Leadership priority	*Sustainability driver*	*Operational topic*
Safety	First, do no harm	
Quality	Corporate responsibility	
Growth	Stewardship	Health information technology
Community	Employee engagement	Waste management
Cost containment	Cost containment	Transportation
Physician recruitment and engagement	Public perception	Food Services
Process improvement	Community benefit	
Employee engagement	Public health	
Patient satisfaction	Competitive advantage/brand	
Future of health	Compliance	

What should every healthcare leader know about sustainability?

FRED: I have no idea. I'm just figuring out what sustainability means. I'd better ask Knox...

(Phone rings)

KNOX: Hello. Knox Singleton.

FRED: Hello, Knox. This is Fred. Got a few minutes for a little advice? The Chairman of the Board keeps sending me his ideas relative to sustainability and I don't know where to start in terms of answering his questions. Frankly, the questions he asks lead me to more questions rather than answers.

KNOX: Okay, Fred. Well that's a good thing. That means you're thinking. What's the question that's giving you trouble?

FRED: I can't figure out what I need to know about sustainability as a leader. What does sustainability mean to *you* as a healthcare leader?

KNOX: I would say that every healthcare leader should appreciate where sustainability falls in terms of customer expectations. At some level, the leader's core responsibility is to understand who her customers are and what their expectations are of her. Customers include patients, clinicians, physicians, community, employees and payers. And then there are also the elected officials. It boils down to understanding what all customers expect in terms of sustainability performance. Then the leader needs to connect those expectations into the strategic plan, budget and culture. That may be quite a lot to learn, actually...

Management tip

In general, what every healthcare leader needs to know about her customers falls into two categories:

* What do customers expect?
* How do I deliver the desired benefits in ways that are effective?

The leader begins by identifying the benefit(s) she wants the customer to experience, such as compassionate and effective treatment for patients, a good place to work for staff, a willing partner and advocate for the community.

Keeping the main thing the main thing

FRED: I understand that even though a program or service may be valuable, that doesn't make it an organizational priority. So I'm still a bit confused as to why I should put sustainability high on the list.

KNOX: There are four overarching reasons why every healthcare leader should care about sustainability. First, the expectations of a lot of customers can't be ignored. Responding to customers is an essential part of what we do as leaders. Second, there are regulatory consequences with regard to sustainability. Several sustainability activities are regulatory requirements—LEED, mercury elimination, waste management practices, etc. [11] [12] [13] [14]

FRED: Breaking the law, or showing up in the news over some public violation of dumping regulations, would not be a pretty picture for me or for Memorial Hospital!

KNOX: Right. In that case, the leader faces liability and legal exposure, in addition to the public relations exposure of failing to protect the health of the public and the environment.

FRED: Like the nuclear industry—that industry has a checkered image because it's sometimes perceived as not having a robust enough safety or environmental record.[15] For the healthcare leader especially—with accountability for public health and community resources—there's liability associated with not aggressively pursuing a sustainability program. That's clear to me.

KNOX: Third,—Am I boring you yet?

FRED: Maybe a little, but keep going!

KNOX: Okay, third, I expect for demographic reasons we'll face another healthcare workforce shortage in the years ahead.[16] For most new healthcare workers, a significant consideration in their employment decisions includes working for organizations that they feel embodies their principles, their belief systems.[17][18] Healthcare workers will have choices between multiple places to work, and sustainability credibility is a factor when choosing a new employer. Fourth, quality management and cost-effectiveness occur primarily in organizations with cultures that embrace process improvement; employees have to be committed to driving waste out of work processes. People who think Lean and act Lean, for example, will naturally be drawn to the sustainability mindset around resource utilization and waste. When deployed effectively, both Lean and sustainability lower long-term operating costs and waste less in an economic sense.[19][20]

The role of the Board

The Board of Trustees principally plays a fiduciary role. It protects the assets that have been entrusted to the organization. To some degree, the Board also protects the community's interests so that the assets are utilized appropriately.[21] Governance is largely about disposition or strategic direction, which usually takes the form of supporting or redirecting the leadership advice of management. Boards usually do not generate strategy, nor do they invent the mission of the organization. They certainly don't create new tactics, at least good boards don't. The Board's principal job is to keep management aligned with the organization's basic purpose and mission while they mitigate risk in terms of protecting the organization's assets. The two key responsibilities the Board has are to:

- protect the assets
- protect the mission.

Figure 1.2 From the boardroom

Translating sustainability values from the boardroom to the management team and into the community

A healthcare leader's responsibility is a 360-degree responsibility. One fundamental responsibility of leadership is to articulate constituents' and customers' expectations to the Board. For instance, patients and the community generally have a clear expectation of a safe environment within a hospital. The patient expects not to be harmed by infections or by incompetent staff. Employees, visitors and patients expect the physical environment of the institution to be safe.

Most healthcare organizations embrace the principle of improving the health and quality of life of individuals and communities. This principal is consistent with embracing sustainability. There is one respect in which sustainability conflicts with the traditional healthcare culture, however. In the treatment-oriented model that dominates healthcare today, more is better. Resource-consuming processes, such as staying in the hospital longer and frequent use of diagnostic procedures, are often equated with perceived better care or outcomes among patients. In sustainability, less is more.

Creating a culture of sustainable health: top-down, bottom-up

The new paradigm of health will be driven by a culture that gets paid for healthy results rather than for producing more treatment.[22] While sustainability may not be perfectly aligned with today's traditional, treatment-based healthcare model, it is a valuable tool for shifting the healthcare culture from its historical roots to a more healthful, society- and environmentally-friendly cultural value set going forward.

The Chief Financial Officer needs to understand and address how to integrate sustainability into the financial program. The Chief Nursing Executive needs to understand how sustainability integrates with nursing practice. The support service professionals must understand how sustainability drives equipment and supply selection, food purchases and other logistics.

A healthcare leader holds colleagues accountable for driving the integration of goals deep into the organization and help every employee to translate sustainability values into their work. Sustainability goals should be driven like financial goals, safety goals, patient experience goals—all will be driven down through department levels and pushed up through grassroots engagement. Fully embraced sustainability goals are driven down to the staff nurse and the billing clerk, and up to the executive leader. Sustainability requires a top-down *and* bottom-up culture-change approach so that leaders at all levels of the organization are engaged.

In a healthcare organization that embraces sustainability, every employee considers himself or herself an environmental agent, and the healthcare organization considers itself an educational resource for the community to learn about sustainable practices.

Educating leaders

The importance of educating present healthcare leaders about sustainability should not be underestimated. For many rising healthcare leaders, sustainability is part of their core ethos, part of their upbringing. But for many "experienced" healthcare leaders, sustainability has not been part of their training, and in some cases may not be part of their personal experience or value system. And yet, sustainability is central to the role of healthcare leaders of all generations—to be informed about sustainability, to understand it, to be able to represent it, and to achieve positions of organizational clout while embracing sustainability as an ethical responsibility and a moral imperative.

Why is sustainability particularly important for healthcare as compared to other industries?

Sustainability is particularly important to healthcare for two reasons. First and foremost, because of the healthcare expectation to "first, do no harm." Failure to meet the mandates of sustainability results in harm to the community. Because sustainability is an integral dimension of health status, it is implicitly or explicitly incorporated into the mission of the organization. Secondly, healthcare is a huge resource-consumer.

KNOX: The provision of health services is a resource-intensive, inherently hazardous activity. In short, healthcare is a resource hog and prolific generator of solid waste. Healthcare is a large and growing segment of employment in the United States and our overall economy. We consume huge amounts of energy, water and other resources. The care process produces a large amount of potentially polluting and dangerous byproducts. We share the environmental impacts of many other large employers, such as employee transportation. We understand our impact in terms of the present and future health of our community. That puts a special responsibility on us.

FRED: Of course. That makes sense.

KNOX: So, above all, both sustainability and the emerging health paradigm focus on culture, mission and values centered on doing only those actions that benefit patients. Sustainability embraces the concept of examining consequences and preventing problems, avoiding downstream sequelae—like unnecessary waste, energy misuse, air pollution and water contamination. Hospitals and healthcare organizations have enormous impacts on communities and the environment. They have large numbers of employees who drive to and from work every day, just to give one example.

FRED: And I guess, like all drivers, they text while driving in construction zones, and have accidents, and place additional burdens on the system.

KNOX: (*chuckling*) Well, that's one way of looking at it. Another perspective is that healthcare is a huge producer of pollution into our natural systems. We detrimentally impact our environment—water, traffic, education, commerce—all of which in turn may have a negative impact on public health. Sustainability, at its core, promotes that preventive, do-no-harm mindset. How do we as a health system perform in those areas of public health impact?

Many hospitals today advocate against secondhand smoke and for a variety of policies and practices that improve the environment for patients. That's one way that healthcare delivery links into public health. Sustainability in healthcare tends to focus efforts on getting the fundamentals right. So if in healthcare delivery we refocus upstream on prevention rather than treatment, life-cycle rather than upfront costs, then by default we embrace public health concerns.

Let's face it, on every healthcare leader's priority list is how to engage physicians around the important priorities of the institution. Everyone is trying to figure out how to integrate physicians into healthcare teams, especially younger physicians, who often are more familiar with new processes and approaches. Connecting with physicians is important around redesigning clinical processes to drive out wasted steps and reduce costs. So we're seeing that the processes of waste reduction and physician engagement line up. They both tie to and parallel sustainability.

FRED: That's an eye-opening way to think about physician engagement. And, of course, you're not only talking about physicians. It applies to all of our employees. It's a new culture.

About this book

This book concentrates on how to focus the attention of the leadership team on sustainability. Frankly, nothing much on the sustainability agenda tends to be on the average healthcare leader's priority list. Process improvement, meanwhile, is on most everybody's list. The notion of driving waste out of the system is where healthcare leader priorities can and do link to sustainability. There is a lot of interest in how reliably to drive waste out of healthcare processes while continuing to deliver necessary, high-quality medical services; how to be cleaner, leaner and now greener. These are key concepts on which the sustainability enterprise is focused.

KNOX: Fred, I wrote a book about the intersection of sustainability and healthcare leadership, a book about how integrating sustainability within our organizational culture has enhanced my team's effectiveness. It makes a great holiday gift!

FRED: Knox, it sounds like you're drinking the Kool-Aid.

KNOX: (*laughing*) The crazy thing is, though, that I wasn't so into sustainability originally. I mean, I understood its value in terms of employee engagement and the other leadership priorities we've been talking about. But I didn't realize how important it would be for me to build sustainability within the scope of our leadership approach and style.

FRED: It sounds like you were in my shoes when you started your sustainability journey.

KNOX: That's exactly right, Fred. When we began writing this book, I perceived the case around cost structure to be a little weaker than the other sustainability drivers. "I'm going to have to disagree with you about cost impact," our Sustainability Director told me. "We've saved over $100,000 in the past two months alone through reprocessing medical devices." I was shocked that we had saved over $1 million that year through another sustainability program. I wasn't really up to speed on the impact of our sustainability efforts. But Fred, I want to leave you with a different perspective that is starting to emerge for me.

Our engagement with sustainability has taught me several lessons, and I'm sure there will be more as we proceed on the journey that is the basis of the book. One lesson is that sustainability is an essential component of the emerging healthcare paradigm that results. Another lesson is that sustainability is a unifying element of our cultures. Everyone appreciates the importance of "Do no harm" as employees try to do good for patients and the community. The ultimate engagement reward is for everyone in the organization to act as stakeholders in sustainability.

The key to this book is the concept that if you, as a healthcare leader, care about physician recruitment and engagement, process redesign, employee engagement, facility investments and cost structure, then let us tell you about why you should care about sustainability. Each chapter addresses top priorities that healthcare leaders care about. Exploring each leader priority and its link to sustainability impresses our main character, Fred, the healthcare CEO. Every step we take toward linking healthcare values with sustainability drivers is intended to enrich leadership around the value of sustainability as we move toward a new paradigm of health.

Practical application: Leadership's role in implementing a sustainability program—Gundersen Lutheran

The imperative

- Create a more sustainable environment for patients
- Decrease the community's environmental burden
- Use sustainability to promote organizational goals such as improved access to care and lower clinical error rates
- Weave sustainability into the organizational fabric
- Fulfill healthcare's moral obligation: "first, do no harm"
- Distinguish the organization as a leader in the field of sustainability.

The initiative

Gundersen Lutheran's spark for sustainability came from the CEO. In his previous role as Executive VP, he had dabbled in a few sustainable initiatives, but found he had little time to pursue these objectives, given the other demands on his time.

Once he stepped into the CEO position, he was able to organize an initial strategy team of volunteers consisting of himself, a VP and a few colleagues who expressed interest in pursuing more sustainable operations. To create a vision of what it would look like to be a more sustainable organization, the sustainability team reached out to key internal leaders who were already involved in such activities. Shortly thereafter, they brought on a dedicated resource whose charge was to improve the organization's sustainability approach.

The new hire reported to the Senior VP (SVP) of Business Services after joining the organization from an outside industry. The SVP brought diversity of perspective to the team and was open to new ideas, all while sharing common priorities of improved quality and lower costs. The CEO routinely met with the newly created sustainability position, the SVP of Business Services and the Director of Facilities to help organize their ideas and set the course for the organization's sustainability program.

The team created several core sustainability work groups that focused on areas such as energy, waste management and purchasing. The sustainability program slowly gained traction within the organization as they created detailed plans and showed continuous progress. By starting small and demonstrating an array of successes, the sustainability team achieved buy-in from the Board to pursue larger projects, which eventually snowballed into the award-winning program that exists today.

The metrics

Quantitative metrics on this topic do not really exist. However, looking at the timeline of project integration is a key indicator of the speed of adoption within the organization. Additionally, qualitative feedback from senior leadership, board members, medical staff leads, patients, employees and senior community members are all excellent gauges of project success.

The lessons learned

- There will never be a way to get everyone fully engaged—there will always be naysayers for one reason or another (often due to competing priorities). So long as they do not try to obstruct integration efforts, it is best to just let them be, and focus engagement efforts on the individuals who want to be part of the program.
- Publicity helps garner engagement. When a leader highlights the value of a sustainability project in terms of what it means for both community and staff, it helps the leader and organization gain momentum for moving forward on other projects. This type of feedback is especially important to board members and investors.
- Framing the sustainability discussion in the language of the organization's mission and responsibilities will help achieve buy-in. Make it—as often and as much as possible—a part of the work of the organization.
- Do not lead with a "we should do this" command. Explaining sustainability in the context of how other organizations have

approached it and what types of outcomes they have realized will decrease knee-jerk reactions to being told what to do.

- Broaden employee and leadership education about what sustainability means by using a multipronged approach on outcomes to increase the likelihood of hitting a touch point.
- Find an executive in the organization to champion the sustainability cause—the more executive the champion, the better. Once this person is identified, use him or her sparingly to help promote sustainability at the appropriate times. He or she will be an important source of insights into the organizational triggers for accomplishing sustainability goals.
- Avoid the "bleeding edge" phenomenon. When just starting out, it is important to do things that will absolutely work, in order to build momentum. Demonstrating early successes will increase the visibility and credibility of the sustainability program, and increase the likelihood that executive leadership will be engaged in and excited about sustainability.
- Be clear from the beginning about what is expected of key individuals and the timeline for achieving goals.

About the organization

Gundersen Lutheran Health System is a physician-led, not-for-profit healthcare system located throughout western Wisconsin, northeastern Iowa and southeastern Minnesota. It is a comprehensive healthcare network including one of the nation's largest multispecialty group medical practices, regional community clinics, hospital, home care, behavioral health services, vision centers, pharmacies, and air and ground ambulances.

Sources

www.gundluth.org
Interview with Jeff Thompson, CEO, Gundersen Lutheran Health System

---

Leadership imperative

The outcomes of improving sustainability go far beyond reducing costs, important as cost is. Sustainability outcomes are a form of community service boasting a long list of societal, community and individual impacts. Sustainability is a core value of our individual and collective professionalism in healthcare. It is appropriate for our institutions and our communities to look to us for leadership in this domain.

Leadership dialogue

1 How can the healthcare leader who wants to learn more about sustainability get up-to-speed on engaging the leadership challenge?
2 What are sources of information on the technical sustainability topics that will be most useful for a healthcare leader?
3 Establishing priorities is a key responsibility of leadership. Which sustainability priorities align with the priorities of healthcare leaders?
4 What, if any, are the benefits and risks of endeavoring to educate the board about the "why" and the "how" of engaging an organization in sustainability efforts?
5 Which values of health service delivery organizations align, or conflict, with the values of sustainability?

Syllabus integration

Overview

The United States healthcare system requires multidisciplinary approaches to address the dynamic field of healthcare sustainability. This lesson explains why healthcare sustainability is important. Students learn about frameworks for sustainability, identify stakeholders and gather evidence-based resources for sustainability management.

Objectives

- Introductions
- Review course syllabus
- Introduce patient, worker and environmental safety in sustainability terms
- Identify key stakeholders and information repositories

Topics

- Issue framing
- Societal interest in sustainability and healthcare
- Current state of knowledge
- Healthcare's environmental impact
- Corporate responsibility and social entrepreneurship
- Triple bottom line
- Community benefit
- Legal considerations

Homework

Global Health and Safety Initiative (2009) *The Eco-Health Footprint Guide: Measuring Your Organization's Impact on Public Health and the Environment*, version 1.2. www.globalhealthandsafety.org

Practice Greenhealth (2009) 'Introduction to the Revised Green Guide for Healthcare Operations Section,' webinar January 23, http://practicegreenhealth. org/membership/strategic-resource-network

Review the mission statements of healthcare organizations committed to sustainability. Create a mission statement for your imagined or real healthcare organization. Record these in your career journal.

Additional resources

Kaplan, S., Orris, P. and Machi, R. (2009) *A Research Agenda for Advancing Patient, Worker and Environmental Health and Safety in the Healthcare Sector*. Global Health and Safety Initiative. October 2009. www. globalhealthandsafety.org

2 From governance to operations

Figure 2.1 Up to bat for sustainability

Executive summary

Sustainability is often discussed in terms of functional disciplines (energy, waste, water, etc.), but sustainability in the context of leadership. Leadership defined through sustainability provides context for strategy, and can be an accelerator of strategy. Leadership exercised through sustainability can be a framework for guiding cultural reinvention within an organization. Healthcare leaders who integrate sustainability into their priority objectives achieve successful outcomes across a portfolio of programs and services. Successful outcomes achieved through sustainability include improved community relationships, lower long-term operating costs and engaged employees. Sustainability is a mindset many employees value and will rally behind, especially younger employees.

Governance dictates the strategic priorities of an organization. A core challenge of the organizational leadership is implementation of strategic objectives set by the board, shareholder or government. External realities, such as sustainability, are a second set of imperatives that leaders must pursue. The leader's starting point for pursuing the board's priorities and sustainability objectives is engaging executive colleagues to answer the questions "Why should I care about sustainability?" and "How can sustainability help achieve business success?" This chapter guides readers from understanding *why* leaders should embrace sustainability to understanding *what* the leader's role in healthcare sustainability should be. By the end of the chapter, readers will be able to make a compelling case for why their organization should invest in a sustainability program. Readers will also gain an appreciation for translating leadership priorities into sustainability tactics with beneficial operational outcomes. The organizing concept is that engaging the principles of sustainability can help healthcare organizations reduce long-term costs, improve outcomes and nurture the environment that influences health.

A told story

After the board meeting, Fred, CEO of Memorial Hospital, returns to his office perplexed. He's past the shock of the board's Chairman suggesting a hospital sustainability program. Fred wonders how to translate the theoretical sustainability construct from governance to operations. Fred decides the only way truly to engage the organization in sustainability is to engage the executive leadership team by hiring a Director of Sustainability to champion the cause throughout the hospital. Fred initiates a conversation with his leadership team on Monday morning. After several leadership team members identify other priorities that trump investing their time in a sustainability program, Denise, the Chief Financial Officer, agrees to be the executive sustainability champion.

FRED: Good morning, team. How is everyone this morning?
LEADERSHIP TEAM: Good morning (*voices lack energy, one person yawns while other colleagues chug coffee*).
FRED: I hope everyone had a great weekend. I'm delighted to be starting the week with you on this fine Monday morning. So, let's go around the table and share our perceptions of the board meeting. I'm curious to hear your perspectives.
(*Each member of the team shares his or her perspectives about the board meeting.*)

DENISE: *(Chief Financial Officer)* So, Fred, what's your perception of the board meeting?

FRED: You'll recall that we discussed the hospital's financial standing, our vision for the future and our strategy for achieving our vision—all the standard elements of governance conversation. But what really surprised me was when the Chairman approached me to discuss sustainability. Our Chairman was insistent about developing a sustainability program at Memorial Hospital. The more I think about the Chairman's rationale, the more I've come to realize that a sustainability program might not be such a bad thing. In fact, it might actually be a good thing, though I have no facts to confuse me. So, who's interested in leading the development of our sustainability program? *(Fred looks to Dr Goldberg, Chief Medical Officer.)*

DR HEDGE: This isn't a good time for me to take on another assignment. We've got Joint Commission coming soon and that's our focus. Besides, getting our medical staff involved in something like sustainability—which they know little, if anything, about—will be very difficult.

FRED: Okay then. How about you, Kadine? As the Chief Nursing Executive, what do you think about championing sustainability?

KADINE: I think developing a sustainability program is a wonderful idea! I really think you ought to lead it, Fred. You're fairly new here, and this is an excellent opportunity for you to be seen as a leader.

(Leadership team roll their eyes at Kadine)

FRED: *(sighs and turns to Denise, CFO)*

DENISE: I don't see how sustainability fits with our priorities and financial strategy. I will say that my kids have been talking about recycling, which I know is related to sustainability. I believe that younger generations care about sustainability. We should think about how we can be proactive in the sustainability arena as we think about recruiting young talent.

FRED: Okay, thanks to all for sharing your perspectives. I'll go back to the drawing board and see what I come up with in terms of accountabilities. *Fred reviews his notes after the meeting and decides that the majority of his team will follow his lead into a sustainability-based initiative, though perhaps with some hesitancy. As usual with the engagement process, there is no "big bang" or dramatic moment of attitude change, but rather the beginning of an evolutionary shift. Each leader approaches sustainability from different perspectives with their own set of operating goals in mind. Leadership's understanding of sustainability and engagement around it is largely determined by those different perspectives.*

FRED: *(Thinking to himself)* I want to respond positively to the Chairman's direction to engage in a sustainability agenda. There's some wisdom in his argument that Memorial Hospital should be at the front of this parade. Our leadership values have to connect with operations. So, then, who are my choices to lead the effort? Dr Hedge, Chief Medical Officer, is only thinking about leading the physicians through Joint Commission review. He's distracted and unenthusiastic—not the way to introduce a new framework for leadership. I think the Chief Nursing Executive, Kadine, is just looking for a way to avoid the job. She's the niece of the Chairman of the Board, so I guess I could think about designating her as our champion, but she didn't show much interest. And like a lot of managers, she'll get on any bandwagon, whether she cares about it or not. But I don't want a leader with so little enthusiasm; I want a *leader* who will make things happen.

That leaves me with Denise, my unlikeliest choice. She's the only one who's got genuine passion for sustainability. She sees the potential connection of sustainability to the community. I have to start somewhere, so maybe Denise is our executive champion for sustainability. I need to schedule a follow-up meeting with Denise. *(Before Fred schedules the meeting with Denise, he checks his email and finds the following note.)*

Dear Fred,

I know I'm "the numbers person," but I have been thinking about our sustainability conversation. I'm not sure yet how this will all play out, but I imagine we've got lots of employees who will likely be interested in a sustainability program. And then there's City Council—we're going to have to take our bonds to City Council next month, and they're always talking about ways to make our environment more sustainable. It's clear that sustainability is a big issue for the Chairman. I'd be willing to think through with you what sustainability might mean for the hospital and ultimately oversee the translation of sustainability from governance to operations.

Perhaps you might consider connecting with Felipe, Vice President of Materials Management, to let him know that much of the ultimate operational responsibility will fall to him. I think this will be a leadership development opportunity for him. I look forward to discussing this important initiative with you.

Sincerely,
Denise
Chief Financial Officer, Memorial Hospital

FRED: (*Thinking to himself*) I'm glad Denise is stepping up to the plate. One of our key challenges will be answering the question, how do we engage employees? Our early adopters are the people with a passion and natural interest in sustainability. How do we inject that passion into the larger group? We find the natural leader who can be a role model that other people will relate to; we let her connect everywhere there is sustainability interest. We need early wins. Early wins will draw in less interested individuals at the outset. Maybe we pick two or three leadership principles we're trying to affect through sustainability, and introduce sustainability to stakeholders in the context of the selected leadership principles. I'll leave it to Denise to pick leaders who successfully engage employees on the broader Memorial team and in the community.

It's unexpected to have the CFO be the sustainability champion, but I think it's a blessing. After all, Denise will understand the fiscal implications of sustainability, and she oversees Materials Management, which will be responsible for implementation of our sustainability program. Thankfully, Denise volunteered.

I think this whole sustainability thing has a future at Memorial Hospital.

The story of sustainability in healthcare—vision and alignment

A number of leading observers of the United States healthcare system have dubbed it "unsustainable."[23] Health outcomes are hardly outstanding when compared with other countries, especially given the high costs.[24] The level of resources consumed by US healthcare has grown steadily, rising from 9 per cent GDP in 1980[25] to 17.3 per cent GDP in 2012.[26] It is a system characterized by poor performance in the area of environmental sustainability as well.[27] From economic, social and environmental perspectives, the US healthcare system is full of waste, and replete with negative side effects for people delivering the care as well as the people receiving it. This scenario calls for healthcare leaders to pursue the "triple bottom line" of economic, social and environmental responsibility.[28]

Who's who in healthcare sustainability

Practice Greenhealth
"Practice Greenhealth is the nation's leading membership and networking organization for institutions in the healthcare community that have made a commitment to sustainable, eco-friendly practices. Members include hospitals, healthcare systems, businesses and

other stakeholders engaged in the greening of healthcare to improve the health of patients, staff and the environment."[29] Practice Greenhealth is a not-for-profit organization that provides visioning support for hospital staff through educational webinars, consulting and other training materials.

Health Care Without Harm
"Health Care Without Harm is an international coalition of hospitals and healthcare systems, medical professionals, community groups, health-affected constituencies, labor unions, environmental and environmental health organizations and religious groups."[30]

Healthier Hospitals Initiative
"The Healthier Hospitals Initiative (HHI) is a US-based coalition of major health systems and three key non-profits that are committed to improving sustainability and safety across the healthcare sector. The HHI agenda is based on the premise that a coordinated sector-wide approach to how we design, build and operate hospitals can improve patient outcomes and workplace safety, prevent illnesses, create extraordinary environmental benefits, and save billions of dollars. HHI utilizes research data on environmental sustainability and community health to delineate a prioritized sustainability roadmap, a method for moving from good ideas implemented by individual facilities to a comprehensive sector-wide adoption of sustainable practices and cost reduction."[31]

Global Green and Healthy Hospitals Network
"Hospitals, health systems and health organizations representing the interests of more than 3,500 hospitals from six continents have come together to form a global network dedicated to reducing their ecological footprint and promoting public environmental health."[32]

Environmental Protection Agency
"The mission of EPA is to protect human health and the environment... When Congress writes an environmental law, [EPA] implement[s] it by writing regulations. Often, [EPA] set[s] national standards that states and tribes enforce through their own regulations. If they fail to meet the national standards, [EPA] can help them. [EPA] also enforce[s] [its] regulations, and help[s] companies understand the requirements."[33]

EPA has resources dedicated to the healthcare business sector, notably Energy Star, "a joint program of the US Environmental

Protection Agency and the US Department of Energy helping us all save money and protect the environment through energy efficient products and practices."[34]

Department of Energy
"The US Department of Energy (DOE) invites healthcare organizations to join the Hospital Energy Alliance (HEA). HEA brings together leading hospitals and national associations in a strategic alliance designed to improve energy efficiency and reduce greenhouse gas emissions of healthcare systems throughout the country. By leveraging access to advanced technologies emerging from the national laboratories, HEA members are creating a national forum for the industry to share evidence-based technology solutions and influence the energy performance of medical equipment and systems."[35]

United States Green Building Council
"The US Green Building Council (USGBC) is a 501(c)(3) non-profit community of leaders working to make green buildings available to everyone within a generation."[36] USGBC provides "green" building tools for the architecture, design and construction community through a credit system called Leadership in Energy and Environmental Design (LEED).

Supporting organizations

The following is a snapshot of some of the health service professional organizations that recognize the importance of sustainability and share sustainability information with their members:

- American College of Healthcare Executives (ACHE)
- American Hospital Association (AHA)
- American Nurses Association (ANA)
- American Public Health Association (APHA)
- American Society for Healthcare Engineering (ASHE)
- Association for the Advancement of Sustainability in Higher Education (AASHE)
- Association of University Programs in Health Administration (AUPHA)
- The Center for Health Design (HCD)

Sustainability: a means to an end or an end in itself?

One of the primary choices a leader must make is whether to frame sustainability as a strategic imperative in its own right or as a means of accomplishing the institution's operational objectives. In recent years, it's become increasingly clear that embracing sustainability can be an economically successful strategy—an effective means of accomplishing cost control because of the reduction in energy utilization, reduction in waste stream and environmentally preferable purchasing, for instance.[37]

At the same time, there's the hospital's societal imperative to serve as a community leader in the campaign to improve health, in part through performance as a sustainable organization. Boards of trustees and community advocates are looking past the role that sustainability can play in achieving operational goals; they are pressing for healthcare to take on the mantle of leadership as a champion of sustainability, both in terms of advocacy and in terms of a model practitioner.

A key task of the healthcare leader who embraces sustainability is to define what excellence in sustainable performance looks like.[38] To start that means developing sustainability mission and vision statements. It also means engaging in sustainability through leadership and program innovation; it requires a long-term commitment to investing resources and personal prestige in sustainability to create a high-performing entity.[39] This concept is no different from the process of establishing one's organization as a top decile performer in safety or finance.

A 2011 survey of 500 business leaders from The Business of a Better World demonstrates the confluence of sustainability and business success. Eighty-four per cent of business leaders surveyed stated that their domestic company will adopt sustainability as part of its core business strategy in the next five years. Respondents expressed optimism that global companies will adopt sustainability within their core business strategies and functions in the next five years, indicating widespread concern about the environment and the strategic positioning of business interests.[40]

The relationship between sustainability and climate change has a strong influence on strategic thinking in the business community. A McKinsey Quarterly report suggests that a significant majority of surveyed corporate executives view climate change issues as a consideration of overall business strategy in terms of opportunities and risks.[41] Specifically, nearly 70 per cent of executives surveyed view climate change influences as key to managing corporate brand, product development, investment planning, purchasing and supply management. Further, roughly one-third of respondents indicate that climate change issues trump most other global trends.[42]

It is important for business leaders to communicate the goals of sustainability initiatives. Within healthcare, people throughout the organization—doctors, volunteers and employees—need to understand at the grassroots level how their interests and personal goals connect to the facility's sustainability objectives. In the final analysis, there must be an alignment between the interests of the hospital's stakeholders and the sustainability program. Stakeholders want to be part of something greater than themselves and sustainability can be the platform.[43]

FRED: (*Talking to himself*) A healthcare organization ought to be a role model for reducing waste, conserving energy, increasing community goodwill and brand equity, employee engagement and physician engagement. The process of managing every one of those critical performance criteria has to be about enhancing health. This means providing healthcare while having as few negative side effects as possible, doing so efficiently, consuming as few resources as we can. Consider what healthcare would be like if we applied the principle of sustainability to every major dimension of leadership.

(*Knock on the door. Ms Crumpmuffet, Fred's executive assistant, sticks her head in to let Fred know that his next appointment is ready. It's Felipe, Vice President of Materials Management.*)

FRED: Good afternoon, Felipe.

FELIPE: Good afternoon, Fred.

FRED: Did Denise connect with you regarding our sustainability conversation?

FELIPE: Yes, she did.

FRED: Very good. Well then let's dive right in. I think there is some element of a moral imperative here when people think about sustainability. There's not only a connection with the environmental goals and outcomes, but a calling to come "join the movement." That should be our message to our employees and staff, supported by suggestions of how to apply it in their daily activities.

FELIPE: That makes sense. I think one of the things I've learned while educating employees about supply chain management is that it's not about trying to give people a lecture or information. In my colleagues' eyes, it's less about our grand goal for the impact on the environment, and more about "What's in it for me?" and "What can I do that's going to make a difference?"

FRED: Of course, of course. Our challenge is to make sustainability something with which every employee, at every level, can have a sense of engagement. It's about creating a culture.

Growing interest

The healthcare industry has seen significant growth in sustainability. Studies show that healthcare is not the only field in which sustainability is of growing interest. An analysis of businesses in 2010 shows that, even during economically challenging times, many companies increased investments in their sustainability activities and made bold new sustainability commitments. The 2011 *State of Green Business Report* shows a dramatic shift occurring in mainstream business—companies are thinking bigger picture and longer term about sustainability than they did in the past.[44] According to Farient Advisors, approximately 10 per cent of Standard & Poor's 100 are currently factoring environmental issues into their incentive compensation plans, either as strategic objectives or as quantifiable goals.[45] *Newsweek* further supported the trend by releasing its third annual US and Global Green Rankings, which are beginning to influence corporate behavior and disclosure.[46]

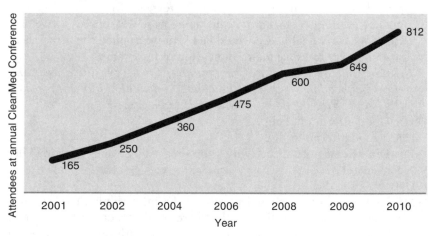

Figure 2.2 Growth of interest in healthcare sustainability

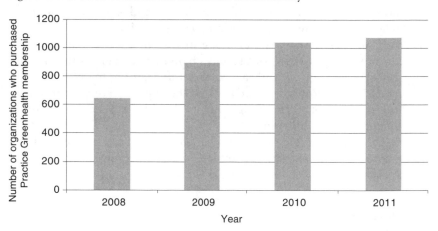

Figure 2.3 Growth of sustainability membership organizations

Sustainability—general facts and figures

- Eight out of the Top 10 Best Colleges in America ranked by US News and World Report have sustainability training programs.[47]
- A recent survey found that commitment to environmental, social and governance issues is becoming exceptionally strong: 93 per cent of CEOs see sustainability as critical to their company's success. Sustainability is strategic priority for executives around the world.[48]
- The majority of Fortune 500 companies now issue a corporate social responsibility report. Global Reporting Initiative-based reports are at an all-time high. The number the number of companies reporting to the Carbon Disclosure Project has increased tenfold in seven years (from 350 in 2003 to 3050 in 2011).[49]
- According to a report produced by Ernst & Young, "In 2010, resolutions focusing on social and environmental issues made up the largest portion of all shareholder proposals. That trend is expected to continue this year: we estimate that half of all shareholder resolutions in 2011 will center on social and environmental issues (Ernst & Young, 2011)."

A growing field

The growing priority of sustainability in business is consistent with trends in higher education. A 2010 survey by the Association for Advancement of Sustainability in Higher Education (AASHE) documents that 260 of

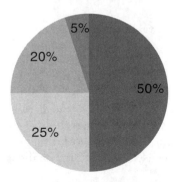

Figure 2.4 Shareholder focus on social and environmental issues[50]

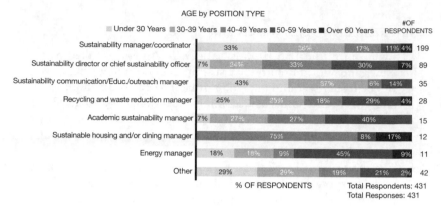

Figure 2.5 Sustainability position type by age

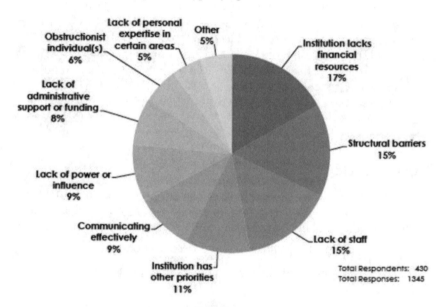

Figure 2.6 Biggest challenges of sustainability positions[53]

the 421 universities surveyed have sustainability positions created since 2008.[51] According to the AASHE survey (2010), just over 40 per cent of sustainability-related leaders had sustainability work experience of five years or less, excluding internships and activism,[52] which is consistent with the theory that many people choosing to work in the field of sustainability represent the future workforce.

The AASHE survey also described the challenged sustainability leaders face, including:

- institutional lack of financial resources (17 per cent)
- structural barriers (15 per cent)
- lack of staff (15 per cent)
- institution has other priorities (11 per cent)
- effective communication (nine per cent)
- lack of power or influence (nine per cent)
- lack of administrative support or funding (eight per cent)
- obstructionist individual(s) (six per cent)
- lack of personal expertise in certain areas (five per cent).

A sustained investment in sustainability—does it make sense?

Asking why leaders invest in sustainability is like asking why leaders invest in brand. It is not about immediate, short-term returns. In *The Seven Habits of Highly Effective People*, Stephen Covey writes that great organizations invest in third-quadrant priorities. There are four quadrants of leadership priorities based on urgency and importance.[54] Focusing on sustainability is a third-quadrant investment along with building brand and satisfying customers, training employees and investing in the next care delivery model.[55] When economic times are hard, successful organizations do not stop research and development, nor do they stop investing in employee engagement. Similarly, tough economic times provide no excuse for ignoring sustainability imperatives.

A Pew Charitable Trust study documents that United States "green-collar jobs"[56] grew by 9.1 per cent between 1998 and 2007, roughly 2.5 times faster than job growth in the overall economy.[57] While the task of defining and quantifying green jobs remains a challenge, the Brookings Institution's report *Sizing the clean economy* estimates that nearly 2.7 million people worked for the "clean economy" in 2010.[58] To encourage momentum in the clean economy, President Obama signed an appropriations act in December 2009 that provides $611.4 million to the Bureau of Labor Statistics for the 2010 fiscal year, specifically targeted to stimulate the production of green jobs, industries and occupations.[59] In other words, society is increasingly focused on sustainability across market sectors.

FELIPE: We have data from other organizations showing that there's a strong financial benefit that can result from a long-term approach to investing in a focused sustainability program. For instance, Inova Health System saved $1 million this year by reprocessing medical devices.[60]

FRED: Sure, that's impressive, but we're a stand-alone community hospital and Inova is a system of hospitals.

FELIPE: Well, there are plenty of examples of community hospitals that are performing well and saving money through their sustainability programs. Gundersen Lutheran is an impressive example of a community hospital that excels at energy management. They partner with City Brewery in La Crosse, Wisconsin to generate three million kilowatt hours per year, turning discharged biogas waste from City Brewery into electricity for the hospital. I contacted their sustainability champion and learned that Gundersen Lutheran intends to lower its energy consumption costs by 20 per cent annually, eventually becoming 100 per cent energy independent by 2014.[61] And they're capturing biogas waste and reducing demand on the power grid.

FRED: Who would've thought a beer distributor would be a sustainability partner? It's ironic that one of my early memories of discussing sustainability is someone telling me, "There's no cash in the trash." The person's point was that if you're only practicing sustainability to save money, that's an inadequate justification. I'm realizing that sustainability does go beyond moral obligation. While we're unlikely to get rich through sustainability initiatives, sounds like sustainability can be fiscally rewarding in some instances. Today, based on what you're telling me about sustainability programs in other systems, there are sustainable practices we could engage in that have positive environmental and financial returns.

If we're going to get serious about practicing sustainability at Memorial Hospital, we need a Sustainability Director. We need someone who wakes up every day and thinks about how he or she will drive sustainability throughout the hospital.[62]

Knock at the door. *(Denise joins the conversation with Felipe and Fred.)*

DENISE: Once our leaders commit to being sustainability-minded, we'll need a steering committee. Perhaps a hub-and-spoke model, to connect our sustainability program to each dimension of our organization. Each of those spokes usually has a leader.[63]

FRED: Why are you suggesting the hub-and-spoke model as opposed to any other organizational framework?

DENISE: One of the reasons to employ the hub-and-spoke model is because there's a grassroots level of interest with sustainability. We hear that people want to be engaged in our sustainability program and they offer a variety of thoughtful ideas. We should connect with the frontline and connect leadership with the good ideas that employees are sharing. There are a lot of people in this organization who care about sustainability. We need to give them vehicles to participate, to connect with the sustainability mission and cultural change projects. I think it will help immensely to have a Sustainability Director— someone to facilitate sustainability progress across the organization.

Management tip

It is a misconception to think that sustainability is mostly a top-down process. Success, whether in sustainability or other domains, is often driven by how talented the performer is and how well he or she performs for the judges. In short, success requires picking projects carefully, connecting with natural leaders, and engaging the broader population of employees, physicians and the community. This combination results in leaders and employees engaging in the hospital's work of sustainability with little further encouragement other than connecting it to the core culture of the hospital.

Implementation: build sustainability into an organization

Sustainability impacts every dimension of a hospital, from purchasing decisions, to nursing care, to facility design and maintenance, food services, operating room regimens, strategic planning, safety standards, quality efforts and community benefit.[64] Data from 2009 and 2010 Practice Greenhealth reports strongly suggest active cross-departmental Green Teams in order to achieve successful sustainability programs.[65] Departmental representation on Green Teams includes:

- administration
- communication/marketing
- engineering
- environmental health and safety
- environmental services
- facilities
- food services
- infection control
- materials management
- nursing
- nutrition
- physician
- risk management
- safety.

Research further suggests that there is a trend toward identifying a sustainability owner for the hospital whose sole focus is to wake up everyday with the intent of promoting sustainability.[66] Healthcare institutions that successfully integrate sustainability within the organizational culture often fulfill the following characteristics:

1   have an environmental commitment statement
2   have a written plan for environmental management of the facility
3   have a Green Team
4   have a designated Sustainability Director
5   have someone on staff who is responsible for sustainability within their job description (but not by title)
6   track their sustainability improvement initiatives in the Joint Commission structure
7   provide new employee orientation on sustainability initiatives
8   provide annual training on sustainability initiatives
9   engage clinicians, including nurses and physicians, in their sustainability programs.

Organizations that embrace these fundamental sustainability program elements are most likely to improve the sustainability cultures of their organizations. Simply put, the emerging role of the Sustainability Director in healthcare is increasingly important.

Practical application: hardwiring environmental stewardship at Advocate Health Care

The imperative

- Harnessing the interest and ideas of passionate individuals.
- Organizing and integrating a sustainability infrastructure.
- Improving the patient experience through engaged, happy employees.
- Creating a culture of sustainability.
- Capturing and maximizing dollar savings opportunities.
- Identifying the role of each employee as it relates to sustainability.
- Aligning employee values and creating a culture of similar/system thinking.
- Maximizing the organization's impact on public health.

The initiative

Advocate Health System takes a multipronged approach to hardwiring environmental stewardship into the core of its operations. This engagement program targets both front-line employees and leadership. It focuses on helping these groups understand both the *why* and the *how* of sustainability, providing engagement mechanisms that allow every stakeholder to take part in achieving the organization's broader environmental stewardship goals.

The role of Advocate's dedicated sustainability position is to help the organization and community understand what opportunities are available and to facilitate their implementation when possible.

Advocate incentivizes employees to engage in sustainability by appealing to their intrinsic desire to do good and by offering ways to be involved. Examples of such initiatives include:

- Green Teams at each facility
- system-level working groups comprised of Green Team leaders to identify priorities and action items
- annual computer-based environmental stewardship tutorials
- Green Advocates Ambassador Program, a self-sustaining program that incentivizes the creation of sustainable workspaces and rewards entire departments for their participation in "greening" their workspaces
- internal awards program for employees engaged in environmental stewardship.

Advocate's efforts in executive engagement focus on engaging top leadership teams to create a setting where participation opportunities are available to every employee. Some of their mechanisms for achieving this goal include:

- Sustainable Operations Council comprising VP-level and above leaders from every site that has a Green Team, as well as key representatives from every department
- Sustainable Operations Index composed of specific environmental goals for the organization, which each person on the System Committee and Sustainable Operations Council carry as part of their own set of goals, and which are rated on in performance reviews
- Quarterly Environmental Stewardship Dashboard summarizing sustainability performance is publicly visible, and distributed to community and council members and all hospital leadership.

The metrics

Although the organizational integration of a sustainability program is difficult to measure quantitatively, certain metrics assist in gauging progress in this endeavor:

- Levels of participation in employee engagement events and training programs
- Responses to sustainability questions on employee engagement survey
- Performance across broad suite of Sustainability Dashboard measures, such as recycling rate, regulated medical waste per adjusted patient

day (APD), construction and demolition recycling percentage, kBtu (kilo-British thermal unit) consumption (with goal of percentage reduction), greenhouse gas emissions, dollars saved in electricity/ energy use, reprocessing savings, paper reduction, etc.

• Overall progress towards achieving organizational sustainability goals identified by Sustainable Operations Council

The lessons learned

• To get help from leadership in driving these efforts from the top down, it is necessary first to translate the concepts into leadership's language and to establish accountability for achieving outcomes.

• Support and passion from key leadership are critical dimensions of achieving successful adoption of programs—work to achieve a "cascading" effect from the top down. Waste less time with the people who are not on board or passionate about the sustainability mission. Instead, tap into the energized individuals, because they are the ones who are really going to unleash the energy that will make things happen. Do not waste your time trying to convince people who do not want to be convinced, especially during the early stages of implementation.

• It is crucial to harness the passion that exists in all staff. This is easiest to achieve when organizational incentives align with employees' professional and personal interests. In the healthcare setting, emphasizing the connection of sustainability and wellness is an alignment worth considering.

• Hiring a person to organize the sustainability efforts and translate between stakeholders will facilitate the implementation of sustainability projects. The individual filling this role will be most effective if she or he has full access to the organization's resources and reports up to as high a rank as possible within the organization.

• Getting buy-in from certain departments may be challenging. Each department's and individual's incentives may be different and sometimes it will be tough to find a champion. Disconnects will exist. Helping each department and individual understand the *why* of sustainability will help cement shared understanding about the purpose and value of sustainability.

About the organization

Recognized as one of the nation's top ten health systems, Advocate Health Care is the largest integrated healthcare system in the state of Illinois. This faith-based, not-for-profit health system offers more than 250 sites of care, including ten acute-care hospitals and two integrated children's hospitals.

Sources

www.advocatehealth.com/body_nonav.cfm?id=1427
Larsen, Mary. Personal Interview. 1 May 2012

Leadership imperative

People who practice sustainability for moral reasons will do so regardless of the financial costs. There additionally exists a business case for investing in sustainability as a practical, "here-and-now" component of healthcare leadership. Leadership has an obligation to build sustainability into organizational mission and vision because of healthcare's commitment to preserve and improve the community's health. Leaders cannot stop at mission and vision; sustainability must also be incorporated into operational performance if its full potential is to be realized at all levels of the organization.

Leadership dialogue

1   Why do you think sustainability should or should not be a core mission and responsibility of healthcare leaders and organizations?
2   Executive team engagement is essential to drive core values throughout the organization. But engaging executive leadership may be particularly challenging in the case of sustainability, which is not a traditional leadership priority. What are some approaches to engaging those leaders who may be most reluctant to get on board?
3   What is most important to identifying an executive sustainability champion, having a high technical knowledge or having a sincere passion for sustainability? Why?
4   Covey's "third quadrant" focuses on priorities that are important but not urgent. Why is it—or why isn't it—appropriate to cite sustainability as an example of third-quadrant thinking?

Syllabus integration

Overview

Healthcare professionals with an understanding of sustainable practices share a unique vantage point of challenges and solutions that cut across all aspects of business. They are positioned to identify problems and opportunities and to broker information. This lesson surveys tools used to measure environmental health system impacts, focusing on innovative solutions that add business value and contribute to an organization's overall strategic business success.

Objectives

1 Facilitate an oral presentation of homework from the previous class.
2 Identify critical interactions between economic, social and sustainable development issues that are important to business activities.
3 Examine the planning, development and implementation considerations taken into account when evaluating sustainability drivers and programs.
4 Learn how to advance business performance through metrics program implementation.
5 Evaluate business benefits, costs and best practices by systematically addressing economic development, social equity and environmental issues.
6 Review sustainability job descriptions.

Topics

1 Plan—do—check—act (PDCA) life cycle
2 Strategic development planner
3 Three safeties
4 Future sustainability employment opportunities.
5 Performance reporting.

Homework

Practice Greenhealth (2009) 'Eco-checklist for operations: how green is your healthcare organization?,' Version 1.0, April.
Imagine you are the CEO of a healthcare organization that is newly committed to sustainability practices. Based on classroom conversation and examples, write an organizational statement of commitment to sustainability to a public community audience. Record in your career journal.
Practice Greenhealth (2012) 'Sample job description: Healthcare Sustainability Director,' Reston, VA: Practice Greenhealth. http://practicegreenhealth.org/pubs/toolkit/greenteam/SampleJDSustainabilityDirector.pdf
Draft a healthcare sustainability administrative job position in your career journal. Include a job title, position description (required skills and experience, core responsibilities), compensation (salary and benefits) and location on the organizational hierarchy.

Additional resources

Environmental Health: Tools for Nurses, United American Nurses, AFL-CIO.
GEMI (2004) *Environment: Value to the Investor*. Washington, DC: Global Environmental Management Initiative.

3 Saluting the captain of the ship

Physician engagement + health information technology

Figure 3.1 Engaging physicians with health information technology

Executive summary

Physicians care about variables impacting health status. A physician's concern is about the health of his or her patients. Any connection that can be demonstrated between clinical or administrative processes that enhance is generally viewed favorably by physicians. Physicians understand the concept of the "health of the community," but prioritize the welfare of their individual patients more highly.[67] Physicians are aware that their patients expect a safe, environmentally friendly healthcare setting. This chapter explores physician engagement through the lens of sustainability in a delivery setting where health information technology is new to the scene.

Storyline

(Director of Marketing and Communication, Fiona O'Malley, is working with Dr Hedge, Chief Medical Officer, on the communication strategy for the roll-out of a new electronic health record called Epic.)

FIONA: Dr Hedge, We are working on the newsletter about the role out of EPIC. I've added the graphics. What are your thoughts? (*Fiona hands the drafted newsletter to Dr Hedge for his approval.*)

DR HEDGE: Am I looking at the right document? I'm seeing a picture of trees and a forest. What do these images have to do with EPIC?

FIONA: Our Sustainability Director told me about the environmental impacts of the new electronic medical record. We'll significantly reduce the amount of paper that's being used today. And you know, the way she explained it helped me understand that reducing paper usage is ultimately about patient health. Reducing paper not only saves trees, but leads to a significant reduction in water use and chemical and greenhouse gases that are used in paper production. Changing our documentation process will have an especially strong impact on our community because we have that pulp mill just outside of town. Think about the air quality around here and what that means for our pulmonary patients.

DR HEDGE: I never thought of it like that. My son's nanny works at the pulp mill part time and I've wondered about the health impacts of working there. I never thought about the connection to what we do here though...

FIONA: Dr Hedge, you might consider meeting with Amalie Dubois, our Sustainability Director. I bet she could tell you more about what we're doing in terms of sustainable practices, and what we could be doing. But in the mean time, I need to get this story out, so what are your thoughts on the newsletter draft?

DR HEDGE: Well Fiona, I like where you're going with this, but let's take it a step further. Could we print the newsletter on recycled paper, or perhaps distribute it electronically?

If IT's important to the patient, IT's important to the physician

Embracing sustainability may add value to the hospital's relationship with the physician if it adds value to the physician–patient relationship.[68,69] To the degree that patients care about sustainability, they may care about the physician's regard or disregard for sustainability. It is felt by many observers that sustainability will increasingly be part of how physicians relate to, and are evaluated by, their patients (Nayler and Appleby, 2012).

The physician, health information technology and sustainability

Mrs Lobatnic enters the hospital to pay a visit to Dr Goldberg. Once again, Mrs Lobatnic has no physical ailments to address during the appointment; she just wants to talk. Today all she wants to talk about is her grandson's science fair project on sustainability. Dr Goldberg listens to Mrs Lobatnic, checks to ensure she's feeling okay, listens to a few stories, and then proceeds to the medical staff meeting. At the medical staff meeting, the Chief Technology Officer, Lucient Uguayo, explains to the physicians that he's been charged with integrating sustainability into Memorial Hospital's technology practices. Lucient communicates to the medical staff that sustainability integration will begin in Women's Services. This news is not received well by the physicians.

Physician: captain of the ship

To engage the team, it is essential to engage the leader. The idea of engaging the team without engaging the leader is an oxymoron. It is like an athletic team with no coach to assign positions and orchestrate the plays. Physician support and participation are integral to achieving almost all priorities of any hospital. To build a culture of sustainability, the healthcare team must carry out "plays," much as an athletic team would. The quarterback of the team is the physician and the teammates are nurses, who are important contributors to and influencers of a hospital's culture.[70]

The physician's role

Physicians are respected members of the community who exert tremendous social influence. The physician's role, in the hospital and in the community, is important to the success of the sustainability effort.[71] It follows, then, that engaging physicians involves making clear how sustainability is important to physician-valued programs in the hospital. Physicians are, of course, also motivated by the economic success of their practice and their often symbiotic economic relationships with their hospital.[72] For example, the anaesthesiologist will be interested in sustainability when the hospital leader demonstrates how the anaesthesia program is, in some fashion, dependent upon sustainability. This alignment of economic interests between the physician's practice and the welfare and success of the hospital is more direct for employed versus independent community practice physicians, but it exists for both groups. The proportion of physicians who are hospital employees or contractors will influence the degree to which this alignment is apparent and leads to an increasing level of physician support for sustainability initiatives.

From the administrative perspective, physicians are the clearly dominant economic customer. If a customer assessing a car for purchase values safety in a car, then safety becomes a priority for anyone selling cars. Similarly, healthcare leaders pay close attention to physicians as customers and usually find that physician values and priorities drive leadership and organizational values. Of course, boards and executive leadership articulate values and contribute to organizational priorities, but it is typically within the "excess space" defined by physician interests as the primary customer of the hospital.

If the goal of the board and executive leadership is to build the organizational cultural value of sustainability, that path must include meaningful engagement with physicians. Therefore it is essential to bring physicians into the sustainability dialogue at the earliest possible point and to identify physicians who will champion the cause and engage their colleagues around sustainability. It is particularly important for leaders to effectively explain why sustainability complements physicians' professional objectives and how it can generate resources for physicians' priorities.

Hospitals are concerned about their public image, that is, how they are perceived by the community. Physicians are visible and influential participants in the community, and are positioned to carry the hospital's sustainability message to constituencies who view physicians as credible voices to be respected in the public dialogue. How can the leader familiarize physicians with the concept and applications of sustainability?

(Fred is having lunch in the physician's dining room with Dr Hedge, Chief Medical Officer, and several other medical staff leaders.)

DR HEDGE: Fred, good afternoon. How's the sustainability initiative going?

FRED: I'm learning how complicated and challenging it will be to accomplish our sustainability vision. I'm concerned about the people on the team and about sustainability's impact on the broader organization. I'm concerned that if we don't have a sustainability program, it will negatively impact the community's perception of the hospital and our priorities. I've got to worry about how the patients and physicians perceive sustainability and experience sustainability. I think about the cost structure of our sustainability program because it'll cost something up front to get the program up and running. Sustainability never came up in my professional education. I learned how to read a balance sheet. I learned how to counsel employees, how to hire and how to resolve conflict. I learned about process improvement and how to promote a culture of safety. That's a long answer to your brief question, but the point is that learning about sustainability is an educational process for all of us for, which I'm not well prepared.

DR RUPEE: *(clinical department chair)* I've never thought about sustainability before and we've never talked about it before as a medical staff. I'm a department leader and I realize that if we're going to succeed, I've got to develop my people in this area.

FRED: Sustainability is an emerging competence that we should address using the same processes we used to address quality improvement and leadership development. The first challenge is to reach the folks who are current health care professionals. The second step is to see to it that people don't come out of education for medicine, nursing, health administration and the other health professions as poorly prepared in sustainability as we seem to be. The health administration programs are strong on medical care quality, finance and general management. The students get some exposure to sustainability issues in public health. But understanding sustainability is nonexistent in most programs, at least the ones I've been exposed to. With your support and role as the Clinical Chair, Dr Rupee, we will make great strides. Every physician, nurse, administrator and other staff member in our organization has to embrace sustainability if we're going to transform our culture. Those who are engaged are learning a lot about sustainability, me in particular.

DR GEHRY: *(Internist)* I'm starting to see the link. If you're going to be a primary care physician, does that mean that you should know something about sustainability?

FRED: I believe sustainability is an indispensable part of the foundation of healthcare clinical and administrative leadership. I have to admit that I've become an advocate.

DR HEDGE: *(CMO)* I think we have the clinical leaders on board, though some are more enthusiastic than others. Physician engagement is challenging on most every subject, not only for sustainability. It's difficult to get physicians to recognize that sustainability—or any other goal indirectly connected to clinical care—is important to the organization. It's challenging, in part, because most of our staff physicians spend their time in their offices. While physical proximity isn't everything, it is generally easier to engage the hospital-based specialists.

DR KUSEK: *(Chair of ob/gyn)* We depend a lot on our regular medical staff departmental meetings, but recognize their limitations. The informal networks are uneven. I am the first to admit that empowering and engaging physicians is the most challenging part of my job. It's not the knowledge or understanding, it's finding ways to actually connect with some of the busiest people I know.

FRED: When I was a young hospital administrator, I spent a lot of time in medical staff meetings. Nowadays there seems to be little physician interest in the hospital activities, especially in those specialties whose practices are largely office-based. I have to admit, I don't know how in the world we can get physicians interested and engaged in sustainability. Any ideas?

DR HEDGE: You know, just yesterday I had a surgeon ask me, "What's the deal with this sustainability program I've been hearing about?" It was a great opportunity for me to connect with her and suggest that she engage with other physicians who've exhibited some interest in the sustainability program. I agreed to schedule a coffee break with them to dialogue about sustainability in more detail. If each of us pull together two or three physicians for a sustainability conversation, we would move the engagement and empowerment balls forward.

Fred and the physicians agree to pursue Dr Hedge's suggestion. As Dr Hedge leaves the cafeteria, he pauses at the trash bin, checks the back of his food plate for the recycling symbol, and appropriately discards his plate in the recycling bin.

DR RENATA: I have enough on my plate. I don't want to have anything to do with sustainability. I care about quality and this new patient care model. I don't want the sustainability thing.

LUCIENT UGUAYO: Don't you see, Dr Renata, there's a strong parallel between sustainability stewardship and stewardship of patient interests?

What does health information technology have to do with sustainability?

Health information technology (HIT) as an electronic medium largely replaces paper-based documentation in the clinical care process. Paper is processed using large quantities of water and energy. Paper is delivered to its intended location using trucks and gas. Hospitals with low levels of HIT implementation consume a lot of paper—paper forms, paper registration information, paper bills, paper records of all sorts. On the other hand, the use of personal computers results in higher energy consumption.[75] There is a counter-argument about replacing paper with HIT that must also be considered due to the large amount of energy consumed by most HIT systems. While it is not always easy to determine the "right" answer in terms of sustainability impact, Turley *et al.*'s study, among others, investigated the environmental impacts of electronic records and concluded that electronic health records have a positive net effect on the environment.[76]

Less paper versus paperless

Even hospitals that use electronic medical records still maintain paper records due to state laws that require a patient records to be stored for years (for example, patient records in Massachusetts must be stored for twenty-five years after the time last used).[73] "Iron Mountain, a data storage and protection company that claims to work with about a third of the nation's hospitals, estimates that the 6,000 hospitals in the US spend about $10 billion a year to store and manage 500 million patient records" and the cost to convert historical files is estimated to be "$1 billion for Johns Hopkins Hospital alone."[74]

Practical application: Kaiser Permanente's HealthConnect

The imperative

- Improving quality of care and service.
- Ensuring and continuously improving patient safety.
- Modernizing outdated systems and obsolete practices.
- Increasing access to latest treatments and protocols.
- Facilitate information-sharing.
- Emphasizing the organization's commitment to preventive medicine.

The initiative

HealthConnect is a comprehensive health information system which includes one of the most advanced electronic health records available. It is an innovative tool that enables Kaiser Permanente to deliver high-quality, safe and efficient care in new and unique ways. It facilitates communication between members and Kaiser Permanente's team of professionals to help make getting well and staying healthy as convenient as possible.

HealthConnect provides a website that facilitates e-connectivity between a patient and the healthcare team. It allows patients to view key components of their medical records and conduct clinical transactions online, and provides them with information so that they can make knowledgeable decisions about their health. At the same time, it allows physicians to contact patients electronically, order consultations, laboratory and other diagnostic work, send prescriptions directly to the pharmacy, provide health literature and set reminders for follow-up appointments.

Kaiser Permanente's HealthConnect was initiated in 2004 and completed in each of the organization's medical facilities in early 2010. It is the world's most widely used personal health record, securely connecting 8.6 million people to their healthcare teams, their personal information and the latest medical knowledge. Over 80,000 members log in each month, sending more than 850,000 secure email message to doctors and care teams.

The metrics

Kaiser Permanente found that a comprehensive electronic health record can increase consumer convenience and satisfaction and provider efficiency, while maintaining clinical quality. Some of the metrics they use to measure the success of this program include:

- rates of outpatient, urgent care and emergency department visits
- external referrals
- scheduled telephone visits
- annual total office visit rates
- website traffic data
- usage of particular website features
- repeat visits
- number of people registered to use the system.

The lessons learned

- It is important to have an economic model that aligns financial incentives with providing effective and efficient care, regardless of how it is delivered. Rewarding care strategies other than face-to-face visits will increase the incentives for providers.
- If face-to-face visits remain the gold standard for measuring quality, care standards will not reflect the preference of consumers for alternative, more convenient modes of care when they are appropriate or reinforce more efficient care delivery options.
- Collaboration among providers, combined with government support, will help advance widespread consumer adoption of online healthcare.
- Electronic health records may increase the time it takes to document patient visits, but since email messaging and scheduled phone visits consume much less time than in-person visits, logic suggests that the efficiency gains offset any increases in documentation time. Temporary decreases in productivity of as much as 15 per cent were reported during implementation.

About the organization

Founded in 1945, Kaiser Permanente is one of the nation's largest not-for-profit health plans, serving more than 8.9 million members, with headquarters in Oakland, California. It comprises the Kaiser Foundation Hospitals and their subsidiaries, the Kaiser Foundation Health Plan, Inc. and The Permanente Medical Groups.

Sources

"Fast facts about Kaiser Permanente," http://xnet.kp.org/newscenter/aboutkp/fastfacts.html

"Kaiser Permanente identifies key elements in successful healthcare information technology implementation," http://xnet.kp.org/newscenter/pressreleases/nat/2009/031009healthaffairs.html

"Kaiser Permanente HealthConnect® electronic health record," http://xnet.kp.org/newscenter/aboutkp/healthconnect/index.html

Leadership imperative

To achieve personal ownership, any individual must answer the fundamental question: why should I care? The best link for engaging physicians in sustainability is the shared imperative around improving patient health. HIT is one example of a metaphor for improving patient health and reducing unintended harm for patients. Similarly sustainability is an upstream solution many physicians can relate to population health.

While the health impacts may be the "hook" to get a physician's attention, his or her interest may be further engaged by the cost-saving opportunities. Projects such as hibernating computers in non-clinical areas when not in use, telecommuting, or moving toward electronic pay stubs yield direct cost savings. For instance, Partners HealthCare saved $54,121.59 between 2002 and 2009, and conserved 2,845,743 of unprinted pages,[77] thanks to their success in connecting HIT priorities with sustainability imperatives and physician values. "Kaiser Permanente's electronic health record system, which covers 8.7 million beneficiaries, eliminated 1,000 tons of paper records and 68 tons of x-ray film, and... has lowered gasoline consumption among patients who otherwise would have made trips to the doctor by at least three million gallons per year."[78]

Leadership dialogue

1 What strategies could healthcare leaders use to help physicians appreciate that their patients and families evaluate them, in part, on how they relate to environmental stewardship?

2 What conditions relating to sustainability might a healthcare leader include in contracts to ensure physicians understand and practice the hospital's sustainability values?
3 How can healthcare leaders help physicians recognize that positive sustainability performance by the hospital supports their professional imperative to improve health?
4 How can leaders use energy-saving innovations involving information technology to engage physicians not only in optimizing clinical care process and convenience, but also in achieving sustainability goals?

Syllabus integration

Overview

Healthcare today depends on information technology, yet not much attention has been paid to sustainable HIT. There will continue to be profound implications for sustainable HIT systems as healthcare transitions from a paper-centric environment to an IT-centric environment. This lesson will introduce opportunities for environmental HIT practices based on case studies.

Objectives

1 Study examples of how benchmarking results lead to implementation of sustainable HIT improvement programs.
2 Provide a format, structure and step-by-step process for a benchmarking study.
3 Introduce a useful total quality environmental management (TQEM) tool.

Topics

1 Infrastructure investment.
2 Storage management.
3 Server virtualization.
4 Print reduction and elimination.

Homework

Brown, B. and Thiry, M. (2010) *Sustainability "How-To Guide" Series*, Houston, TX: IFMA Foundation.
Practice Greenhealth (2008) 'Responsible purchase of computers with a Kaiser Permanente case study,' webinar December 19. www.practicegreenhealth.org

Additional resources

EPEAT® the definitive global registry for greener electronics: http://www.epeat. net/

Nimpuno, N., McPherson, A. and Sadique, T. (2009) *Greening Consumer Electronics—Moving Away from Bromine and Chlorine.* Göteborg: International Chemical Secretariat and Spring Brook, NY: CPA (North America). www.cleanproduction.org/library/GreeningConsumerElectronics.pdf

Practice Greenhealth (2009) 'Greening operations series: change is good! Using change management techniques to improve environmental performance—with a case study on paper prevention,' webinar October 16. www. practicegreenhealth.org

4   Waste not, want not

Process improvement + waste management

Figure 4.1 Waste, waste, waste and more waste

Executive summary

It is ironic that hospitals are places of healing and also producers of substances known to harm the public's health. When healthcare leaders speak of waste, they're often referring to inefficiencies in time or resources, as opposed to solid waste. Applying Lean methods to process improvement is increasingly popular inside healthcare organizations. Parallel efforts inside most hospitals to reduce tangible waste—such as solid waste and sanitary sewer effluent, to name but two—are emerging.

Healthcare leaders have the potential to help employees and patients improve individual health through clinical processes while improving community health through waste segregation and alternative off-site waste management services. Wasting less intrinsically means saving more—a combination of waste reduction and prevention strategies is saving millions of dollars annually at healthcare organizations across the

United States.[79] This chapter explains why process improvement, when combined with waste management practices, can improve efficiencies and reduce operating costs.

A told story

Upon realizing how many resources Memorial Hospital throws away after each patient procedure, Georgia Trohv, a nurse in surgical services, takes action. Georgia is passionate about the environment and has just completed Lean process improvement training. She discovers that regular trash is being thrown into the regulated medical waste bin because the bin is large and convenient for nursing staff. Georgia works with Environmental Services and Materials Management to obtain smaller regulated medical waste containers that are appropriate for the amount of regulated medical waste generated daily. Georgia also works with her unit director, Franco Popellero, to conveniently locate the municipal solid waste bins (regular trash) and to place the regulated medical waste bins where they are easy to access as a second stop. These changes result in proper waste sorting through right-sized containers and well thought-out receptacle placement. Ultimately, the changes lead to less costly waste management practices. When Georgia communicates with Franco and her nursing colleagues in other units, they too are excited to "do no harm" from both patient and environmental perspectives. This success story eventually gets to Fred, CEO of Memorial Hospital, who meets with Felipe, VP of Materials Management, to better understand the process improvement strategies in use.

Change the system: linking Lean

The core concept of reducing waste is fundamental to both sustainability thinking and Lean thinking. Similar to waste management, Lean is a management technique whereby work processes are redesigned to increase efficiencies and reduce waste. According to the Lean Enterprise Institute, "Lean means creating more value for customers with fewer resources."[80] Linking the Lean approach with organizational values, such as sustainability, is an important step. Lean focuses on efficiencies along the entire process, from concept to implementation to understanding customer needs. Lean works horizontally through an organization as well as along process verticals.[81] Like Lean, sustainability can improve a healthcare organization's competitive outcomes by reducing waste and operating costs.[82]

The history of Lean process improvement

Process improvement has a long lineage that stems back to the concept of interchangeable parts conceived by Eli Whitney. This milestone was followed by the work of industrial engineers in the 1890s. Henry Ford contributed further to process improvement by introducing manufacturing strategy. Society's current understanding of Lean is largely rooted in the Toyota "just in time" process.[83] As Toyota incorporated the Ford production model into its own production process, Toyota discovered opportunities for improvement. The work of Taichii Ohno and Shigeo Shingo recognized the value of human capital beyond physical labor in terms of quality improvement, concepts captured by James Womack in his highly regarded book on the subject, *The Machine That Changed The World.*[84] While Lean has a history in the manufacturing industry, the fundamentals of Lean are built on the premise of improving processes and quality. Lean principles have been applied to the healthcare setting in an effort to improve both clinical and non-clinical work process outcomes and the patient experience.[85]

What does waste mean in terms of process improvement?

As the graphs in Chapter 2 illustrate, healthcare sustainability as a movement has grown significantly since Practice Greenhealth initiated its Environmental Excellence Awards in 2002. Despite the positive progress, many healthcare organizations have yet to fully embrace sustainable practices, evidenced by the 7,000 tons of waste produced daily by the healthcare industry.[86] Waste reduction strategies often provide a starting point for health organizations newly energized around sustainability, because waste management can be highly visible (e.g. recycling) and there is a clear business case for sustainable waste management.

What a waste!

"The second largest expense on a hospital's balance sheet (following labor) is supply chain costs. As reported in 2009, the average hospital provider spends more than $72 million a year on supply chain functions, nearly one-third of its annual operating budget. The majority of the materials procured by a hospital ultimately become waste, resulting in $10 billion annually in disposal costs across the healthcare industry. By instituting waste management programs along with changes in material consumption patterns, a healthcare facility can reduce the amount of waste it generates and thus its waste handling and disposal costs as well as its environmental impact."

citation: http://www.sustainabilityroadmap.org/topics/waste.shtml

Sustainability is no different from any other process measure outcome: improving sustainability relies on process improvement, as does cost reduction, quality and service improvement. That is why "Linking environmental goals to business values is an important step towards promoting sustainability."[87] The greatest potential for improvement in any process is achieved when the boundaries of the process are expanded upstream and downstream so that the "upstream steps" and the "downstream impact" are studied across the entire continuum.[88] Improving processes across boundaries is challenging, as healthcare is often siloed along professional, departmental or facility lines. Healthcare culture is generally focused on making improvements within departments or service lines, as opposed to across the system, where the greatest opportunity for improvement lies.[89] The remainder of this chapter discusses process improvement in terms of managing tangible waste, taking the topic a step further to examine financial implications and *de facto* alignment of process improvement for sustainable waste stewardship.

What does waste cost?

According to the Joint Commission Environment of Care Standards, "Hospitals lose money due to regulated medical waste management costs. Simple management changes recoup 10% to 50% of costs (and reduce pollution)."[90] There are a variety of reasons to reconsider waste management practices, including increased federal regulation, public pressures and increased costs. A major reason to think differently about waste management is that many current models of waste segregation result in wasted money. "Throwing away non-contaminated waste into the regulated medical waste stream (red bags) may increase regulated medical waste volumes by as much as 50 per cent! Encouraging proper waste segregation and selecting products that don't wind up in the trash can safely reduce regulated medical waste volumes and save 40 to 70 per cent on waste disposal."[91]

Waste management can be a community health benefit because it reduces the spread of toxic chemicals. But what is the cost of not managing waste sustainably? Historically, no-one gave much thought to the opportunity cost of ignoring waste management. But in today's economic environment, healthcare organizations are looking for ways to cut costs and make care more affordable. A healthcare organization that reduces its physical waste stream reduces its waste disposal costs.

Table 4.1 reflects average costs of waste disposal by waste stream as of 2010. Table 4.2 reflects waste costs by region of the US as of 2010.

FRED: You're telling me that if we sort our waste properly and manage how we dispose of or recycle the different waste streams, we'll reduce costs?

FELIPE: That's right. You might be surprised to learn that our competitor saved $1.2 million last year by reprocessing medical devices.

FRED: What are a few examples of items we can get started on with regard to reprocessing?

Table 4.1 Average cost of waste disposal by waste stream in the USA (2010)*

Waste stream	Solid waste cost per ton ($)	Recycled cost per ton ($)	Regulated medical waste cost per ton ($)	Hazardous waste cost per pound ($)
Average	121	68	963	4.02
Maximum	404	445	3243	45.58
Minimum	31	−1133 (revenue)	141	0.15
Number of respondents	87	70	81	73

*Brown, J. (2010) Benchmarking Sustainability in *Health Care Awards Benchmark Report.* Reston, VA: Practice Greenhealth. www.cleanmed.org/2010/downloads/presentations/C4/Brown.pdf

Table 4.2 Waste costs by US region*

	Average costs by region ($)						
	California	Northeast	Midwest	Southeast	Southwest	Mid-Atlantic	Northwest
Solid waste per ton	158	122	90	53	109	136	150
Recycled per ton	51	41	88	82	−29 (revenue)	83	25
Regulated medical waste per ton	1,111	1,765	821	552	461	729	1,618
Hazardous waste per pound	4.99	4.66	1.91	0.27	1.76	3.32	6.61
Number of respondents	12	13	21	2	3	11	11

*Brown, J. (2010) *Benchmarking Sustainability in Health Care Awards Benchmark Report.* Reston, VA: Practice Greenhealth. www.cleanmed.org/2010/downloads/presentations/C4/Brown.pdf

FELIPE: One of the most financially lucrative items is a harmonic scalpel. Other commonly reprocessed items are orthopedic burrs and bits and, in general surgery, laparoscopic surgical devices, pneumatic cuffs and ultrasonic scalpels. Some of these are solid metal devices that are otherwise thrown away after just one use.

FRED: My guess is that most of our employees recycle at home, so recycling at work would be natural for them.

FELIPE: I think there's a natural alignment between the cost strategy and the sustainability strategy. If you cared not a whit about sustainability, and you were solely focused on driving down the cost profile of operations, then you should be concerned about waste management. The cost of waste sorting for the entire hospital comes to an average of a quarter of a million dollars each year. Granted, waste management is just a small percentage of the total operating budget, and that percentage of our total costs hasn't changed much over the years. But, there is no reason to throw cash in the trash. I suspect there's a lot beyond the cost implications that you probably care about with regard to waste management.

FRED: I think the conversation about waste goes something like this: high waste means low quality and high cost. Every leader I know wants high quality and low cost. So we want to drive out waste. Now I tend to be a cynic, and I think, from a sustainability point of view, that reducing waste is a means of reducing cost. But I understand that for some of our employees, sustainability is an end in and of itself, rather than a means to an end.

FELIPE: (*Thinking to himself*) I wonder if there will come a time when sustainability as a program isn't a cost neutral cost center... I wonder, if sustainability becomes a cost center that isn't cost neutral or isn't saving money, would it still make sense to have it?

Opportunity costs

There simply isn't enough human or financial capital to invest in every leadership opportunity. When leaders establish priorities, they effectively deny a focus on other opportunities. When healthcare organizations choose not to manage waste, it is worthwhile to examine the consequences. For instance, consider the implications of no waste management on construction and demolition debris (CDD) and its associated cost. During major capital improvements, hospitals face the decision of recycling CDD or letting it go to solid waste landfills. CDD is typically the largest volume of waste that goes into landfills.[92] When healthcare organizations divert waste, they not only have the opportunity to recycle resources, but many hospitals make donations to less developed countries. This practice benefits the recipients while keeping waste out of the landfills.[93]

Commonly donated items from CDD include:[94]

- clinical items
- medical equipment
- furniture
- computers
- linens
- books.

Given the relative ease with which these items can be donated, leaders ought to be asking themselves: what is the opportunity cost of not implementing waste management, not just for CDD, but across all operations?

FRED: Sustainability accomplishments aren't necessarily going to serve cost reduction goals, right? I mean, there's a chance that doing the right thing for the environment could actually cost us more, I presume. And, let's face it, many sustainability projects require some upfront resources—whether it's time, attention or money. So what's the rationale for sustainability goals?

FELIPE: Well Fred, we're used to thinking of a single bottom line: cost. But sustainability is about a triple bottom line, as you know: environmental, social and fiscal responsibility. In today's competitive healthcare marketplace, we often make decisions based on cost and safety. The trouble is that when we focus solely on cost, we often miss the opportunity to achieve a triple bottom line, and we overlook potential solutions that incorporate environmentally or socially responsible practices. Driving our decisions based on cost alone may be the most fiscally responsible thing to do from a narrow perspective, but we miss out on serving our goals for social and environmental responsibilities in the process. And those social and environmental outcomes have consequences and costs for all of us as members of the global community.

FRED: We rarely drive decision-making by focusing solely on cost, Felipe, despite how it may appear.

FELIPE: Of course, Fred, I understand that. Let me make clear that I don't think it's okay to neglect cost efficiencies to the benefit of socially and environmentally responsible operations. Sustainability is about optimizing and balancing the intersection of all three bottom lines—social, environmental and fiscal. Focusing on one bottom line at the expense of the others won't help us much long term.

FRED: I see. I gather that when the benefits of two of the bottom lines outweigh the third bottom line, it could still be a high-value proposition from a sustainability perspective.

FELIPE: Potentially, Fred. That's right.

Human impact of waste management

Waste management has gained a level of sophistication in the past decade. Modern food service would be a good metaphor, which requires not just managing food production, but also managing safety, nutritional value, customer service and cost. Twenty-five years ago, hospital food was a utilitarian exchange with less of a focus on taste.[95] If employees or hospital patients were actively dissatisfied, that was a problem. But expectations for food management were very low. Today, patients and employees expect the food to be part of what drives a positive patient experience.[96] Similarly, waste management is experiencing a shift in how it is perceived. Patients and visitors expect to see recycling bins. A leader can do everything else right in terms of sustainability, but if he or she does not have recycling options, there is an image exposure in the public's eye. Recycling is the most visible and emotionally connecting element of environmental sustainability because individuals are engaged at a personal level.

There is no clear definition of where sustainable waste management accountability lives within the modern healthcare organization, though Environmental Services most often owns it. Outsourcing trends across a variety of hospital departments may result in gaps in management oversight.[97] Waste management is no exception, particularly as Environmental Services is often outsourced.[98] Sustainability is an essential component of the way every healthcare organization is operated, and can not be an optional part of the process for leadership. Hospitals are responsible, both legally and socially, for their waste.[99]

FRED: I can't say I've ever given much thought to waste sorting, but we spend an average of a quarter of a million dollars on waste management each year.[100][101] If we could get a fraction of that cost out, that would be pretty good. If we bought new supplies and then reprocessed them, we could save another chunk of change. I think we have to find 3 to 5 per cent in our overall structure just in waste management. I can't remember a time when we turned to waste management to help defray overall operating costs. That's a big change, and a big plus for sustainability.

FELIPE: Our hospital model for the longest time has been that prices went up, volumes went up, and expenses went up. So we weren't exactly forced to find cost savings. Meanwhile our friends in the airline industry, banking and telecommunications had to find 5 or 10 per cent each year to keep consumer pricing competitive.

Clearly an unsustainable model hence the current focus on cost reduction in healthcare

There are several waste streams in most hospitals, as Figure 4.2 illustrates. There are best practice standards for each type of waste stream (Table 4.3)[102]:

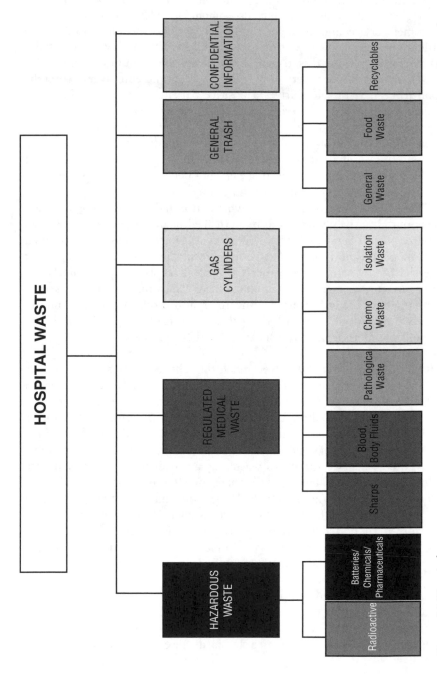

Figure 4.2 Hospital waste streams

Table 4.3 Waste streams and best management practices

Waste stream	Best practice (percentage of total waste weight)
Solid or non-regulated medical waste	60
Recycling	30
Regulated medical waste	10
Hazardous waste	<1

WASTE STREAM COSTS:

$ ⟹ $$$$

R E C Y C L I N G   G E N E R A L   T R A S H   C O N F I D E N T I A L   R E G U L A T E D   M E D I C A L   H A Z A R D O U S

Figure 4.3 Relative waste stream costs

Waste measures include[103]:

- average pounds of total waste per adjusted patient day (APD)
- average pounds of total waste per licensed bed per day
- average pounds of total waste per staffed bed per day.

Getting paid for process improvement

The fiscal savings from waste management incentivizes leaders to champion sustainable management practices. When leaders realize the cost savings of optimal waste disposal, the social and environmental goals that are equally important to the triple bottom line of waste management suddenly seem more achievable as well.

Most innovation is not about having ideas—it is about empowering

They say that only a baby with a dirty diaper likes change. The truth is, no-one much likes change. For years, successful healthcare organizations have been rewarded for making incremental change.[104] That is especially problematic for organizations that are used to success, because they are likely the ones that need to change most if they are serious about engaging a new model of health.

How does a leader effectively engage employees and physicians in innovative waste management practices and get positive results? Most innovation and positive change does not come about because people have new ideas, but when employees and leaders are empowered to act upon those ideas. Leaders have to be explicit about empowering innovation around sustainability. The reality is that very little about waste management is truly innovative. But an organization's approach can become increasingly sustainable by making it easy for employees to experiment with and implement new approaches to sustainable waste management.

Leaders must involve employees to weave sustainable waste management practices into daily operations. Employees have a responsibility to study and improve the processes in their department and teach colleagues sustainable waste disposal practices. Only after building connections with employees based on shared values (like sustainability) can changed practices begin to be hardwired into the organizational culture. At that point, sustainability becomes a purposeful element of everybody's job.

Sustainability accelerates strategy

There are a growing number of examples of healthcare leaders who have successfully hardwired sustainability into their organizations.[105] Several of these organizations are highlighted in the practical applications within each chapter. Among these leading organizations, some are known for sustainable food practices, while others are known for sustainable facility design. But all of the leading organizations share strengths in properly managing and segregating biohazardous from non-biohazardous waste materials. Red bag waste reduction is an area of focus for sustainability efforts that not only reaps financial savings, but is also the socially and environmentally responsible thing to do. Single-use device reprocessing, reusable sharps container programs, and pharmaceutical waste management have recently become top priorities for leaders as an increasing number of hospitals implement programs to handle these complex waste streams properly. Hospitals have especially intensified their efforts to understand how to dispose of both hazardous and non-hazardous pharmaceutical waste sustainably.[106] A model pharmaceutical waste program is described below[107].

1 Implemented a pharmaceutical waste management program.
2 Hired an outside vendor to help set up your program.
3 Separate pharmaceutical waste at the point of generation.
4 Send pharmaceutical waste back to pharmacy for proper segregation.
5 Collect all pharmaceutical waste at the waste collection point and sort in a satellite accumulation area.
6 Treat all pharmaceuticals as hazardous waste.

FRED: Please have copies of the pharmaceutical waste management process for Monday morning's meeting so that we can facilitate an introductory conversation.

FELIPE: Sure thing.

FRED: Felipe?

FELIPE: Yes, Fred.

FRED: I suppose we ought to do the sustainable thing and send the document electronically instead of printing paper copies.

FELIPE: Will do, Fred.

Embedding the concept of waste

A key leadership role is to help colleagues understand alternative practices that are more sustainable than existing practices. "The top five most highly recycled materials in 2010 were batteries, fluorescent lamps, mixed paper, computers and electronics and, likely, cardboard. In 2009 the list looked the same, except that toner cartridges replaced mixed paper. These lists highlight the efforts hospitals are making to segregate their Universal Wastes in order to reduce their hazardous waste stream and associated costs."[108] Roughly half of the organizations that lead the healthcare industry in recycling practices make money off of their recycling programs (best case was over $181,000 annually). The other half of best practice hospitals for recycled content lost money (worst case, almost $88,000).[109] Regardless of the cost savings or expenditure, hospitals with developed waste management programs generate less waste than their counterparts at about a 30-per cent rate.[110]

Dioxins

Dioxins (waste by-products of industrial processes) are a community health concern because they can cause cancer, weaken the immune system, interfere with the endocrine system and reduce fertility. "The United States Environmental Protection Agency's 1995 dioxin emissions inventory estimated that medical waste incineration was the nation's third largest dioxins source, emitting 15 per cent of all the dioxins on the national inventory."[111]

Table 4.4 Recycled materials sorted by the highest occurrence of recycling*

Cardboard	Food waste (composting)
Batteries	Foam peanuts
Fluorescent lamps	X-ray film
Paper, mixed	Shrink wrap
Computers/electronics	Plastic, #6 PS
Toner cartridges	Solvent distillation
Oil (coking)	Plastic, #5 polypropylene
Pallets	Single stream recycling
Cans, aluminum	Glass, colored
Equipment donation	Blue wrap
Co-mingled recycling	Linens (reused for rags only)
Ink jet cartridges	Glass, clear
Paper, white	Boxboard
Newspaper	Plastic, #1 PET
Single-use device reprocessing	Glass, mixed
Reusable sharps containers	Plastic, #2 HDPE
Cans, steel	Plastic, mixed
Steel (listed as steel cans in 2009)	Oil (motor)

*Brown, J. (2010) *Benchmarking Sustainability in Health Care Awards Benchmark Report*. Reston, VA: Practice Greenhealth. www.cleanmed.org/2010/downloads/presentations/C4/Brown.pdf

Low waste means high quality and low cost

In the United States, only 11–14 per cent of electronic waste is sent to recyclers and the rest is dumped or burned.[112] Even electronic waste (such as computers, monitors and medical devices) that is sent to recycling services may not be properly handled. According to e-Stewards, recyclers send an estimated 70–80 per cent of their electronic waste to less developed countries, where they are burned in large piles for metals, exposing people and the environment to a host of toxins.[113] To avoid environmental and human health hazards, ask for e-waste recyclers or ask group purchasing organizations for e-waste recyclers that have taken additional steps to be environmentally responsible.[114]

Electronics are not the only recyclable product for which leaders ought to find new options. There is also substantial opportunity in the area of reusable linens.[115] Other reusable items in healthcare facilities include:

- surgical drapes
- surgical gowns
- incontinent products (underpads and briefs)
- isolation gowns
- scrubs
- surgical packs (sterile and nonsterile).

Know before you throw

Red bag reduction continues to be an area of focus for sustainability efforts. Hospitals that reap savings from these efforts report that they:[116]

- engage in a regulated medical waste education and reduction program
- post waste segregation posters at red bag collection areas
- use a fluid management system in operating rooms
- use the fluid management system exclusively in orthopedic operating rooms
- use single-use device reprocessing
- implement a reusable sharps container program.

Figure 4.4 is an example of a waste segregation poster for a red bag collection area, available free online.[117]

FELIPE: You know, Fred, I went to the supermarket the other day, and when it came time to pay, the lady working the cash register asked if I'd like to make a dollar donation to a good cause. She asked the person ahead of me in line that same question. It struck me that the brilliance of this fundraising tactic was that it was hardwired in the checkout process. In other words, it was excellent product placement and logistically feasible.

FRED: You mean you could make a positive contribution to society while paying for groceries?

FELIPE: That's right, Fred. The supermarket made it easy for me. They made me feel like I was part of the solution. I think those are the two main reasons why I donated. I don't even remember what the cause was that my money went to.

FRED: So maybe if we put the recycling bin in easy-to-access, line-of-sight locations, our employees will be more apt to recycle. Do you think that might work? I'm convinced we'll have better results if we make it easy for our employees and visitors to think about managing waste sustainably. One of our biggest challenges will be getting the entire physician and employee population to build sustainability into the way that we operate. They're so used to doing it one way.

FELIPE: How about this—I'll walk the entire hospital and ask the stakeholders, our nurses, physicians and employees, what they throw where. We'll see if we can come up with a hardwired solution to sort our waste properly.

FRED: Sounds like a plan to me!

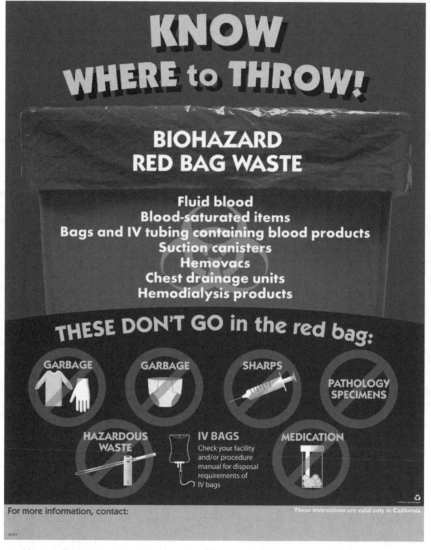

Figure 4.4 Regulated medical waste educational signage

Practical application: Providence's blue bag recycling program

The imperative

- Increasing recycling rate.
- Decreasing waste management costs.
- Circumventing restrictions on what local jurisdictions would accept from hospitals.
- Providing employment to underemployed social group.

The initiative

Before Providence Health & Services began its focus on recycling, the system's hospitals were recycling small amounts of materials here and there, but lacked a comprehensive program. They hovered right around a 15 per cent recycling rate, but had aspirations of achieving a rate of over 50 per cent. However, they could not find a vendor who would provide a unilateral, single-stream recycling service to their hospitals.

The individual in charge of the system's sustainability initiatives took the issue to a local consortium of hospitals and industry vendors, through which they were able to develop an internal system for self-sorting the materials. They then partnered with a local organization that worked to provide jobs for developmentally disabled adults, using these individuals as helpers in sorting the recycling waste from its commingled containers. The hospitals would package the separated materials themselves and sell them to local vendors, receiving a modest profit per bale.

After establishing this behind-the-scenes system, the focus turned to the front line. In order to increase the amount of materials being recycled, it was necessary to engage and educate the staff about Providence's recycling program. This was achieved through a number of mechanisms:

- presenting at large department meetings
- placing clear, visible signage on containers or right above them
- providing peer-to-peer education and pressure from Green Team members
- putting together presentations highlighting specific problems when sorting issues occurred
- highlighting dollar savings from programs
- focusing on nursing staff, who do most of the sorting
- auditing, evaluating and correcting placement of containers to make sorting easier.

The key individuals involved in implementation of this project included property managers, the Director of Hospitality (who oversaw environmental services), Green Team members, quality practice councils, infection control, public relations and the nursing staff.

The metrics

- Recycling rate
- Quantity of material recycled (lbs, tons, total bags).
- Dollars saved due to landfill diversion.

The lessons learned

- Sharing what colleagues are doing and the positive results they are seeing in order to garner administrative and clinical support.
- Engaging peoples' competitive edge challenges colleagues to reach further than they otherwise might in achieving sustainability goals.
- Highlighting what will be "left on the table" if the organization does not pursue the sustainability program can spur a positive reaction
- When implementing a commingled recycling program, education is key. Help staff understand what is and is not recyclable by sharing consistent information in as many different formats as possible— particularly related to problem areas such as what to do with HIPAA (Health Insurance Portability and Accountability Act)-protected information and opened/unused supplies. This is the most effective method to combat contamination issues.
- It may be difficult to find a vendor who will accept a commingled stream of all the recyclables found in the healthcare setting. If this occurs, reaching out to other local hospitals or meeting groups for the healthcare industry for ideas is a good next step. Every state and virtually every country has these groups—they often have online forums for idea-sharing and they also often invite vendor partners to participate.

About the organization

Providence Health & Services is a not-for-profit Catholic healthcare ministry committed to providing for the needs of the communities it serves—especially for those who are poor and vulnerable. The health system spans five states—Alaska, California, Montana, Oregon and Washington—and includes twenty-seven hospitals, 214 physician clinics, senior services and supportive housing, a health plan, a liberal arts university, a high school and many other health and educational services.

Sources

www2.providence.org/phs/Pages/default.aspx
Interview, Mike Geller, Providence Portland Service Area Sustainability Coordinator

Leadership imperative

A healthcare organization may have the most environmentally progressive program, but the program will likely go unnoticed until employees and patients actively participate. Employees and patients alike relate to what is immediately identifiable. Beyond employee engagement, why should a healthcare leader care about waste management? Sustainability effectively translates to the executive level when it is integrated into the business goals of the organization. Using Lean as a vehicle for integrating sustainability will improve processes, in part, by helping to set and monitor targets and milestones that allow leadership to gauge sustainability progress. Lean helps make visible to leadership both the goal and the performance process.

Leadership dialogue

1 Why and how does process improvement, when combined with waste management practices, improve efficiencies and lower operational costs?
2 Why is it important to promote sustainability by linking sustainability goals, such as waste management, with business values?
3 Why does Lean thinking naturally align with waste management?
4 How can leaders effectively link the Lean approach with sustainability values for employees who do not recognize the natural alignment?
5 How can leaders improve waste management processes across professional, departmental and/or facility boundaries?

Syllabus integration

Overview

This lesson introduces an overview of process improvement as related to solid waste regulations, risk assessment methodologies, solid waste collection, and disposal practices and recycling. Students will learn about waste minimization and pollution prevention, treatment of hazardous waste and remediation.

Objectives

1   Participate in a process improvement exercise.
2   Explore major sources and types of healthcare waste.
3   Identify opportunities to reduce waste and avoid risk.
4   Evaluate costs and benefits of proposed waste management practices.
5   Analyze gaps in current knowledge concerning waste management.
6   Discuss current legislation and regulation regarding waste issues.
7   Debate when it is safe to reuse disposable items.

Topics

1   Types of waste.
2   Waste subtopics.
3   Halogenated anesthetic gas exposure.
4   Pharmaceutical waste management.
5   Reduce, reuse, recycle, prevent.

Homework

Washington State Department of Ecology (2005) *Best Management Practices For Hospital Waste*. Hazardous Waste and Toxics Reduction Program.

Practice Greenhealth (2009) 'Mind Your Ps & Us! Managing pharmaceutical waste, including an update of the 2008 10-step blueprint for healthcare facilities in the US,' webinar May 15. www.practicegreenhealth.org

One of the most challenging efforts of healthcare sustainability is selecting a starting point. Reflecting on classroom discussion, assigned reading and webinar content, identify where you would begin as a Sustainability Director located at a regional medical center, and why you chose that starting point. Record in your career journal.

Additional resources

Practice Greenhealth (2007) 'Waste volume reduction strategies in the operating room,' webinar September 14. www.practicegreenhealth.org

Chen, I. (July 6, 2010) "In a World of Throwaways Making a Dent in Medical Waste", *New York Times*, available online: http://www.nytimes.com/2010/07/06/health/06waste.html?pagewanted=all&_r=0 (accessed 10/22/2012).

Harhay, M.O., Halpern, S.D., Harhay, J.S. and Olliaro, P.L. (2009), "Health care waste management: a neglected and growing public health problem worldwide". *Tropical Medicine & International Health*, 14: 1414-1417.

McRae, G., Shaner, H. and Leach-Bisson, C. (1993) *An Ounce of Prevention: Waste Reduction Strategies for Health Care Facilities*, American Society for Healthcare Environmental Services of the American Hospital Association (ASHES). See www.sustainablehospitals.org/HTMLSrc/WasteSort.html

5 The long and winding road (leads me home)

Employee engagement + transportation

Figure 5.1 Commuting to a hospital

Executive summary

The outcome is predictably positive when leaders connect their organization's interests with the existing interests of key stakeholders, such as employees, physicians and the community. Those interests can be as diverse as the stakeholders themselves. Engagement is critical to empowering employees and other key stakeholders in fulfilling the sustainability agenda. Ultimately, sustainability is about personal health, community health and the health of the environment. This chapter explains why it is important to engage employees in the sustainability journey and how to do so, using transportation as the sustainability vehicle.

A told story

Gregor, the Director of Safety and Security at Memorial Hospital, lives far from work and is plagued by rising gasoline prices. He arrives at work stressed from sitting in traffic.

GREGOR: Gas prices are getting higher and my commute is not getting any shorter. There has to be a better way to commute. Either that, or I need to find a job that is closer to home.
  (The next day, Gregor sees a shuttle for a company drive by with one of his neighbors onboard. After work, Gregor stops by his neighbor's house to ask how his company came to provide the shuttle service. Gregor learns that the local county government is committed to reducing traffic and provides funding to create shared ride programs. Gregor takes this knowledge to Denise, Chief Financial Officer, during a meeting about construction of the new building.)
GREGOR: I learned that the county is requiring us to have a plan to manage the traffic congestion that is going to be associated with the construction. It's required as part of the building approval we obtained through the rezoning process. I think part of the overall problem is that we aren't making it easy for employees to be sustainable about their commuting options. I for one am rather envious of my neighbor, who gets to ride to work each day. His company worked with the county to get funding for a shuttle from their community.
DENISE: Well, that's interesting. Sounds like you've just found yourself a new project! Why don't you take the lead on researching what our options are for more sustainable transportation?

Employee engagement is a leadership priority

When a leader commits to sustainability, one of the immediate next steps is to build ownership among the leadership team and among as many employees as possible. Building ownership involves finding something that employees care about and embedding sustainability into that employee interest. It is only when employees perceive that there is a "win" for them, or an alignment of interests between the hospital and themselves, that ownership starts to occur. Learning what employees value is a somewhat counterintuitive place to start when operationalizing a sustainability agenda, but it is an important first step for the leader seeking alignment between employee values and organizational priorities.

At Inova, for instance, 99.1 percent of the 545 employees randomly surveyed responded that "Environmental Sustainability ('Going Green') is important to me

A different mindset

FRED: Do you think that a sustainability program would attract new employees? I could envision an applicant would interview at Memorial Hospital, hear about the sustainability program, and say, "Gee, that's different. I've been applying to jobs right and left and the sustainability program at Memorial Hospital really stands out as forward-thinking. I think our values align."

FIONA O'MALLEY: It's a possibility. Sustainability as a value may or may not be desirable from a recruiting point of view. We'd have to ask HR.

FRED: The notion that it's new and therefore progressive is probably a very good thing. Sustainability attracts people who are looking to progress in their worldview, people who have relatively high tolerance for ambiguity and figuring things out. It's people who are progressive and change-friendly who largely define innovative organizations, because they create improvements that customers value faster than organizations that don't have change-friendly environments.

Embedding sustainability in leadership priorities

Any given hospital employs hundreds, if not thousands, of employees who move to and from the hospital each day. Visitors are also a major source of transportation impact. Less visible, but no less consequential for the community, is supply chain transportation. The leader who can align organizational priorities with employee interests will enlist valuable allies (e.g. reduce the cost or time required for daily work commute). The ultimate goal, from a sustainability perspective, is to find tactics and approaches that improve the triple bottom line outcomes of lowering cost, improving the community's health and improving sustainability.[118]

(Fred and Lori Prince of Human Resources engage in conversation.)

FRED: Are we wrestling with transportation issues for transportation's sake, or are we're talking about transportation in terms of employee engagement? Our employees care deeply about how they get to work, in terms of time and cost. Frankly, it's a major source of dissatisfaction. I'm wondering if we can think about transportation in the context of sustainability.

LORI PRINCE: I don't think I've heard any of our leaders talk about transportation in the context of sustainability before. I respond to employee complaints about insufficient parking, but that's about it.

FRED: One of our shared priorities is to strengthen employee engagement. What do you think about using sustainability issue A to help us achieve employee engagement goal B?

LORI PRINCE: I think it's worth a shot.

Besides employee engagement, transportation naturally overlaps with energy efficiency and cost reduction, clean air and related health effects, reduction of supply chain and waste disposal costs, and other environmental, fiscal and social issues. But the key point for the purpose of this book is that there's a clear and explicit overlap between transportation strategy, employee engagement and sustainability.

My employees care about how they get to work

Recruitment has been a major issue historically and, given demographic trends, will likely continue to be an issue. "Our nation already suffers from shortages of a range of health professionals, made worse by geographic maldistribution... The shortages are expected to worsen as 78 million baby boomers begin to hit retirement age in 2011 and require more care for chronic illnesses... Many predict there will be a shortage of up to 200,000 physicians and 1 million nurses by 2020."[119] Access to transportation is a key part of the recruitment equation in today's society. Public transit stops, highways and bike access influence the accessibility of the hospital to the workforce as well as patients.

Another trend that is impacting healthcare transportation in a significant way is the transition to home and ambulatory care.[120] [121] Home health is

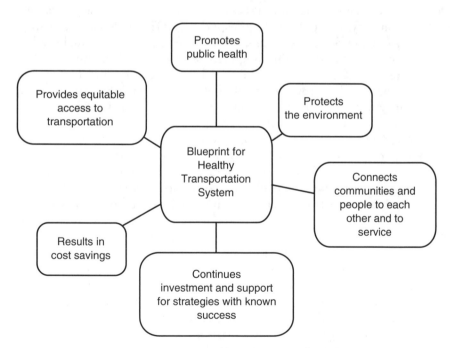

Figure 5.2 Blueprint for a healthy transportation system[126]

the fastest growing sector in the healthcare industry, with an anticipated growth of 66 per cent over the next ten years. Over seven million patients are served in home health settings each year. It is often the lowest-cost option for delivering healthcare services that would otherwise be provided in the hospital setting.[122] [123] Primary care, in particular, is increasingly retail-oriented and located outside of the hospital for optimal patient access.[124] That means that more services will be physically located in the community, rather than at the hospital. Fewer people will be venturing to the hospital as more people transition to ambulatory care sites. One example of an expanding ambulatory program is the Program of All-Inclusive Care for the Elderly (PACE), a comprehensive service for enrollees that includes transportation of enrollees from their homes to the PACE site.[125] Alternatively, what are the transportation implications of moving large numbers (in small groups) of healthcare workers out to patients' homes? With an inadequate transportation system, delivering ambulatory and home healthcare will be affected and will likely lead to both dissatisfied employees and patients. As hospitals across the country embrace ambulatory and home healthcare models, it is an ideal time to incorporate sustainability into the transportation system.

LORI PRINCE: Have you given any thought to where we should locate our ambulatory care sites and how smart growth plays into that decision?

FRED: I don't know enough about smart growth to have an informed opinion. But I have to say that, based on my limited knowledge, my reaction to smart growth has been negative. I mean, the basic concept of smart growth makes sense, you know, purposefully developing where people live and work in a contiguous space. But the way smart growth translates so often has sort of been against building roads or having any sort of investment in surface transportation. I never really understood how to apply smart growth to our interests.

LORI PRINCE: Well, Fred, I'm no expert on smart growth, but I thought it was more about building density and public transportation. Proponents of smart growth are not against roads. It's more that they realize that once we screw up land-use planning, that is, unless we grow adequate density, public transportation won't make economic sense. And all that pollution will make all the pulmonary patients flock to the emergency department (ED).

FRED: I'm out of my depth on that topic, but I never thought about it that way before.

To the degree that leaders engage employees in community issues such as transportation policy or air pollution rules, it is likely a relatively small, but growing piece of the total policy agenda. Support for sustainability, one could argue, is really not much different from support for child safety seats, because they are both topics that everyone—patients, families, employees, physicians, etc.—is touched by. Improving transportation is directly related to improving health.

What is Smart Growth?

According to the US Environmental Protection Agency (EPA), smart growth is "development that serves the economy, the community, and the environment." It changes the terms of the development debate away from the traditional growth/no-growth debate to "how and where should new development be accommodated?" Smart growth is development that simultaneously achieves economic development and jobs, strong neighborhoods and healthy communities.

Create connective opportunities

There are a wide range of higher-order values that people care about. It could be finding a cure to cancer or religious faith, or it could be sustainability. Regardless of the topic of interest, connecting people with each other around higher-order values is key to creating a culture of employee engagement. As sustainability becomes increasingly prevalent in healthcare organizations, employees will want to connect with each other and their leaders who embrace sustainability values. The challenge, then, is for leaders to connect their sustainability agenda with employees in a meaningful way.

What matters to employees? One objective of every nurse is to understand the patient's and family's value system. What will drive the family's behavior and the patient's compliance to manage health or follow the treatment plan? During the process of understanding the patient and family value system, it is likely that there could be direct alignment between employees and patients who share a belief that sustainability matters. One can imagine a time when the nurse–patient conversation goes something like this: "Hello. Please confirm for me your name and date of birth. We are going through this process for your safety. What you would like in terms of your diet? Was public transportation available to you? I am asking you these questions because we are trying to reduce our environmental footprint. These supplies you see are all recycled and meet the highest quality standard." When employees articulate their motivation(s), whether it is safety or sustainability, they add value in the eyes of their patients and families. The patient thinks, "Hmm, my nurse cares about my safety, she cares about sustainability, she cares about me actually improving my health." Aligning values builds relationships and also builds trust. In this hypothetical situation, it is the core value of the caregiver, rather than the action taken, that provides the basis for alignment.

What is employee engagement?

Employee engagement is "a force that drives performance outcomes."[127] Successful organizations realize that, more often than not, their most valuable resource is their workforce. Additionally, lost productivity has a cost, and a high one at that (Harter, *et al.*, 2010, see also Gallup, n.d.)[127]. In 2008, an estimated $300 billion in the United States and €226.5 billion was lost in productivity due to disengagement. In light of cost alone, employee engagement is a leadership priority. Surveys show that the greatest success factor in getting employees engaged is through interaction with their management team (Murlis and Schubert, 2001).

Transportation is a health issue

The way a community is designed and built has a lot to do with the future health of that community. The growth of suburban areas created lack of access to walking corridors and safe bicycle riding routes, resulting in more automotive transportation. The additional burden and stress of sitting in traffic has an impact on health. Land use planning and transportation planning are key components of the social determinants of health. Much of the land planning over the latter half of the twentieth century was based on the premise that people would own cars. The current reality is that many people cannot afford cars, choose not to use cars in many urban settings, people spend three hours on round trips for groceries.[128] Lack of connectivity and access to healthy foods and food deserts have added to the obesity epidemic.[129] Well planned communities are built around these access points.

In 2008, the government of the United Kingdom set out a strategy, "Healthy weight, healthy lives," that tied land planning with increased physical activity thorough walking and cycling.[130] Also published in 2008 was a Public Health Guidance-PH8, which offered "guidance on the promotion and creation of physical environments that support increased levels of physical activity."[131] Of the seven evidence-based recommendations provided in this guidance document to the National Health Service (NHS), four focused on transportation access-related items.[132] The US Department of Transportation (DOT) has also recognized transportation as a public health issue. In 2010, DOT Undersecretary Roy Kienitz reinforced a statement about the impact transportation policies have on public health.[133]

How can transportation improve employee health?

Increasingly, healthcare employers seek to reduce their benefit costs and improve employee retention and productivity.[134] [135] Often, employers attempt to achieve these goals by improving the health status of employees. Johnson & Johnson "leaders estimate that wellness programs have cumulatively saved the company $250 million on healthcare costs over the past decade; from 2002 to 2008, the return was $2.71 for every dollar spent."[136] A component of many organizations' strategies is to embed opportunities for exercise into the work environment and work processes.[137] Is there a way to connect the dots: transportation issues, exercise opportunities and employee health?

FRED: We have physicians and employees who bike to work every day. We know that the employees who exercise by virtue of transportation, whether it's biking or walking, tend to be healthier than their colleagues. I think that when transportation is considered more broadly, it can be something as simple as walking. Take internal transportation, for instance. Our employees could walk up the stairs instead of taking the elevator. I met recently with a Kaiser executive who told me that leaders at Kaiser are not permitted to use the elevators at their Oakland, California headquarters. Talk about a transportation policy!

LORI PRINCE: Do you know what employees receive the most complaints about from our patients?

FRED: No, what? These questions get harder the deeper into this we go.

LORI PRINCE: It happens before they even get inside the hospital! Our patients and visitors complain most often about our parking area. They complain that there isn't a covering from the garage to the hospital itself.

FRED: Maybe if we provided a covering, folks would be incentivized to walk. I see so many people take the shuttle option even though the garage is right across the street.

LORI PRINCE: I'm telling you, Fred, we probably get more complaints about how hard it is to get in and out of the hospital than anything else. Patients don't want to encourage their friends to visit them because the transportation and inaccessibility is so tough. That's one of the first messages our employees hear from our patients when they arrive at the hospital.

FRED: What do you think about labeling environmentally preferable parking spots in the garage, you know, for carpools and hybrid vehicles? I realize that doesn't solve the problem we were just talking about, but it does make our commitment to sustainable transportation visible to the community.

LORI PRINCE: I think that's a neat idea. What made you think of it?

FRED: Well, it was proposed originally as a way of encouraging people to buy hybrid vehicles. You know, there are a lot of people, especially younger employees, who are concerned about our posture *vis a vis* the environment. It's really all about Richard Florida's creative class principle. Have you ever read his book about the rise of the "creative class"? He says that the creative, bright, often highly educated people are attracted to organizations and communities that nurture the things that they find important.

LORI PRINCE: I know the type. Some of the things that this creative class finds important is individual liberty. They are sort of spoiled and they like individual customization. Employment policies, like having flexible work-at-home arrangements and open benefit structures that accommodate diverse lifestyles, are very important to them.

FRED: The point is that now I see how a small thing—like a parking spot—has symbolic value. Beyond that, it's an alignment of employee values with organizational sustainability objectives. One of the things that attracts the creative class is a clear commitment to sustainability and the environmental ethic.

Pursuing sustainable policies, transportation policies included, tends to be an employee satisfier. For many younger employees, engagement in sustainability practices is a minimum expectation of their employment.[138] Healthcare organizations that have bike racks, offer car pooling, shuttle options or other transportation alternatives will engage a meaningful number of employees.

Figure 5.3 Lining up for sustainability
Courtesy of Jamie Huffcut

What are the health impacts of traffic?

Transportation health impacts are both local and global in scope. On a local level, transportation impacts air quality, which can have regional effects on airborne infections. On the global level, the potential exists for impacting the balance between the atmosphere, oceans and the Sun, weather effects and effects on vegetation.[139]

Transportation has a wide-reaching impact on public health. For the average citizen, driving is his or her most air-polluting activity.[140]

Given their ubiquitous nature, air and water are two elements that have the largest impact on human health. In fact, the US EPA has predicted the prevention of 230,000 early deaths by 2020 as a result of the Clean Air Act between 1990 and 2020.[141] An added benefit includes a projected $2 billion in savings from direct benefits of the program. Table 5.1 highlights some of the health areas of impacts from air pollution:

Table 5.1 Predicted reduction in health-related impacts from the Clean Air Act*

Health impact	Predicted number of cases	
	2010	2020
Adult mortality—particles	160,000	230,000
Infant mortality—particles	230	280
Mortality—ozone	4300	7100
Chronic bronchitis	54,000	75,000
Heart disease—acute myocardial infarction	130,000	200,000
Asthma exacerbation	1,700,000	2,400,000
Emergency room visits	86,000	120,000
Lost school days	3,200,000	5,400,000
Lost work days	13,000,000	17,000,000

*US EPA (2011) 'Benefits and Costs of the Clean Air Act: Second Prospective Study – 1990 to 2020,' Washington, DC: Environmental Protection Agency. www.epa.gov/air/sect812/prospective2.html

Practical application: Cleveland Clinic's Alternative Transportation Program

The imperative

- Increase patient and employee satisfaction by eliminating traffic backups.
- Address environmental and health impacts of transportation.
- Reduce demand on automotive parking infrastructure.
- Minimize the commuting cost burden for employees.
- Pursue cost savings related to taxes on stormwater discharge and congestion in parking structures.

The initiative

Before Cleveland Clinic's transportation program evolved into the comprehensive program it is today, it consisted of a variety of individual initiatives under the control of different groups within the organization—wellness promoting bike ridership, parking services promoting a carpool program, human resources promoting pre-tax public transit benefits.

Each initiative was independently overseen until the Chief Operating Officer and Chief Security Officer co-identified a large gap between growth projections and available supply of parking spaces. They initiated a cross-functional work group to evaluate ways to reduce demand. Restructuring the organization's transportation program was a joint effort between protective services, the office for a healthy environment, the design and construction team, and the real estate team.

The current program consists of three major components:

- Providing commuting alternatives with the goal of increasing the value and the benefit of Cleveland Clinic's public transit program so it would be more attractive for employees to participate. Examples of such programs included auditing and installing new bike racks, hosting transportation fairs promoting public transit options, and subsidizing public transit through a pre-tax public transit benefits program.
- Creating a sophisticated infrastructure by updating the technology used in garages, leveraging parking-related programs, and building greener facilities. Examples of such initiatives included automatic vehicle identification (AVI) technology, pay-on-foot technology, creating flexible work arrangements to eliminate peak demand days, installing flexibility in parking rates to encourage part-time alternative commuting, and installing permeable pavers, bioswales and rain gardens to reduce the burden on stormwater discharge.
- Addressing fleet management issues to increase overall fleet efficiency. Examples of such efforts included developing purchasing standards

encouraging the use of fuel-efficient or advanced technology vehicles, and developing anti-idling policies.

The metrics

Cleveland Clinic measures success across these three areas in a variety of ways, including:

- overall fleet efficiency
- pounds of CO_2 emissions avoided due to wait and idle time reduced
- wait time coming out of buildings
- results of commuter surveys
- quantity of people enrolled in carpool program and public transit program
- audits of bike racks to understand which are under- and over-utilized.

The lessons learned

- Identifying an executive champion—such as the head of the transportation services team—is a crucial factor in achieving significant gains in overall fleet efficiency. Additional leadership involvement and commitment will help drive momentum and create visibility.
- In many places without a sophisticated public transit infrastructure, shifting away from the "driving culture" is a tough sell. Communicating with people in a way that makes sense to them and providing incentives that are appealing to them are great ways to get around this issue. Communicate the *why* and *how* of using public transit, and then make it as easy as possible to participate by walking employees through the process step-by-step.
- It is difficult to cascade the message within the organization so that it gets internalized with all the other noise. It is essential to find inventive ways to convey the message. Messaging about the health impacts of transportation in a way that is tied to your organizational mission is a particularly good way to make this topic resonate with employees.

About the organization

Cleveland Clinic is a nonprofit multispecialty academic medical center that integrates clinical and hospital care with research and education. It consists of nine regional hospitals, sixteen family health centers and twenty-six institutes for specialized care.

Sources

http://my.clevelandclinic.org/about-cleveland-clinic/default.aspx
http://my.clevelandclinic.org/Documents/About/facts-figures-2010.pdf
Interview, Chris Parkinson, Project Manager at Cleveland Clinic, Office for a
    Healthy Environment

Leadership imperative

Sustainability was first introduced in this book by highlighting the triple bottom line. Every sustainability principle and most organizational priorities have a social, environmental and fiscal component. While transportation impacts employee engagement. Additionally it also connects directly with supply chain management, an existing priority of most healthcare organizations. Supply chain management is another area that points out the need to make explicit the invisible character of sustainability for those who consume supplies. Leaders tend to pay less attention to the transportation of materials, in part because the sustainability dimension is invisible to patients and employees. Today, buses powered by natural gas often feature signage displayed prominently on the vehicles to make the environmental benefits visible to passengers and people passing by. The same is true of hybrid vehicles that feature a prominently placed hybrid brand decal. Healthcare leaders can imitate these successful practices for supplies and equipment, thereby making otherwise invisible sustainability practices visible to stakeholders. The key is to not only to make sustainable transportation processes visible, but to also connect with employees so that they are engaged in the organization's shared values.

FRED: Like I said before, the more visible the sustainability benefit, the better. For instance, you know that free-range coffee we have in the cafeteria? The point is that it has the sticker to indicate that the coffee is ethically sourced
HR: Free-trade coffee.
FRED: Right. Free-trade. Give me some slack.

Leadership dialogue

1　Sustainability policies and practices within healthcare organizations are often compared with sustainability policies and practices of other industries. What metrics should healthcare organizations use to benchmark sustainability progress?
2　Employee engagement is driven by a number of factors, including organizational culture and leadership expectations. Imagine these two

elements are not aligned as the leader implements a sustainability-oriented transportation policy. What is the impact on employee engagement?

3 Who should influence sustainability-oriented transportation policies? The Board of Trustees? Management? The community? Elected officials? Employees? Why?

4 Are affinity groups (such as environmental interest groups) useful to engage employees in transportation and general sustainability issues? What are the pros and cons of encouraging affinity group development?

5 Why might a board be concerned about leaders becoming involved in community policy issues regarding the relationship of transportation and health? What are some possible implications for the hospital?

Syllabus integration

Overview

Students will assess and analyze issues related to sustainable transportation programs. The class will watch sustainable transportation video footage and will debate the ethics of sustainable transportation programs.

Objectives

1 Describe the environmental significance of transportation management.
2 Identify opportunities to efficiently manage transportation resources.
3 Explain why public/private partnerships are important to achieve sustainable transportation.
4 Assess why and how the community benefits from transportation management.

Topics

1 Factors that influence transportation operations.
2 Risk categories of transportation management.
3 Practical application promoting transportation management.
4 Factors that influence the adaptability of sustainable transportation programs.

Homework

Practice Greenhealth (2009) 'Greening operations series: worker commuting options and incentives,' webinar December 18. www.practicegreenhealth.org

Additional resources

NICE (2008) 'Guidance on the promotion and creation of physical environments that support increased levels of physical activity,' London: National Institute for Health and Clinical Excellence. http://guidance.nice.org.uk/PH8

Ross, A. (2010) 'Planning, transport, and health inequalities – a recent history and future progress,' London: Local Government Association. www.idea.gov.uk/idk/core/page.do?pageId=23454074

US Department of Transportation (2010) 'Transportation is a public health issue; DOT doing its part to keep kids moving,' *Fast Lane* July 16. http://fastlane.dot.gov/2010/07/dot-doing-its-part-to-keep-kids-moving.html

6 Good-bye fried chicken, hello healthy, sustainable food

Patient satisfaction + sustainable foods

Figure 6.1 A prescription for health

Executive summary

Promoting community health starts with promoting individual health.[142] One of the most rewarding health promotion tactics a hospital can practice is serving healthful, sustainable food to its patients, visitors and caregivers. Research indicates that nutrition is intrinsically linked to health; nutritious foods support healing and prevent disease.[143] The environmental and financial impacts of using sustainable foods are also worth noting. Locally sourced, fresh produce is frequently the healthiest choice of food on the market, and requires less energy consumption for transportation compared with foods shipped from distant locations.[144] This chapter guides healthcare leadership through the transition from the existing food paradigm to one that is focused on "healthy" foods in healthcare. Healthy food in healthcare is based on a framework of purchasing local, seasonal foods harvested in a sustainable manner with verified sourcing. Good-bye fried chicken, hello healthy, sustainable food.

A told story

Fred, the Memorial Hospital CEO, receives a letter from a dissatisfied patient, Julie Schmooly, about the food she and her family were provided with during Julie's hospital stay. The care was great, according to Julie, but the food was so bad, Julie isn't sure she'll return to Memorial Hospital, should the need arise. Poor food quality detrimentally impacted Julie's patient experience and perceived quality of care. Reflecting on Julie's letter and his own opinions about hospital food, Fred approaches Liam Ludwig, Memorial's Director of Food Services about starting a healthy, sustainable foods program for patients, families and employees. Fred asks Liam to partner with the Sustainability Director, Amalie DuBois, on the project.

April 28, 2012

Dear Mr Fred,

I am the proud mother of a baby girl, Louise, after giving birth at Memorial Hospital. I couldn't possibly ask for a better support system. My parents and my husband's parents came to the hospital, along with some of my closest friends and cousins. The nurses were also a wonderful support team. They were attentive to my needs and expressed sincere concern for my well-being; I felt as though I was their only patient, knowing full well that couldn't possibly be true. Dr Gandhi prepared me well and I felt the delivery went as smoothly as it could have.

The food served at Memorial Hospital, however, was just awful, both for me and for my family. If you can't put together a healthy plate of food, what makes me think you can put together a healthy person? I stayed overnight at the hospital, but barely made it on the canned, chemically-laden, fatty, frozen foods that came my way. I actually felt bad about having my guests visit the hospital because there wasn't any place to get healthy, fresh meals. My husband ended up going to the nearby McDonald's to get me food, and that's really not what I had in mind for kicking off my post pregnancy health diet. Have you sampled the food you serve to patients and families?

Mr Fred, I request that you look into alternative food options for patients and families alike, food that is healthy and fresh and helps prepare patients to return to daily living and engage in healthy habits.

Sincerely,

Julie Schmooly
Memorial Hospital Patient

An insightful conversation

FRED: Liam, I received a negative letter from one of our patients. The patient wrote that her clinical care was excellent, but the food we served her and her family did little to aid her healing process. We know that eating fresh foods and vegetables is one of the keys to staying well and regaining one's health, so maybe we ought to examine our food selection.[145]

LIAM LUDWIG: *(Director, Food Services)* The double cheeseburger and fries combo is on sale today in the cafeteria.

FRED: Are you serious?

LIAM LUDWIG: Yes, I am serious.

FRED: Wow, that's not good, especially since we just launched our "Fight Obesity" campaign. What do you suggest we do about that?

LIAM LUDWIG: Well, I think the hospital has a role in promoting healthy food options. We should be a model of health for our community and our patients. It's just that the cheeseburger sells.

FRED: I understand that. But if we've got patients with congestive heart failure and they're in the hospital for the sixth time, it's probably not a good idea to serve the triple whooper with a week's supply of fat and salt. That'll just make their recovery even harder.

LIAM LUDWIG: Point taken.

Leading the way

The public generally believes that most features of hospitals are the result of intentional decisions by leadership.[146] This is not a happy fact when considering that patients, visitors and employees wonder what people in leadership are thinking when they see the hospital providing onion rings, fried chicken, and one slice of pizza drowned in four servings of cheese.

One of the most useful functions sustainability-oriented leaders can provide is to focus on telling the story about sustainability efforts for which there is no debate. Evidence-based practices that positively impact health and the environment should be visibly leveraged with regard to food choices.

The changing healthcare paradigm is about the individuals taking more responsibility for managing themselves in every dimension of health. Incentives are increasingly offered for employees to improve their diets and enroll in exercise regimens, and employee health benefits are increasingly discounted for not smoking.[147]

New nonsmoking hiring policy at Cleveland Clinic

To take further steps in preserving and improving the health of all its employees and patients, Clinic has recently implemented a nonsmoking hiring policy requiring all job applicants and individuals receiving appointments to take a cotinine test during their pre-placement physical exam. This is a pre-employment test only. The cotinine test will detect the presence of nicotine in all forms of tobacco. Beginning September 1, 2007, appointments that have been offered to prospective residents and fellows who test positive will be rescinded. Individuals who test positive will receive a referral to a tobacco cessation program paid for by Cleveland Clinic. Those individuals testing positive who test negative after 90 days may be reconsidered for appointment at the discretion of the program director should the residency position remain vacant.

(See: http://my.clevelandclinic.org/Documents/Urology/Non-Smoking_Hir
ing_Statement.pdf)

When employees adopt healthy habits, they achieve reduced health insurance premiums.[148] According to Dr Dean Ornish, President and Founder of the Preventative Medicine Research Institute, "Many people tend to think of breakthroughs in medicine as new drugs, lasers, or high-tech surgical procedures. They often have a hard time believing that the simple choices that we make in our lifestyles—what we eat... can be as powerful as drugs and surgery, but they often are. Sometimes even better."[149] Wellness and patient health are inherently tied to sustainability.

When behaviors are presented as contributors to a desirable vision, many individuals will embrace the desired new behaviors, even if they have some emotional discomfort associated with behavior change.

Fried chicken tastes great to many people. But a vision of community and health speaks about giving people healthy food options and supporting local agriculture. It is about promoting a healthy childhood, even if the child prefers sugary drinks. Sustainable foods are about preventing cavities and chronic illness in children. There is one inexplicable question for most leaders: why would you promote a smoke free environment, or ensure everyone gets a flu shot, and then offer unhealthy foods? Effective leaders pay attention to casting the vision of health promotion and tie it to the organization's mission of health. Effective leaders also articulate values, vision and the rationale for change.[150] It is all about making the vision visible and explaining the rationale for the leadership actions taken.

It is easy to tell key constituents that eating fresh and local is part of the healthcare leader's mission to achieve a healthy community. The good news is most employees and patients already believe strongly in the organization's vision and values. That shared vision is what most employees believe is worth some inconvenience and limited restriction in their choices. They might be willing to pay a little bit more for healthy, fresh, local foods. For instance, Whole Foods Market raised its fiscal 2012 outlook after reporting profits of $118.3 million, or 65 cents a share, up 33% from earnings in the same period last year (see http://articles.marketwatch.com/2012-02-08/markets/31040775_1_sales-share-grocer). The truth is that leadership and telling the "*why*" of the vision is important for getting support from stakeholders affected by such changes.

How did we get to where we are?

Historically, food was produced locally. Food was grown at home or in the immediate vicinity, resulting in communities that understood the production process and where food came from. In the early 1900s, much of America was a rural landscape with food produced and consumed locally.[151] Today, people are generally less connected with their food because food production is often managed by large, global businesses or cooperatives. In fact, two companies are responsible for 50 per cent of exported grain; three companies are responsible for 80 per cent of the meat slaughtered; and four companies control 90 per cent of the cold cereal production.[152] Being removed from the process has greatly reduced the individual consumer/purchaser's awareness of the positive health impacts of food choices, as well as the type and impact of food production methods.[153]

Healthy food tends to be more sustainable fiscally, socially and environmentally.[154] And healthy foods have a positive impact on human health. Research shows that, compared with the people who consume the least fiber, people who consume the most fiber have 40–50 per cent reduced risk of colorectal cancer. Similarly, those who consume the most vegetables have a 52 per cent lower risk of colon cancer.[155] From environmental and fiscal perspectives, food that's purchased locally generally costs less to transport than food purchased from great distances.[156] Local food retains its nutrients better because it's traveling a relatively short distance over a relatively short time period, and can be picked at a time when it is fully matured.[157] In other words, purchasing local foods is the socially responsible, environmentally friendly and healthy thing to do.

Lack of understanding of what makes food healthy and sustainable is a major issue, as evidenced by staggering obesity rates. The Centers for Disease Control and Prevention (CDC) estimate that 35.7 per cent of America's population are obese.[158] The cost of treating obesity-related diseases is anticipated to reach $550 billion by 2030.[159] Many healthcare organizations have been slow to recognize the clear connection between their mission of health and providing healthful, sustainable meals. The growing global population and accompanying strains on our environmental resources make a case for highlighting the connection between responsible production and purchasing of healthful local food and health.[160] From a fiscal perspective, "Americans spend 9–14 per cent of their disposal income on food, as compared to about 30 per cent in 1950." Based on these statistics, it is natural to wonder whether perhaps the quality of the food purchased helps explain the lower food costs. Researchers and health professionals argue that lower costs do not compensate for the costs of negative downstream health impacts, or the downstream costs of production methods that cause environmental degradation.[161] [162]

Sustainable food is a leadership issue because the average person is not thinking about food as a direct health, environmental or financial issue. Healthy food has a vital place in the realm of individual well-being and is also a central feature of a sustainable model of societal health.

Understanding local versus sustainable

There is sustainable, and then there is local. Local food is often defined as being sourced within a 100–400 mile radius.[163] On the average American food plate, food comes from about 1600 miles away.[164] That is why the concept "buy fresh, buy local" is a powerful two-for-one deal in terms of impact[165]—the "buy local" is about supporting our local economy in ways that promote minimal environmental degradation. And the "buy fresh" is about fresh foods—it is the alternative to food with lots of sodium often found in canned vegetables, or packaged with preservatives or sugar. Dishes with plants and fruits are most sustainable because they reduce environmental damage and have positive public health impact.

Why healthy, sustainable foods matter to healthcare

Hospitals were not traditionally paid for keeping people healthy.[166] That is why most hospitals and most health professionals are paid to treat sick people. But with the new incentives provided by many insurers to penalize hospitals and doctors for unnecessary readmissions, times are changing and so, too, are attitudes. Hospitals need to feed patients healthy, sustainable foods so they do not return to the hospital. Part of that new responsibility includes teaching patients not to go across the street to a fast food restaurant for high-fat, high-calorie food when they leave the hospital. It would often be outside most health providers' individual economic interests to attempt to promote healthful behaviors. The old cliché that "care follows the dollar" is true in many circumstances.

Most hospital leaders have come to understand that they are trapped in a model that will eventually collapse precisely because it focuses too much on sickness instead of health. All that fried chicken is like fins on a 1957 Chrysler. That was the model feature that made perfect sense at the time. Today, dealers find that fins have extra weight and, with mileage going down and the high cost of gasoline, fins are a problem. Similarly fried food is making people sick and healthcare will increasingly be paid to keep people healthy.

A changing paradigm

"In 2010, almost $20 billion was spent on statin drugs in the United States. The potential cost savings of reducing the need for statin drugs by changing diet and life style is of great interest."[167] Indeed, a shift in attitude in the public is underway. Healthcare is transitioning to a new paradigm in which the goal is to focus on the health and well-being, preventing people from needing to enter the hospital until absolutely necessary.[168]

The new mantra recites healthcare's obligation to have a positive impact on individual health. There is some disagreement in the policy debate about the connection between sustainability and health promotion, but the problem is that everything from housing to clothing to education to public safety impacts health.[169] This chapter helps focus the scope of health on food, a key ingredient of individual, family and community well-being. What is the role of leadership in helping patients, families and health professionals understand the critical role that sustainable, healthy food has in optimizing the individual's health status and quality of life?

To start, leaders must encourage individuals and the healthcare system at large to think differently about food. Healthy food is part of our mission and our responsibility to model the sustainability and healthful character of the food served.

A leadership dilemma, challenge or opportunity?

Healthcare administrators at best practice organizations are influencing food vendors to make different selections when it comes to food services. Best practice organizations such as Kaiser Permanente, Cleveland Clinic and Vanguard Health Systems host farmers' markets and engage physicians in promoting healthy, local food habits for their patients. They're eliminating sugary drinks and serving healthy foods in the cafeteria, among other food strategies.

Kaiser's and Vanguard's sustainable food practices deserve praise. But what about the rest of the healthcare industry? Many organizations are advocating for a balanced menu to be implemented right away, which means increasing the average amount of fruit and vegetables on the menu of healthcare organizations.[170] This is just one example of a small but meaningful step that healthcare leaders can take to embrace sustainable foods and healthful living.

Healthy food, healthy economics

> "One quarter of what you eat keeps you alive. The other three quarters keeps your doctor alive."—Egyptian saying

One dilemma in leadership is the challenge of balancing customers' desires with the vision and mission of the organization. The vision of a healthy, sustainable community and happy, satisfied individuals sometimes conflicts with the habits and perceptions that both the community and patients embrace. For instance, some hospitals pride themselves on offering whichever foods patients request. The problem with that approach is that when hospitals ask patients, "Would you rather have the tofu patty with steamed broccoli or a double order of fried chicken with a side of buttered potatoes?" well, you know what people pick. That is why so many patients end up in the hospital in the first place, with a variety of illnesses linked to obesity.[171]

At face value, the optin is the higher purpose—health and well-being, or the short-term pragmatic gain a happy fried chicken customer. If sustainability and health are two of healthcare's higher purposes, then leaders have to make these priorities visible and explicit. Leaders make priorities clear and then align the leadership around them by communicating the priorities to everyone in the organization. Leaders who succeed will be clear about the role that healthy, sustainable foods play in keeping employees healthy and helping patients optimize their health and the health of their families.

Dear Julie,

Thank you for bringing to our attention the difficulties you encountered during your visit with Memorial Hospital. As always, our team strives to provide the highest quality care to our patients and we truly appreciate your feedback. We view your concern as an opportunity to improve the services we provide.

Since receiving your feedback, I met with Memorial Hospital's leader of Food Services to discuss why and how to integrate sustainable foods for patients, employees and visitors alike. Memorial Hospital now has a plan to ensure that food is part of how we provide excellent care for future patients.

Should you be in the area again soon, we'd be delighted if you'd come visit our new onsite farmers' market that supports local agriculture while promoting healthy, fresh eating habits or take some of our new cooking classes focused on healthy sustainable foods. We're also in the process of revamping our cafeteria dining options to incorporate and incentivize employees and visitors to consume more healthful foods. Patients, similarly, will have access to foods that optimize health and well-being.

Again, we are truly sorry that you were not completely satisfied with your visit to Memorial Hospital and we hope that you will continue to use our facility for your family's future healthcare needs. It is through feedback like yours that improvements are made throughout Memorial Hospital.

Sincerely,

Fred
Chief Executive Officer
Memorial Hospital

Practical application: eliminating sugar-sweetened beverages in healthcare

The imperative

- Foster a culture of health and wellness within healthcare organizations.
- Fulfill organizational mission related to improving the health of patients, employees and communities.
- Reduce rates of obesity and chronic illness as well as their associated healthcare costs.
- Increase public and community goodwill towards the organization.
- Capture financial incentives of healthier foods programs, including national grant opportunities.
- Create and capture opportunities for publicity.

The initiative

Healthcare organizations across the United States are working with government and non governmental agency (NGO) partners to develop hospital food service programs that promote health and wellness. A major focus of these efforts has been on the reduction and/or elimination of sugar-sweetened beverages (SSBs) within healthcare facilities, since this type of beverage has been shown to be detrimental to public health.

Several industry-leading healthcare organizations are acting on this mission, each at a different point along the path to complete elimination of SSBs within their walls. They are targeting all beverages to which a caloric sweetener—including sugar, high-fructose corn syrup, cane sugar, glucose, sucrose, honey and brown sugar, among others– is added. Beverages on the target list include sodas, sweetened tea and coffee drinks, sports drinks, energy drinks and fruit juices.

Programs to eliminate SSBs often consist of a phase-out schedule, which generally includes the following steps:

1 create a project task force with representatives from multiple departments, including food services, patient care, leadership, etc.
2 conduct a beverage audit to identify availability and consumption levels of both SSBs and public drinking water within each facility
3 develop a healthy beverage program outline with input from the project task force (the outline should identify specific action item such as removing SSBs from vending machines, adjusting pricing structures to incentivize healthier beverages, increasing visibility of non-SSBs, etc.), create a timeline for achieving the goals, and establish accountability for outcomes

4   adopt a healthy beverage policy that includes purchasing specifications for future contracts

Initiatives aiming to eliminate SSBs from the healthcare setting are often part of an organization's larger program promoting healthy food and beverage consumption habits. Additional components of such programs may include efforts such as:

- eliminating fried foods,
- expanding salad bar offerings,
- replacing unhealthy options with healthier choices in vending machines and cafeterias,
- developing a pricing structure that makes healthy choices more financially attractive, and increasing labeling and education efforts in locations where food is sold.

The metrics

Measuring progress towards achieving elimination of sugar-sweetened beverages can be achieved by tracking:

- total sales of SSBs in cafeterias, vending machines, catered events, etc.
- total availability of SSBs in cafeterias, vending machines, catered events, etc.
- placement of SSBs versus non-SSBs in most visible retail locations
- number of public water sources (with or without filters)
- results of food service surveys regarding attitudes, knowledge and opinions of SSBs.

The lessons learned

- Do not be alarmed by initial drops in sales—several organizations that have implemented a complete ban on SSBs saw drops in sales after initiating the ban, but later recouped in full any initial losses experienced.
- Increasing public access to free water—and ensuring that water is appealing to consumers—is a crucial component of shifting beverage consumption habits. Try adding filters to existing water machines, installing additional filtered water machines, creating signage and educational materials, providing reusable water containers, or financially incentivizing the consumption of water over SSBs.
- Several steps can be taken to make the consumption of healthier beverages a no-brainer for consumers, including making healthy beverages cheaper than SSBs, adjusting the amount and location of

shelf space given to SSBs, highlighting healthier beverage options, and creating educational materials highlighting the health and environmental impacts of high consumption of SSBs.

- Facilitate implementation at the procurement end by establishing a general contract with beverage vendors. Such contracts will not specify a percentage of SSBs sold, so the facility is able to select which beverages it wishes to offer.
- Before taking any action, it is crucial to gain buy-in from hospital administration and clinical advocates. This level of backing creates an environment of social support and will help head off any potential pushback from consumers.
- Education and communication are critical when implementing initiatives that require consumers to change their behavior patterns. Ensure staff and other consumers have adequate time and mechanisms to provide feedback before rolling out the program. Creating messaging that highlights the health impacts of the initiative will also help to facilitate buy-in.

About the organization

Healthcare organizations such as Vanguard Health Systems, Cleveland Clinic and Fairview Hospital are leading the way nationwide in the shift towards healthier beverages in healthcare. They are supported by initiatives such as Health Care Without Harm's Healthy Beverage Project and the CDC's Rethink Your Drink campaign, among other projects.

Sources

http://articles.chicagotribune.com/2012-04-24/business/
    ct-biz-0425-hospital-sugar-ban-20120424_1_sugar-sweetened-beverages-
    drinks-hospital-group/2
http://chicagohispanichealthcoalition.org/wordpress/?p=268
www.noharm.org/lib/downloads/food/Hydrate_For_Health.pdf
www.noharm.org/lib/downloads/food/Fairview_Hospital_Beverage_Best_
    Practices.pdf

Leadership imperative

One goal of the inpatient care team is to prepare a patient and their accompanying family to resume their lives and maintain health once they return home. In the hospital, patients are surrounded by nutritionists, nurses, pharmacists and therapists—it is like football training camp where there are many expert coaches surrounding the players before they actually play the game. In the game, there is no coach on the field, there's no weightlifting guru, there's no nutritionist. Likewise, when an inpatient, it is training camp, it is practice—the hospital tries to build a model that bridges between the patient and independent community citizen. At home is real life. The way to keep score is the quality of health.

When a patient and family are in the hospital, they have the opportunity to be explicitly educated or "coached" in terms of what to eat, how to prepare healthy food and how to select foods as part of building their health. The foods hospitals serve patients, the ways hospitals educate families about healthy, sustainable food habits, the tools that hospitals give patients and families about healthy eating—when and how much— are all about optimizing individual and community health. The incentives to keep people healthy have been coming for a long time. Now the incentive is changing: good-bye fried chicken, hello sustainable foods.

Leadership dialogue

1　What strategies can healthcare leaders use to educate employees and caregivers on the role a healthful diet plays in preventing disease and speeding recovery?
2　Lack of knowledge about the importance of sustainable food in both patient and employee settings can lead to resistance when introducing healthier, more sustainable alternatives. What can leaders do to overcome such resistance?
3　One of the most difficult cultural elements to change is persuading patients to take accountability of their health and food choices. How should leaders support physicians in their efforts to encourage patients' healthful, sustainable food choices?
4　Community leaders increasingly encourage leaders in hospitals to "walk the sustainability talk." Why should—or should not—hospitals continue to offer sodas and sodium-rich snacks in their visitor vending areas?
5　A patient's time spent in the hospital is time spent preparing for "real life" after discharge. How should leaders encourage employees and physicians to empower patients to select, prepare and expect healthy food choices after they return home?

Syllabus integration

Overview

Students will assess and analyze environmental issues related to local, nutritious food procurement in the healthcare setting.

Review case studies that demonstrate how the current healthcare food supply and distribution system can be modified to comply with sustainability aims.

Objectives

1 Identify factors that pose a risk to the operations of daily sustainable food procurement.
   (a) Food safety objectives
2 Explore incentive programs structured to advance sustainable food objectives, including local procurement and healthy eating habits.
   (a) Menu of change

Topics

1 Food sourcing
   (a) Farmers' markets and nutrition
   (b) Carbon footprint
   (c) Green chemistry
2 Case studies
   (a) Pitt County Memorial Hospital
   (b) Children's Hospital and Regional Medical Center, Seattle

Homework

Health Care Without Harm (2008) *Menu of Change: Healthy Food in Healthcare, A 2008 Survey of Healthy Food in Healthcare Pledge Hospitals*. Health Care Without Harm.
Texas Department of State Health Services (n.d.) *Farm to Work Toolkit Resources*. www.dshs.state.tx.us/obesity/pdf/F2W_toolkit_resources.pdf
Submit a one-page proposal to the Board of Directors outlining a proposal for sustainable food procurement. Record in your career journal.

Additional resources

Practice Greenhealth (2006) 'Healthy food in hospitals,' webinar October 6. www.practicegreenhealth.org
Practice Greenhealth (2009) 'Greening operations series: food services waste prevention and composting,' webinar January 16. www.practicegreenhealth. org
http://www.nems-v.com/NEMS-VTools.html
http://www.cdc.gov/nccdphp/dnpao/hwi/programdesign/wellness_committees. htm
http://healthierhospitals.org/hhi-challenges/healthier-food
http://www.ncpreventionpartners.org/dnn/

7 Through the looking-glass

Cost + energy management

Figure 7.1 Hospital energy options

Executive summary

Healthcare ranks second among industry sectors in energy consumption.[172] Hospitals examining ways to manage costs will find that energy projects provide new opportunities. This chapter highlights why and how hospitals seek to reduce operating costs through energy efficiency and energy reduction while maintaining high quality of care in existing clinical programs.

Storyline

The Chief Medical Officer, Dr Hedge, and the Director of Facilities, Sandy Smith, are waiting in the cafeteria line. Dr Hedge turns to Sandy Smith and initiates a conversation.

DR HEDGE: I can't believe it. We just received our monthly CMS [Centers for Medicare and Medicaid Services] quality measures report, and we're below the midpoint again. Every time this happens, we get calls from the health reporters asking why clinical quality is suffering.

SANDY SMITH: You think that's a problem! We just got a letter from the electric company letting us know that we're one of the largest energy users in the entire state. Just wait until our elected officials get a load of that information and decide to do something with it!

DR HEDGE: Well, Sandy... That actually makes a lot of sense. After all, we do so many CT scans, and we do a lot of MRIs too. The truth is that we could probably do physical therapy or take other measures that are less resource-intensive instead of doing all those tests. Let's face it, the tests cost a ton of money and use an immense amount of energy.

SANDY SMITH: Well, Dr Hedge, the last time I looked, your CT scans were my number one energy consumer during the 9–5 shift. (*Phone makes a "ping" noise, indicating that a new email message has been received. Sandy Smith checks his phone and sighs.*) Memorial Hospital just got listed in the lowest category in the governor's energy efficiency list. We're in trouble now.

Why leaders do what we do

When you started as a healthcare leader, no-one asked you to think through sustainability practices as part of your leadership responsibilities. So let us pause and ask you now, why do you do what you do? Why do you have all of the lights on in your office, especially in the parts of the office that you are not in most of the time, like the kitchen or the print room? Why do you leave the lights on when you are gone for half the day? Why is the computer on when you are absent for extended periods? While we are at it, why do not we ever empty the recycling container? Most of our behavior is not intentional; we just do what we have always done, mostly because we are creatures of habit.[173] Effective leaders are intentional about their personal behavior as a strategy to align leadership teams and to communicate desirable change. Modeling is one way of making desired behaviors visible and instigating change.

Who turned off the lights?

In a typical healthcare facility in the U.S., lighting represents 42 percent of electricity consumption, not including its impact on cooling loads. Posting 'Please turn the lights off when not needed' stickers above light switches will remind both staff and visitors to do so

(see www.touchstoneenergy.com/efficiency/bea/Documents/Hospitals.pdf).

Modeling desirable behavior is the role of the leader

DR HEDGE: I think the vast majority of behavior is imitative. It's not rational, thought-driven behavior. Why do you wash your hands instead of using hand sanitizer? Or why do you use hand sanitizer instead of washing your hands? We don't typically have a good answer to those questions.

I always tell people that 90 per cent of personal development will come from simply emulating successful people. It won't be an intellectual exercise. If you're hanging out with people who eat fried foods, what do you think you're likely to do? The easiest thing to do is eat what everyone else is having, so I guess I'll have fries and pizza. That's not the way we like to think about ourselves, though. We like to think we leaders are so independent and intentional. But I don't care how smart or how driven you are, imitating the behavior of others is the way most people act. So, in truth, picking who you are with and who you work for and respond to is your practical destiny.

SANDY SMITH: So how can leaders use that thought process to effect change? Is there a way that leaders can leverage the sustainability mindset to drive change? Perhaps by modeling sustainable behaviors?

DR HEDGE: That makes sense to me.

SANDY SMITH: If turning off your light became habitual and everybody slowly started to witness the change, conserving energy would become the norm. You know, Dr Hedge, you send messages all the time that you may not give much thought to, messages that are purely based on your behaviors, your habits. Those messages could be about sustainability or anything else.

DR HEDGE: You're right, Sandy. I unwittingly send a lot of messages based on my habits. Leaving the lights on is what I tend to feel most comfortable doing. I do it day-in and day-out, and I don't really think about the message I'm sending because I never bother to ask why I leave the lights on in the first place. I suppose I leave the lights on because it's the easiest thing to do and, quite frankly, I never before gave much thought to sustainability as a leadership imperative. There's certainly a positive power associated with being a role model for good.

How do you lead, if you don't know anything?

Leaders often assume the mindset of "I'm transferring some of my superior knowledge to my subordinates or team members I lead. I'm going to determine how we do things around here." But the successful leader eventually realizes that he or she does not know as much as the team members closer to the action. As the leader communicates with her team, she is educated by her team.

DR HEDGE: You're educating me, and I'm learning as you give examples of energy management—I knew nothing about energy management when we started this conversation. And the thing is, I didn't know I didn't know. Well, I kind of knew I didn't know anything about sustainability.

SANDY SMITH: You probably know more thank you think you do. Do you recycle at home? Do you use glasses or Styrofoam cups at your house? Do you leave your home kitchen lights on overnight?

(Fred joins their table with a tray including chips, a candy bar and a cupcake.)

The power of reducing power

According to the US Environmental Protection Agency (US EPA) program:

- Every dollar a nonprofit healthcare organization saves on energy is equivalent to $20 in new revenues for hospitals or $10 for medical offices.
- Some for-profit hospitals, medical offices and nursing homes can boost earnings per share by a material amount by simply reducing energy costs by 5 per cent.[174]
- According to the World Health Organization, in the USA the health sector's use of electricity adds over $600 million per year in direct health costs and over $5 billion in indirect costs.[175]

What is Energy Star?

Energy Star is a joint program of the US EPA and the US Department of Energy. The joint program helps Americans save money and protect the environment through energy-efficient products and practices. In 2010, Energy Star helped Americans save about $18 billion on utility bills in an effort to avoid greenhouse gas emissions.[176]

According to the Department of Energy, reducing the energy use of healthcare facilities offers several benefits[177]:

- improved profitability
- reduced impact of volatile energy costs
- lower operations and maintenance costs
- improved environmental performance

- reduced carbon footprint
- healthier healing and work environment
- healthier communities.

Putting it in perspective

FRED: It's the notion that I have the power to model sustainable practices because a bunch of people work for me, and they want to mimic the behaviors that I model. That's just the way it works, right? If I don't pause for that period of purposeful introspection before I act, I may well be an unintentional negative influence on the people I lead.

SANDY SMITH: I guess most of the time it's negative messages that are sent by leaving the lights on. If I walk around here, I assume we're not concerned about energy costs at Memorial Hospital because we keep the lights on overnight, and we leave the lights on in rooms where people aren't even present. We don't have any signs posted asking people to shut the lights off when they exit the kitchen or the restroom. So I'm making a negative assumption, based on the facts I'm presented with.

DR HEDGE: I see.

SANDY SMITH: You know, Fred, when I got my computer set up, I had my reusable water bottle on my desk—the one you call "that canteen thing." And the IT specialist came to help me set up my work station. I had two computers at my desk—one that was a desktop monitor and the other was a laptop. I told the IT specialist that I only needed the laptop and he could take away the monitor. And the IT specialist replied, "Oh, I get it, you're conserving energy." And I said, "Yes, well, I guess that's true." That wasn't my intention, to be completely honest. I just didn't want all that electronic clutter on my desk. So, you know, it was a completely unintentional, positive message that I gave the IT specialist because when she looked and saw the reusable water bottle on my desk, she assumed all of my behaviors embodied a sustainable underpinning.

DR HEDGE: In your case, you sent a positive message. That's not often the case *chuckling*.

SANDY SMITH: Right. I think unintentional positive messages are sent a lot less frequently than the negative messages that get articulated. Your position in the organization influences how much your habits are studied. That's why it's so important for leaders to practice sustainability habits—because when the leader demonstrates sustainable behavior, others will follow.

Did you know?"

A typical 200,000-square-foot (ft²), 50-bed hospital in the U.S. annually spends $680,000—or roughly $13,611 per bed—on electricity and natural gas.

The average cost of power per ft² for hospitals in North America is approximately $2.84 for electricity and $0.94 for natural gas.

(see www.touchstoneenergy.com/efficiency/bea/Documents/Hospitals.pdf).

Make the link explicit between wasted energy and improved work processes

Operational processes should be designed to produce as little unintended by-product as possible. The more people think about waste as a general concept, the better for process improvement and the better for sustainability. We can waste energy, we can waste physical resources, we can waste intellectual capabilities, and we can waste creativity. Embedding the concept of waste and the processes that result in sustainable operations maximizes leadership in all dimensions—leaders cannot engage in any meaningful area of their work without encountering the principles of sustainability when thought about this way.

Lean thinking, process improvement, sustainability—call it what you will—we are using a variety of words for the same idea. It is the notion that we need to look for efficiencies in a holistic manner while tackling our business goals.

Figure 7.2 Benchmarking energy usage

You can not manage what you can not measure

Success can be hard to define, especially if it is not clear what the parameters to measure progress are. Given the fluctuations and general trend for increased cost for energy usage, energy efficiency offers an untapped potential for savings. The Energy Use Index (EUI) is a commonly used indicator which is the total amount of energy used by a building per square foot on an annual basis.[178] The EUI is a tool for understanding where energy management opportunities exist and for establishing measurable goals based on industry benchmarks.

FRED: We're very early in that process. Sure, we have a Director of Sustainability, a content expert, but our challenge is that we're relatively immature about integrating sustainability into the organization. My goal is for nurses to think about sustainability as part of their daily routine, the same way that the average nurse thinks about clinical quality or safety. Today, the average healthcare employee doesn't know much about sustainability or what it means to work for a sustainable hospital. We need to train our people in Lean thinking and the sustainability mindset to drive waste out of everything we do. We need to integrate sustainability with our key organizational goals like cost reduction.

DR HEDGE: The key for us is that we need to make that explicit link. A lot of people don't make the link at all.

FRED: Once upon a time, no-one gave much energy—no pun intended!— to the ongoing cost of ignoring sustainability leadership. I wonder, what does wasted energy cost anyway?

DR HEDGE: I thought you were going to ask that question. After all, you're going to have to answer it for the Board when we ask them for capital investment funding. Can't say I envy you...

How much does a hippo weigh?

As hospitals reduce their energy impacts and save dollars in the process, the way the story is communicated plays a critical role in the success of continued employee engagement and public relations success. The average stakeholder will not have an understanding of energy usage terminology such as kilowatt hours and carbon tons. Highlighting the success in relation to known parameters—such as number of cars removed from the roadways, or energy usage saved in relation to a number of houses or how many pounds of waste in 'hippos' they have saved—tells a more effective story.

Energize your leadership priorities

The reality is that energy management has not always been on the leadership's radar—if it gets picked up at all.

FRED: Well, energy is definitely on my radar. When I look at things like natural gas or oil, those energy sources have tremendous variability—I bet in the past five years there's been 100 per cent or maybe 200 per cent variation. You know what natural gas costs today? Oil consumption has gone way down in total, but the price has gone way up, and I don't understand why that is. Four years ago, it was about fifty bucks a barrel. Now it's about one hundred-something.

SANDY SMITH: Fair enough, but if you look at the total operating budget of a hospital in terms of energy, it's only a few per cent. Large sums of money, but small percentage. The percentile of the total costs probably hasn't changed very much. So why is energy management important now? Is it important because we're in a different economic state?

FRED: It probably has more to do with the state of our national security. We live in a country that's dependent on foreign energy sources, so politics, wars and natural disasters bring on spikes in the cost of energy.

SANDY SMITH: Yep. And so my point is that we can insulate Memorial Hospital from all that as best we can. We can reduce our dependence on volatile energy input prices and insulate ourselves, to some degree, from the variation in the energy cost structure. If we're curtailing our energy use and cutting our cost structure, we know that, down the road, we'll be in a better spot financially than we would otherwise be. That strategy would make our cash flow more predictable.

FRED: Wouldn't that be nice! We have a general sense of where our reimbursements will be headed over the next few years. With energy, though, we don't have that security because it's so volatile.

(Phone rings. Fred checks to see who's calling on his cell phone and decides not to answer.)

Hospitals are hogs

Today's young professionals were raised with an appreciation of recycling and other sustainable lifestyle choices.[179] As incoming generations enter the workplace with this mindset, sustainability will become increasingly meaningful in healthcare. And yet, in today's healthcare environment, leadership is just beginning to appreciate the benefits of sustainability. Why are healthcare leaders starting to care? That is because most leaders are worried about the economic future of their organization.

Few leaders cared about sustainability or energy efficiency when their revenue increased by four–five per cent year after year during the 1990s. Leaders could apply increased dollars toward energy costs, facility expenses and labor inflation, and still invest three per cent more on other costs of production, especially since many healthcare organizations were experiencing annual volume increases as demand expanded as well. In short, the economic model was stable and favorable for most healthcare providers.

SANDY SMITH: We've hardly scratched the surface of energy management. I don't even think we realize how much opportunity we have if we make it a priority.

FRED: You're right. I think we're headed in the right direction, though.

SANDY SMITH: You know, Fred, we received a letter from the utility company that was going to the state commission. We were named on the list of top energy users. Not so good for us to be on that list.

FRED: Agreed. I certainly care about how Memorial Hospital is perceived by the community. If (lack of) energy management is tarnishing our brand in a material way, then it becomes something we have to pay attention to. I think our challenge is difficult. I understand that much of the energy efficiency of our facility is built into the building when it's designed. So if you build it inefficiently in the first place, you have limited options later on. But I think the scoring mechanism and the reporting concept are interesting and probably useful for drawing more attention to energy efficiency as an issue. Do we have a sustainability section on our website? I thought that might be a good idea.

SANDY SMITH: Yes, yes we do.

FRED: Well, I mean, aimed at our patients and our customers where you…

SANDY SMITH: Yes, we do. We have videos up there for people to see what they can do to help Memorial Hospital be sustainable. And we have links to additional information, in case the public is interested. One of the things I would like to do on a regular basis is share our actual numbers—for instance, our energy savings. I think that doing so will be a good effort in terms of transparency and interdepartmental alignment.

FRED: Well, Sandy, as usual you're way ahead of me.

Opportunity cost

There is a wonderful alignment between cost strategy and sustainability strategy as they pertain to effective energy use. If you, the leader, care only about driving down the cost of energy utilization, you would likely still be concerned about sustainability. Healthcare leaders want high quality at low cost. High waste means low quality and high cost, so healthcare leaders are concerned about all kinds of waste, including wasted energy. From a sustainability point of view, reducing waste is a means to an end; from a cost reduction point of view, sustainability is an end in itself.

Certain outcomes that serve a sustainability purpose are not necessarily going to serve cost, safety and quality outcomes. Such sustainability goals still require resources, whether that means time, attention or funds. What is the rationale for these "sustainability only" goals? The rationale is founded on opportunity cost.

(Dr Hedge and Sandy Smith part ways. Sandy Smith enters into a meeting later in the day where Fred is present. At the end of the meeting, Sandy Smith catches Fred and follows up on the sustainability conversation with Dr Hedge.)

FRED: Hi Sandy. Good to see you.

SANDY SMITH: Nice to see you too. You know, Fred, I've been thinking about our earlier conversation about sustainability. And there's one question that I want to make sure I understand. I've been wondering whether there will come a time when sustainability isn't cost-neutral, as it often is today. If sustainability became a cost center that wasn't saving us money in operational costs on an annual basis, would sustainability be a program that makes sense to maintain?

DR HEDGE: I like this topic of energy management a lot. I can see so many ways that it applies to leadership, now that we've had a few conversations about it.

FRED: There are programs today, here and now, that are not about making money. It's about providing a service to the community that inherently makes the big picture better. For instance, our pediatric services are necessary, but lose money year after year. It's not enough to bankrupt the system, but its central to serving the community's needs.

SANDY SMITH: Some benefits to the community are high-value propositions, even though we lose money. So is sustainability any different from the pediatric programs you describe? Do the social and environmental benefits outweigh the costs to make it a high-value proposition for the community?

FRED: I think that, as a not-for-profit entity, it's clearly our responsibility to invest in those social and environmental components in a fiscally responsible manner. It's a bit more challenging if you're an investor-owned or commercial enterprise. But I think it's a no-brainer for all organizations with a mission of health, and especially one that includes community service.

SANDY SMITH: I think you're on to something.

FRED: You know, Sandy, you manage to instigate change without making anybody mad. I mean, you're very artful at making stuff happen even when most people don't want to go along. Take that as a compliment. You know, leaders get people to do what they want them to do, and be happy about it. You have that leadership skill.

Practical application: energy excellence at New York Presbyterian

The imperative

- Managing long-term risk from rising energy costs.
- Achieving visibility as a leader within the industry.
- Spurring innovation from employees.
- Reducing costs.
- Improving health by reducing air pollution.

The initiative

New York Presbyterian Hospital (NYPH) first introduced its award-winning energy management program in 2003, and has since become an energy leader both inside and outside the healthcare industry.

NYPH started its energy journey by establishing a structure for managing the organization's energy initiatives. These efforts consisted of:

- creating a full-time Energy Programs Manager position dedicated to maximizing the hospital's energy savings
- establishing the Office of Energy Management
- forming an energy team, consisting of representatives from key departments
- adopting an energy policy
- becoming an Energy Star partner.

Once the structure was established, the organization's energy teams focused on identifying and pursuing key energy-saving opportunities. After performing several energy audits, NYPH implemented a variety of changes:

- performed heating, ventilation and air conditioning (HVAC), controls system, lighting and central plant upgrades
- with the help of a grant, built a combined heat and power plant that achieved millions in annual energy cost savings and generated enough electricity to meet between 60 and 100 per cent of electricity demands
- developed policies for identifying and exploring cost-effective purchasing solutions and energy-efficient practices for employees

- purchased a fleet of Energy Star-rated computers
- created engagement tools, such as a hotline number for calling in energy-saving tips and ideas, a reward program for employees who identify opportunities for energy efficiency improvements, a series of events to boost awareness with public and staff, and a communications package for educating and sharing successes with employees.

These changes, along with many other energy conservation initiatives, helped NYPH achieve its status as a national energy leader.

The metrics

Energy performance is most easily benchmarked using tools such as Energy Star's Portfolio Manager, which are designed to track indicators such as:

- quantity, type and cost of energy consumed (total and per square foot)
- quantity, type and financial impacts of renewable energy produced on-site
- site energy intensity
- energy performance over time
- avoided greenhouse gas emissions from green power sources.

The lessons learned

- Forming a dedicated energy team is extremely helpful when working to develop a comprehensive energy management program. Capitalize on the organization's diverse intellectual resources by including experts from departments such as real estate, IT, engineering, facilities development, strategic sourcing and HR to develop the most comprehensive vision possible.
- Bring vendor partners and other industry experts to the table for at least one energy planning session to add a unique perspective to the dialogue—most will be actively interested in helping the organization pursue its energy goals.
- Recognize that grassroots engagement is key to ongoing awareness and long-term success of the energy program. Developing fun, interesting opportunities to get involved is crucial for achieving employee visibility and buy-in.
- Showing commitment from the top goes a long way in adding credibility to and creating hype around energy efficiency initiatives.
- Make the energy mission easy for everyone to understand and agree with, by putting it in terms that are familiar to them—explain how it

helps to achieve existing priorities such as cost containment, increased efficiency and long-term risk management.

- Understanding current and past energy use is how many organizations identify energy performance improvement opportunities and prioritize investments in less efficient facilities. Performance can be gauged by comparing facilities with each other, to peers or to top industry performers.

About the organization

New York Presbyterian Hospital is the nation's largest nonprofit, non-sectarian hospital, encompassing thirty-three buildings and 8.6 million square feet. It is a leading academic medical center affiliated with two of the nation's leading medical colleges: Columbia University College of Physicians and Surgeons, and Weill Cornell Medical College. New York Presbyterian Hospital delivers comprehensive medical services to residents of New York City and its surrounding boroughs. It was the first healthcare system to earn the Energy Star Partner of the Year Award three times: twice for Excellence in Energy Management (2005 and 2006) and a third time in the Sustained Excellence category (2007).

Sources

www.energystar.gov/index.cfm?c=healthcare.bus_healthcare_ny_presb_hospital
https://www.premierinc.com/safety/green-link/green-corner/NYP_
    GreenCorner-07122010.pdf
http://nyp.org/news/hospital/co-gen-plant.html

Leadership imperative

When leadership embraces sustainability, there is a beneficial impact on the health of the community, the environment and the planet. When sustainability was first introduced to healthcare in the 1990s, it was mostly a religious calling. People embraced sustainability because it was the right thing to do. So any discussion about the sustainability program costing money or fighting with economic objectives was dismissed by fervent believers. The idea was that if you are into sustainability for the money, you're probably in it for the wrong reasons.

That mentality has changed. In today's landscape of the triple bottom line, it is encouraged and even expected to save money through sustainability practices that concurrently benefit the social and environmental dimensions of the community health. In fact, anything short of that would not serve the triple bottom line. There is a sophistication to management that did not exist five, ten, twenty years ago. That newfound sophistication helps explain the high level of activity around exploring different service and operational models. For instance, many hospitals are outsourcing operations outside the scope of their core services. They are migrating to a contractual model with pure-play businesses that expertly deliver higher quality, same-or-lower-cost services than what the hospital could otherwise provide.

Leadership dialogue

1 Sustainability is often an area of a leader's "conscious incompetence" when it comes to modeling leadership behaviors that are environmentally friendly. Why should leaders learn about the behaviors related to energy conservation and make a point of practicing such behaviors in private as well as publicly?

2 How should leaders deal with members of the leadership team who don't support the team's efforts to reduce energy consumption and the hospital's carbon footprint, arguing, "energy costs savings are not material enough to bother with"?

3 Measuring tangible indicators of energy consumption is a force for team cohesion when metrics are made visible for all to see. What are example strategies that leaders can use to make energy metrics transparent and visible to both leaders and employees?

4 Sustainability-related solutions in energy management are sometimes "out-of-the-box" options that require transformational change. How can leaders encourage transformational thinking when focusing on team efforts to implement energy-impacting innovations?

5 The triple bottom line consists of fiscal, social and environmental responsibilities. Which bottom line is most often neglected by healthcare leaders in pursuing efforts to change organizational energy practices? Why?

Syllabus integration

Overview

Typical capital budgeting evaluations do not include environmental costs and savings, resulting in decisions that may prematurely dismiss energy management projects, despite potentially significant long-term environmental and financial savings. The capital budgeting evaluations described in this lesson will be applied to a variety of energy management approaches.

Objectives

1   Raise the economic valuation of energy management projects to a level that is worth considering in addition to alternative options.
2   Discuss key components needed to ensure use of an energy management approach and how the approach can be institutionalized.
3   Utilize tools to measure, calculate and assess organizational energy usage.
    (a) Quantify and allocate energy resources across appropriate business functions and activities.

Topics

1   1 Guidelines for energy management
    (a) Energy Star
    (b) Energy Impact Calculator
    (c) Energy savings
2   Senate Energy Bill

Homework

2010 Healthcare Sector Energy Efficiency Indicator. Institute for Building Efficiency, Johnson Controls. www.institutebe.com/Energy-Efficiency-Indicator/2010-Healthcare-Sector-Energy-Efficiency-Indicator.aspx

Practice Greenhealth (2008) 'Operations series: energy use in hospitals,' webinar October 24. www.practicegreenhealth.org

Describe how to employ the Energy Impact Calculator. Record in your career journal.

Additional resources

Practice Greenhealth (2010) 'Greening operations series: purchasing tools and strategies to reduce energy and maintenance costs,' webinar January 15. www.practicegreenhealth.org

GGHC (2007) *A Prescriptive Path to Energy Efficiency Improvements for Hospitals.* Austin, Texas: Green Guide for Health Care. www.gghc.org/documents/Reports/GGHC_PrescriptivePath.pdf

Reed, C.A. (2005) *Increasing Hospital Energy Performance with Energy Star®*, available online: www.energystar.gov/ia/business/healthcare/IncreasingHospitalEnergyPerformance0105.pdf (accessed 10/22/2012).

US Department of Energy (2011) available online: http://apps1.eere.energy.gov/buildings/publications/pdfs/alliances/hea_plugloads.pdf (accessed 10/22/2012).

8 Before a baby's first breath

Safety + chemical management

Figure 8.1 Safer chemicals in healthcare

Executive summary

Healthcare organizations are high-stress, high-stakes environments in which safety is of primary concern to both patients and employees. Building a safety culture is part of building a sustainability culture. There are numerous examples of unsafe healthcare products that contain chemicals known to have negative health impacts. Kaiser Permanente developed a Sustainability Scorecard to vet the safety of such products, and made it freely available to the public.[180] Equally concerning are the chemicals used in healthcare whose interactive effects have yet to be studied. Increased awareness of environmental safety hazards places additional scrutiny on healthcare leaders to assure that healing environments are safe. Beyond direct patient impact, there are safety concerns related to the use and disposal of toxic materials.[181] This chapter helps readers understand when and how to use sustainability as a tool to mitigate safety risks related to potentially dangerous chemicals.

Storyline

Fred reads an article in Modern Healthcare *that he tears out of the magazine. The article features a story about a nursing group that questions adequate protection from chemicals in the workplace. Fred thinks, I need to share this with Kadine (Chief Nursing Executive) and Lori Prince (Vice President of Human Resources). The following day, Fred has an opportunity to do just that. Kadine and Lori read the article and unanimously respond, "We follow all the applicable guidelines and safety protocols." Fred scratches his head, puzzled.*

FRED: But we don't have any downstream or follow-up studies. In other words, we don't have any data to know how our nurses have done *vis a vis* chemical exposure. I understand that these exposures are rare, but they could have a devastating impact if our nurses end up with cancer related to an exposure.[182] This isn't just about meeting regulations. It's a concern that our employees may be exposed to harmful chemical agents. The safety of our people goes beyond regulation.

(Fred, not getting the reaction he's looking for, tells his assistant he'll be "right back" and goes off to visit with Lorenzo, Director of Environmental Services.)

There is nothing more important to patients than safety

LORENZO LOPEZ: (*Director of Environmental Services*) Fred, what made you be concerned enough to tear out that article from *Modern Healthcare* magazine, or even pause to read the article? I know you must get bombarded with items to read.

FRED: I generally scan everything and express concern if I think most people would be concerned about a given topic or issue. My first job was running a big oncology clinic and, at the time, the nurses—nearly all women—had to gown and double-glove to give some of our chemo patients their medicines. And they found later that double-gloving didn't do the job it was supposed to do. So they were exposed to all those toxic substances. This was a few years ago, and now I find myself asking the same question: are we adequately protecting our employees? Here's the deal: safety is really a big issue for me.

Before a baby's first breath

Humans are exposed to hundreds of chemicals every day. Chemicals exist in the foods we consume, in the clothes we wear and in the pillows we sleep on.[183] Does the average person pause to wonder what they are exposed to, and what the long-term impacts of the exposures are? What chemicals are bio-accumulating in humans, and what impacts are passed down from mother to child? The latter question was the subject of a study called *The Body Burden* conducted by the Environmental Work Group. In this study, the core blood of ten minority newborns was studied for the presence of chemicals including bisphenol-A (BPA). BPA has become known for linkages to disorders such as cancer and obesity, and is also considered an endocrine disrupter.[184] In addition to the presence of BPA, 232 chemicals were found in the core blood of these newborns.[185]

'Please don't kill me'

The effective healthcare leader will increasingly be seen as a champion of patient and employee safety. At an elemental level, safety is the most important value to everyone. Freedom from iatrogenic harm is a core priority for patients. The equivalent priority for employees, including nurses and physicians, is personal safety—the notion of a safe and healthful work environment. Only after having a backdrop of patient and employee safety can employees focus on patient care.

Safety of the community: low incidence, high impact

Think about the worst things Memorial Hospital could do. The clinical team could operate on the wrong leg, or the wrong person, or leave a sponge in the body after surgery—no patient or community wants to hear that story. But safety translates beyond individual patients and employees. The community also tends to be upset when red bag waste is improperly disposed to in the regular landfill, because that waste has implications for the entire community. That is the worst fear at some level—in a very real way, there is a collective sense of, "don't poison us." Chemical management entails asking, "What does exposure to chemicals mean to my health, the health of our employees and our community?"

LORENZO LOPEZ: The link between chemicals and disease is becoming increasingly clear because of the increase in cancer and asthma rates.[188] Fred, are you aware of the potential impacts of the chemicals used at Memorial Hospital?

FRED: To be honest, Lorenzo, that's a level of detail that the average executive leaves to other people. Now, if I was directly responsible for employee health, if I'm Kadine, the CNE, if I'm the occupational safety compliance officer with OSHA [the Occupational Safety and

Health Association]… if I'm in your position as the environmental health leader, then the answer would probably be "yes," because it is your business. Your job is built around those concerns.

LORENZO: (*Thinking to himself*) I think employee and patient safety as shared responsibilities of everyone on the hospital team.

Making people sick while making people healthy

Healthcare is often referred to as a calling rather than a job. Pursuing this calling may require risky behaviors at times. It's a simple fact of daily work that healthcare professionals are dealing with drugs and chemicals in treating the illnesses of their patients. The impact of the exposure to these chemicals, such as chemotherapeutic drugs, by caregivers is coming into question.[186] A study produced by Physicians for Social Responsibility investigated the exposure of healthcare workers to chemicals. The results highlighted that, amongst other chemicals of concern, bisphenol A, phthalates, polybrominated diphenyl ethers (PBDEs) and perfluorochemicals (PCFs) were found in all individuals tested.[187]

Think about where you're going, rather than where you are today

(*Fred re-reads the article from* Modern Healthcare *magazine about a nursing group that questions adequate protection from chemicals in the workplace.*)

FRED: (*Talking to himself*) I'm trying to deal with what I think might be coming rather than where we are today. Is chemical management evolving into something that we ought to be more aggressive about tracking? Is the evidence pointing to chemical management a more serious danger to our nurses? Those are the questions I am trying to explore. And the answer I get from our leaders was, "We're complying with all of the current rules and regulations. We're doing everything that the law requires." (*Sigh*) Well that's great, but if we're doing what we're required to do, but are trading on the health of our employees, shouldn't we do more than what the law requires? I want to know why and how we're going to impact our employees in the future, not just today. Once upon a time, people were smoking in the staff lounges. Now we prohibit smoking on the entire campus. Why did we make this a smoke-free campus? We—along with other healthcare organizations—prohibited smoking before any law to prohibit smoking existed, because it was the right thing to do.

LORENZO LOPEZ: Was that the only reason why we prohibited smoking on campus? Today, there's evidence demonstrating that smoking causes cancer and kills people and that second-hand smoking is bad for other people, not just the smoker. Did we prohibit smoking on the campus because of all the mounting evidence that smoking is unsafe and unhealthy? Maybe we should approach chemical management the same way.

FRED: Yes, there was mounting evidence that smoking was harmful to health, but that had nothing to do with the decision to eliminate smoking on campus.

LORENZO LOPEZ: Well then, why did we make that change?

FRED: You know, Lorenzo, the most persuasive argument for eliminating smoking had everything to do with the other healthcare campuses that migrated to a no-smoking policy. That was the most persuasive argument: everyone else is already doing it and various professional organizations recommended it. If we didn't have groups like the American College of Physicians recommending smoke-free campuses, very few organizations would follow through, because few leaders and physicians are going to individually make the decision to change.

That's the same reason why there's a tipping point around sustainability (Gladwell, 2002). Once it gets to a point where organizations across the country start adopting chemical management as a safety imperative, leaders will say, "The other leaders and physicians are doing it, the accrediting bodies recommend it, the nurses are for it, the Joint Commission thinks it's a good idea. We better adopt the new standard." But until the chemical management issue makes its way into professional associations and accreditation standards, culture change is unlikely.

LORENZO LOPEZ: That all makes sense, Fred. But there are people on the front line who are early adopters. For instance, Dr Bea and Dr Cohen came to me the other day asking why we're not managing our chemicals more proactively and what they can do to kick-start the process.

Chemicals of concern in healthcare

Below is a list of eleven chemical types that cause asthma:

- cleaners, disinfectants, sterilants
- natural rubber latex
- pesticides
- volatile organic compounds
- baking flour

- acrylics
- fragrances
- phthalates
- environmental tobacco smoke
- biologic allergens
- drugs.

Sacred trust

Physicians have a "sacred trust"—the notion that they have been given talent and training to care for people at their most vulnerable stages of life. With that sacred trust comes a tremendous power and personal accountability, because patients put their lives in clinical hands. This is where most clinicians define the limit of their personal accountability in terms of accountability to the individual patient. Issues of equity or group fairness are often perceived to be beyond the traditional scope of a clinician's responsibility. This reality explains why focusing on safety as a leadership priority is necessary for the health and well-being of society.

One of the realities of modern healthcare is that there has been, and still is, scientific support for only a fraction of the treatments and practice employed today. Data is what informs evidence based medicine, but there simply is not statistically significant data for every care process. Clinicians take patients' lives into their hands knowing full well that is the reality of the situation. That is why medicine continues to be a wonderful mixture of art and science. It breeds a cautious conservatism that is foundational to medical practice.

The relative lack of iterative processes in medicine explains the relative lack of change in clinical processes used in caring for patients. Some clinicians may not agree with that statement, though many would agree that there is not much room for error in medicine. Physicians would say that they learn from experience and personalize care by making tweaks to the processes they were taught in school. In truth, it is hard to see much change in the fundamental approach to medical practice as compared with fifty years ago.

FRED: I know that, as the leader, I'm responsible at some level for that lack of progress.

LORENZO LOPEZ: I can be slow, but still faster than 90 per cent of the crowd I hang out with. The "cream of the crap," as I like to say.

FRED: I was speaking with a friend of mine from graduate school who is leading a healthcare organization in the Midwest. She told me an amusing story. She was sitting in on a physician meeting. This young physician appealed to his peer group of pediatricians, trying to convince them that toxic chemicals can be a tremendous hazard to children. He said that physicians had a responsibility to ensure that parents prepare their home environments to be toxin-free to the extent possible, prior to taking home a newborn. That could be a new business line, now that I think about it...

Toxic Substance Control Act

The US EPA has been pushing for reform of the Toxic Substance Control Act. Current regulations do not require disclosure of chemicals used in many healthcare products.[189] Additionally, the EPA does not have the authority to establish safety standards related to chemical management.[190]

Professional associations set the default for practice change in medicine.[191] When in doubt, clinicians typically reach out to their professional associations to determine the ethical and/or practical way(s) forward. Otherwise, most clinicians are incentivized to act on individual decision-making authority, driven by doing what is best for the patient, in their judgment.

Let us look at a how the Joint Commission helps determine healthcare culture. For many years, the Joint Commission published an extensive book of requirements. Periodically, the Joint Commission evaluates a given hospital's performance in terms of patient safety. There is a set of prescriptive procedural requirements, and the task is to fit each one of those procedural requirements into operations to create an environment that prioritizes safety and quality. This system promotes a culture of working to standard and not one of continuous improvement. Working to standard does not incorporate the concept of innovation, but rather the simple discipline of faithful repetition.

Leaders ought to prioritize

Engagement—the notion of everyone being connected to the change—is a key driver of culture change. Engagement is the opposite of the traditional command-and-control mentality that defines much of the current healthcare culture. Engagement is about being team-oriented; it is about empowerment for innovation and change; it is about trying new things. Engagement is not only about institutionalizing sustainability practices, but also about how we design healthcare work processes and ask questions. Look at General Electric or Apple, two successful companies known as innovative businesses that deliver exquisite products. The values of teamwork, innovation and empowerment are defining values of both companies.

It is that type of culture that empowers employees and physicians to ask, "What is the best way to keep people safe?" Maybe chemical management is part of the answer. Regardless of where chemical management falls in the leadership priority list, safety as a leadership priority is certainly at or close to the top.

Promoting an iterative learning culture ought to be on the leader's priority list as well. Excellent leaders are not afraid of change and, in fact, aggressively promote change that moves the organization into alignment with its customers' priorities.[192] Leaders empower teams to create a high rate of change, that is accretive to customers. When organizations have physicians in leadership roles, they are often culturally sophisticated enough to lead change more rapidly within physician populations.

In short, the professionalization of leadership drives the best leaders to be the best change agents, whether in respect to toxic chemical management, or clinical process improvement, or patient safety. Upon taking a closer look, leaders do not make changes. Rather, they engage and empower others to be change agents.

FRED: The people in Occupational Health, for instance, know we ought to be worried about it. They know the challenges that are on the horizon. They know the chemicals that are really bad. My job as the leader is to communicate with our Occupational Health professionals and infuse them with a cultural bias that causes them to say, "You know, we ought to get rid of these harmful chemicals."

LORENZO LOPEZ: How do I empower people to make chemical management a safety priority?

FRED: Let's say the evidence mounts that toxic chemicals are bad. They're bad for our patients, bad for employees and bad for the community if we don't dispose of them properly. The evidence of these realities mounts to the point that employees come forward to you and to Occupational Health recognizing that chemical management is an issue. How do you then empower that message to be delivered and changes to be made?

LORENZO LOPEZ: Well, um...

FRED: Let's go back to where we started this conversation, with the article from *Modern Healthcare* magazine about the harmful chemical agents. I was looking to the future of where this issue is going, rather than where we are right now. Sharing that article about chemical and nurse safety sent a message that I thought it was important. I didn't empower our colleagues to do anything about it, though. I didn't make it clear enough to Kadine (Chief Nursing Executive) or Lori (Vice President of Human Resources) that chemical management is an organizational priority.

Management tip

One key job of leadership is to change the culture so that changes percolate up from the people closest to the problem, rather than depending on top-down policy pronouncements. Creating a culture where people close to the problem feel empowered requires the articulation of priorities, with safety being high on the list. Once the safety priority is articulated, the next step is to empower employees to engage the safety value within their sphere of influence.

Effective leaders create a culture of accountability where employees and physicians feel accountable to make changes happen within their sphere of influence. With a culture of empowerment and accountability, employees will promote sustainability, just like safety, if sustainability is a community priority. To date, healthcare chemical management issues and concerns are not sufficiently defined to evoke a regulatory response.[193] Those standards that exist are largely outdated and lack the environmental perspective.

Practical application: Nordic Swan for Healthcare Targets Polyvinyl chloride/Di(2-ethylhexyl)phthalate

The imperative

- Driving the market for alternatives to products containing chemicals of concern.
- Reducing toxicity of healthcare waste.
- Minimizing risk to human health.
- Fulfilling the organizational mission to protect public health.

The initiative

In the global market, the Nordic Ecolabelling organization has developed one of a few "eco-standards" that target chemicals of concern in medical products. The primary objective of this label is to help healthcare organizations in the Nordic region identify products that reduce chemical exposures at every stage of the product life cycle.

Manufacturers and distributors of disposable bags, tubes and accessories for healthcare who mark their products with the Nordic Swan Ecolabel commit to eliminating polyvinyl chloride (PVC), harmful plasticizers and a variety of other chemicals that are harmful to health. They also commit to reducing packaging waste and ensuring consistent levels of safety, quality and performance in their products.

Though standards such as these do not yet exist in most countries—including the USA—many other resources exist for targeting chemicals of concern in healthcare products. Sample questionnaires can be used to help spur a dialogue with vendors; sample safer chemicals or environmentally preferable purchasing (EPP) policies can help specify purchasing priorities; and case studies can help provide insights into the key success factors in implementing a Safer Chemicals program.

To help guide this process, experts in chemical safety in healthcare have also identified a priority list of chemicals to target for elimination, based on environmental and health impacts:

BBP:

DBP:

DINP:

DNOP:

- mercury
- persistent bioaccumulative toxics
- lead
- potentially endocrine-disrupting plasticizer phthalates (DEHP, n-butyl benzyl phthalate (BBP), Dibutyl phthalate (DBP), Diisononyl-phthalate (DINP), Di-n-octylphthalate (DNOP))
- halogenated plastics, including PVC
- flame retardants (halogenated, chlorinated, brominated)
- carcinogens, mutagens and reproductive toxics
- Bisphenol A (BPA)
- volatile organic compounds
- latex.

The metrics

Measuring the progress of a safer chemicals program can be achieved by tracking:

- qualitative metrics: presence of a safer chemicals policy, existence of a value-add in purchasing process for products with reduced chemicals
- quantitative metrics: total dollars spent on safer chemicals products, percentage of safer chemicals products purchased (total, within a product category, within a department), total number of chemicals of concern targeted.

The lessons learned

- Nordic Ecolabelling has stated that it will consider including requirements regarding energy, recyclability of materials, labeling and design, process contaminants and residues, and working environments in future criteria, alongside its current criteria focusing on safer chemicals. This alignment highlights the close connection between developing a safer chemicals program and an Environmentally Preferable Purchasing program—the two are closely connected and can be built together into policies, purchasing practices and conversations with suppliers.

- Several groups within and external to the healthcare industry are working to identify chemicals of concern in hospitals and the products that contain them. Examples of such groups include the United States Department of Labor, Physicians for Social Responsibility, Kaiser Permanente and Health Care Without Harm. Targeting the areas where work has already been done is the easiest place to start.
- For organizations that are unsure where or how to start implementing a safer chemicals program, there are several easy-to-use tools to help healthcare organizations identify chemicals of concern, track the products they are in, and develop a plan for eliminating them.
- Engaging the hospital's purchasing department in the planning process and educating them extensively about the safer chemicals program is crucial. Talk about the chemicals being targeted, including their health impacts and what products they are found in, so that the entire purchasing team is knowledgeable and capable of communicating about the program with vendors.

About the organization

The Nordic Ecolabel is the official Ecolabel of the Nordic countries, and was established in 1989 by the Nordic Council of Ministers with the purpose of providing an environmental labeling scheme that would contribute to a sustainable consumption. Covering 63 product groups, it is a voluntary, positive ecolabelling of products and services.

Sources

Nordic Ecolabel for disposable bags, tubes and accessories for healthcare: www. nordic-ecolabel.org/criteria/product-groups
Guide to Choosing Safer Products and Chemicals: www.noharm.org/lib/ downloads/chemicals/Guide_to_Safer_Chems.pdf

Leadership imperative

Safety should be on every healthcare leader's priority list. Similarly, sustainability should be on every healthcare professional's priority list. Sustainability improves individual and communal safety and, in cases such as chemical management, prevents harm. It is the leader's responsibility to create a culture where employees and physicians know that chemical and environmental safety is an organizational priority.

In productive, safe organizational cultures, employees are encouraged to break down silos and work across boundaries to address issues of safety and sustainability. In these cultures, two things happen. First, employees and physicians feel accountable for identifying issues related to toxic chemicals or similar problems. Second, employees and physicians understand enough about leadership to socialize chemical management, thus bringing about change in the professional setting.

Many leaders reflexively turn to top-down solutions because they are looking for a quick and easy short-term solution. They wait for the law or regulation to influence chemical management practices in healthcare long term, which tends to be the least efficient or affective method due to lack of employee engagement. The leadership learning embedded in this chapter is that chemical management is not on the leader's priority list, but safety certainly is. Leaders will turn to organizational experts for specific guidance about toxic chemicals. As evidence mounts that healthcare needs to improve chemical management processes, leaders will increasingly recognize that—like any other sustainability topic—chemical management is really about safety, accountability and facilitating a culture of empowerment.

Leadership dialogue

1 What are possible sources of camaraderie and tension between leaders in healthcare and leaders in sustainability over environmental policies and procedures?
2 Hospital safety programs are largely concerned with patient, employee and visitor safety. These are the foci of advocacy for sustainability, as well as the safety of the community. In what ways do these safety concerns align and diverge?
3 Why should—or should not—leaders wait until substances are listed on the regulatory "proven dangerous" list before taking action?
4 How does a leader create employee and physician accountability for sustainability within a healthcare organization?

Syllabus integration

Overview

Review product evaluations, specifically focusing on their documentation of quality impacts as well as workforce safety and health. Students will familiarize themselves with the numerous examples of unsafe healthcare products that contain chemicals known to have negative health impacts.

This class helps students understand when and how to use sustainability as a tool to mitigate safety risks related to potentially dangerous chemicals.

Objectives

1 Reconsider chemical management to incorporate sustainability and public health values.
2 Study how chemical management affects community relationships and business relationships with physicians, manufacturers and product suppliers.
3 Understand why safe chemical management supports prevention and wellness goals.

Topics

1 What to do in worst-case scenarios
2 Key safety concerns of chemical management.
3 Green cleaning:
   (a) Clinician perspective.

Homework

Chase Wilding, B., Curtis, K. and Welker-Hood, K. (2009) *Hazardous Chemicals in Healthcare: A Snapshot of Chemicals in Doctors and Nurses.* Washington, DC: Physicians for Social Responsibility.
EWG (n.d.) '232 toxic chemicals in 10 minority babies,' Environmental Working Group. www.ewg.org/minoritycordblood/home

Additional resources

Markkanen, P., Quinn, M., Galligan, C. and Bello, A. (2009) *Cleaning in Healthcare Facilities*, Health Care Without Harm and the Global Health and Safety Initiative, available online: www.sustainableproduction.org/downloads/ CleaninginHealthcareFacilities.pdf
US EPA (n.d.) 'Essential principles for reform of chemicals management legislation,' Washington, DC: Environmental Protection Agency. www.epa. gov/oppt/existingchemicals/pubs/principles.html

9 Downstream without a paddle

Quality + Environmentally Preferable Purchasing

Figure 9.1 Environmentally Preferable Purchasing—the front door to sustainability

Executive summary

The community's quality of health is, in part, dependent on keeping the environment free of toxic chemicals.[194] Waste management and chemical management both touch on this subject. They are downstream mitigation methods once toxic substances have already been used and have the potential to create negative impacts. Environmentally Preferable Purchasing (EPP) is the front door to sustainability because it prevents toxic substances from entering healthcare facilities in the first place. The healthcare industry has the opportunity to act as an agent for change in environmentally sustainable market trends by employing its large purchasing power. Across the country and the world, hospitals are partnering with group purchasing organizations (GPO) and manufacturers to eliminate toxic chemicals from healthcare products and facilities. This chapter is a resource for leaders to explore why and how EPP opportunities are a means of achieving quality goals.

A told story

(*Fred has a bi-weekly mentoring meeting with Felipe, Vice President of Materials Management at Memorial Hospital, during which he discusses how to successfully integrate core elements of sustainability into the hospital culture. During this conversation, Fred and Felipe discuss how to engage employees in understanding the impact of EPP on their work.*)

FRED: Felipe, how is your day going?

FELIPE: Frustrating! My car's check engine light went on. I had to take it to the shop again. This is the third time in as many months. I'm starting to wonder about the quality of the car.

FRED: Huh, that's interesting. Imagine that instead of repairing your car after repeated incidents, the mechanic taught you how to prevent the check engine light from going on in the first place.

FELIPE: I wish that would happen, but that's not reality. The car mechanic told me, "Preventing the light from turning on is not my problem. My problem is that we need to fix the car quicker, faster and cheaper. We have a business to operate, you know."

FRED: I see. So the mechanic is mostly incentivized by the volume of car fixes. And now you're wondering about the quality of his work because you've visited so frequently. I use a mechanic who fixes the root problem. Now that's a quality mechanic!

FELIPE: I see what you're saying about targeting and fixing the root problem, but I have to admit, I am not sure what the mechanic has to do with anything... other than perhaps I should find a better mechanic.

What is EPP?

Environmentally Preferable Purchasing is the procurement of products and services that, through their life cycle, do not cause harm or cause less harm to the environment, to the patient, to the employees or to the community at large.

Quality process, quality outcomes

Quality improvement and quality outcomes are driven by the quality of the process that produces the product or service.[195] The two principal drivers of the quality of the process are the degree to which:

- The process is visible and incorporates features that can prospectively identify and optimize the function of the process
- Leadership can use a process to prevent a problem entirely versus mitigating it downstream.

Sustainability is founded on the principle that prevention is superior to downstream mitigation, treatment or rehabilitation. A visible process combined with a sustainability-oriented mindset, empowers leaders to anticipate, prevent and reduce negative outcomes through process improvement. That principle can be applied to clinical quality processes as well as EPP processes. For example, designing a transparent clinical process enhances the likelihood that the clinical team will prevent an error from occurring because there is active involvement and participation by team members. It also enhances the degree to which the team can continuously improve the process because its visible to all participants.[196]

These same principles may be applied to EPP processes. For instance, the healthcare leader may decide to stop purchasing single-use devices, instead opting for products that can be reprocessed. This decision focuses upstream to reduce waste from the supply chain process because the purchasing process is visible and therefore can be continually improved over time.

The front door to sustainability

A successful environmental sustainability program will not only consider how to dispose of waste responsibly, but will look upstream to eliminate waste before it is generated. By choosing to bring materials into a facility that are created using less toxins, that do not emit volatile organic compounds, that use less energy and create less waste, hospitals can enhance healing environments and support healthy communities.[197]

Organizing concept: health, not just healthcare

Most purchasing decisions are incentivized by the prospect of short-term cost savings. The trouble with this approach is that short-term savings are not always aligned with the organization's long term interests in community health. For instance, if Felipe, Vice President of Materials Management, is charged with reducing departmental costs, he will likely base his purchasing decisions on cutting down immediate or first costs to reduce this year's budget. That approach contends with aligning Felipe's incentives around long-term savings and sustainability's triple bottom line.

Figure 9.2 Warehouse of supplies

Supply chain

The supply chain is a sequence of activities that takes place as raw materials are converted into products by manufacturers, purchased in bulk by distributors, and then purchased by providers in smaller quantities (Chopre and Meindl, 2004). EPP has many layers of complexity, beginning with understanding the impacts of a given product or service along its life cycle. A life-cycle analysis assesses the impact(s) products have at every step along the supply chain. EPP meets supply chain at the outset of the supply chain process where decisions are made to incorporate environmentally preferable products.

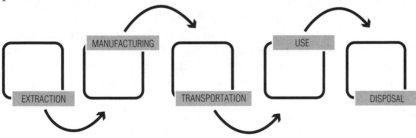

Figure 9.3 Supply chain process

(Denise, Chief Financial Officer, and Felipe, Vice President of Materials Management, congregate in Denise's office to review Felipe's annual budget and cost reduction targets.)

FELIPE: I understand that I need to reduce our departmental costs in order to make budget. But I'm at a loss about how to make financially savvy decisions that don't undermine our sustainability goals. Would you please give me some advice about how to balance short-term budget goals with long-term sustainability savings?

DENISE: (*Pauses while thinking how best to answer Felipe's question. Felipe gets a bit uncomfortable and fidgets in his chair due to the unusually long silence.*) I guess one answer is that you need to use metrics for both performance management and performance incentives, metrics that reflect long-term organizational goals. You know, Felipe, history is littered with organizations that managed quarter to quarter and made a lot of appropriate short-term decisions that positioned them for long-term loss. That situation is not only relevant to supply chain management purchasing decisions, but we're seeing a similar trend in other departments. For instance, during the recession, admissions fell and we laid off a number of employees, remember?

FELIPE: Yes, how could I forget?!

DENISE: We may lag in the recovery because we made poor short-term decisions. By letting go of experts who are important during times when the economy is more robust, we sacrificed longer and medium-term opportunities to gain more market share in the short term. My guess is that it'll be hard to fill those positions with the comparable level of expertise, as evidenced before the economy tanked.

Long-term consequences of our decisions often get lost in short term thinking and that's the real risk of not thinking sustainably—we make short-term sacrifices that aren't in our community's long-term interests.

Knowing where to start

EPP can be separated into two key components, each having its own set of goals, tasks and measurement of progress.

The first EPP component is determining which products are purchased. The point of this component is to ensure the specified product is not polluting the environment through the product life cycle—from manufacturing, to the direct impact on patient health, through to the disposal process.

The second EPP component is exploring the EPP profiles of suppliers, ideally before contracting with them. The goal of this component is to work with suppliers to influence their sustainability-oriented procurement and manufacturing processes through the hospital's purchasing power. Think about this EPP component like a traditional background check—a leader does not hire an employee, consultant or vendor without researching the individual or business history. Why should suppliers be any different? The supplier background check should be complete before contract negotiation begins so that EPP can be worked into documentation. Please refer to the appendix for a sample letter to a GPO requesting less toxic products. This letter was developed by the Minnesota Center for Environmental Advocacy's Polyvinyl Chloride (PVC) Task Force and provided by Minnesota Technical Assistance Program (MnTAP).

Global perspective

Many more hospitals in Europe are managed by government entities than in the United States, where hospitals are largely not-for-profit or for-profit.[198] Because of the ownership structure, various dimensions of healthcare management in Europe focus on longer-term efficiency as compared with United States healthcare management models. European hospitals frequently receive global payments versus payment for specific services (WHO, 2011). In other words, they are economically incentivized to optimize prevention and reduce utilization of healthcare restoration services. They are paid a fixed annual amount per patient, and if they can find cost-effective long-term purchasing strategies or facility development methods, hospitals save money on their global budget. The United Kingdom's National Health Service pays regions a fixed budget that is a capitated rate, similar to the Canadian health system (WHO, 2011). The power of this model is that both European and Canadian hospitals look upstream to impact prevention and reduce utilization of treatments and facilities over the long term.[199] The European sustainability mindset extends from processes to facility design, where the sustainability mindset is particularly visible.

Understanding the true cost of a purchase

Cost is one of the greatest perceived sustainability barriers. However, cost considerations often do not consider the total cost of ownership. The total cost of ownership includes all costs related to the extraction, manufacturing, transportation, use and disposal of materials throughout the supply chain.

EPP in the marketplace

To formulate an EPP strategy, it is important to first create benchmarks by evaluating and measuring current purchasing practices in all operational departments. This process provides a basis for identifying opportunities for which EPP policies and targeted goals can be developed. Opportunities exist to integrate

EPP while working with existing contracts as well as while initiating new contracts. New contracts afford the opportunity to insert sustainability performance indicators. Such changes can be formalized by developing policies to support sustainability purchasing decisions in future contracts.

Practical application: Sweden's Industry Initiative for Sustainable Procurement

The imperative

- Achieving cost savings by capturing economies of scale.
- Creating an information-sharing forum to lessen the learning curve within the industry.
- Pressuring suppliers to improve environmental and social impacts of healthcare products.
- Promoting the mission of healthcare to "first, do no harm."
- Reducing consumption today so that resources needed for continued operations are available in the long run.

The initiative

In 2006, a group of city and regional councils in Sweden conducted an impact analysis of the regions where major healthcare products were produced and services procured, in terms of quantity and dollars spent. They used the results of this analysis—an examination of economic, ecological and social development issues within regions across the globe—to identify seven healthcare product categories that generally require closer monitoring up the supply chain due to their impacts:

1   instruments and stainless medical products
2   operating products, disposable
3   gloves
4   dressings
5   textiles
6   pharmaceuticals
7   IT.

Most of the products identified, as well as their component materials, are produced within eastern and southern Asia. Business, labor and environmental laws in these regions are less restrictive of practices that are prohibited elsewhere in the world. Healthcare organizations belonging to the city and regional councils that conducted the analysis support and promote sustainable procurement practices within these priority areas in two main ways:

- subscribing to a common code of conduct that addresses issues of environmental, ecological and social development up the supply chain; subscribing to a common code of conduct that targets the upstream impacts of priority procurement area manufacturers, parts suppliers and service providers
- implementing a follow-up model for priority procurements, consisting of:
  - dialogue with suppliers: inviting existing and potential suppliers at least annually to discuss compliance with code of conduct and review opportunities for improvement on an annual basis, if not more frequently
  - observance of the code of conduct: requiring suppliers to show, on demand, that all components of the products and services they are providing have been produced in compliance with code of conduct; for those that fail to meet the requirements, also involves taking corrective actions up to and including contract termination
  - formal follow-up process: sending a self-assessment form to priority procurement area suppliers and assessing responses to determine where more detailed follow-up is needed; following up in further detail via requests for meetings with suppliers, remedial actions or live audits at the manufacturer; requiring an action plan for addressing any environmental, social or quality issues, with occasional spot checks in production; inviting suppliers to seminar to review audit results and any action required.

The metrics

Although it may be tricky at times to track the specific impacts of environmentally and/or socially preferable purchasing efforts, there are ways to monitor progress:

- quantity of products targeted as priority procurements
- quantity of and dollars spent on priority procurements
- number of suppliers who have/haven't met criteria
- specific product characteristics targeted to avoid (e.g. mercury-free, reduced packaging).

The lessons learned

- Several industry organizations have developed and made publicly available in-depth vendor questionnaires that specifically target certain chemicals, products and business practices. Using tools such as these helps standardize the sets of questions being asked of vendors from organizations across the industry, making it easier for them to understand exactly what types of information and products they are looking for.

- Since healthcare organizations share many of the same suppliers, there is great potential to standardize the industry's approach to procurement and purchasing. Working together with other healthcare organizations to implement vendor evaluations, supply chain investigations, or industry-wide discussions makes accomplishing the task more impactful than each institution individually.
- Suppliers are often national companies with subcontractors abroad. When conducting a supplier or product analysis, it is essential for follow-up to extend all the way up the chain of production to ensure all supply-chain impacts are identified and considered.
- Certain product groups are more vulnerable than others to environmentally or socially harmful practices during the production process. Start small by developing an environmentally preferable purchasing program that targets these product groups, rather than trying to build a comprehensive program from scratch.

About the organizations

Since 2006, Stockholm County Council, Skåne Regional Council and Region Västra Götaland have been working together to promote social responsibility and sustainability in procurement. Together, the group developed a common code of conduct and follow-up model for suppliers. The county councils and regions in Sweden are primarily the principal authorities for healthcare, and also for public transport and sustainable growth in their respective regions.

Sources

Stockholm County Council et al. (2010) *Social Responsibility in Procurement: Code of Conduct for Suppliers*. Sweden: Stockholm County Council, Skåne Regional Council and Region Västra Götaland. www.vgregion.se/upload/Regionservice/Inköp/Miljöhänsyn/Social%20responsibility%20in%20procurement.pdf

---

Leadership imperative

Like every other dimension of sustainability, EPP points to leadership and leadership's role in promoting sustainability as a core component of value for the organization. Creating a successful EPP program is contingent on leadership. Leadership is crucial to having EPP within an organization, and is equally imperative when facilitating EPP relationships with industry partners. It is the leader's role to make it clear to individuals in decision-making positions that sustainability and prevention are core values. It is the leader's role to empower leaders at all levels of the organization to make purchasing decisions based on life-cycle cost and triple bottom line sustainability criteria. This chapter highlights some of the challenges and solutions of EPP, both of which are morphing as the EPP industry develops.

(*Fred and Felipe are conversing in the hallway before a meeting begins.*)

FELIPE: Okay, Fred, so we've instituted a hospital-wide EPP policy and it's really starting to show results. We're saving energy because we bought the environmentally preferable lights and now our engineering folks are delighted—fewer light bulbs to change. The operating rooms nurses are happy too because we've been using EPP to source the inter venous fluid management system. Now the nurses have minimized exposure risk because they no longer need to handle bodily fluids—the machine takes care of it all while not throwing away a bunch of canisters for every OR case, the way we used to before we purchased the fluid management system.[200]

FRED: Well, I'm starting to feel good that we did the EPP thing.

(*Fred's phone rings. It's Mrs Crumpmuffet, Fred's assistant. Mrs Crumpmuffet tells Fred that the Mayor is on the phone. Fred speaks into his cell phone.*)

FRED: (*To the Mayor*) This is Fred speaking.

MAYOR: Good morning, Fred. This is the Mayor here.

FRED: Good morning, sir. What can I do for you today?

MAYOR: Well Fred, I understand that Memorial Hospital purchased new lighting technology that can be retrofit, which ultimately saves energy for the community. I would appreciate if you would come by so that we can discuss those projections.

FRED: (*thinking to himself*) Thank goodness I saw the light before the Mayor showed up.

Leadership dialogue

1   Quality and environmentally preferable purchasing share common underlying principles, and leaders often find resistance to both topics. What are the causes of resistance?

2   Why do—or why do not—leaders have to make a choice between healthcare (retroactive; healing the sick) and health (proactive; preventing harm)?

3   Why is the "true cost" of purchasing situation-specific?

4   When the leader brings an environmentally preferable purchasing proposal to the Board of Trustees, it may be subject to criticism because

of the short-term financial impact on the institution. How can a leader help the board to understand the true cost to the hospital of short-term thinking versus the long-term perspective associated with sustainability?

Syllabus integration

Overview

We will examine best practices for preferred purchasing practices that document efficacy, infection control, environmental and human life-cycle impacts from manufacture to waste, and effective capital and maintenance costs.

Objectives

1 Evolve supply chain management from a traditional focus on purchasing and logistics to a broader, more integrated emphasis on contributing to value creation.
    (a) Identify and illustrate opportunities to enhance supply chain performance by creating business value in the procurement supply chain.
2 Study how sustainable supply chain management affects business and relationships with manufacturers, suppliers, clinicians, managers and practices.
    (a) Detail how companies in other industries derive business value from sustainable sourcing.
3 Understand how cleaning practices support prevention and control goals.
4 Link occupational health to healthcare sustainability.

Topics

1 Drivers of environmental health and safety successes
    (a) National Institute for Occupational Safety & Health (NIOSH)
2 Key questions of the environmental health and safety supply chain
3 Environmentally preferable purchasing
    (d) Group purchasing
    (e) Business process improvements
    (f) Environmental and social benefits

Homework

GGHC (2007) *Toxic Reduction through Environmentally Preferable Purchasing Technical Brief* version 2.2. Environmentally Preferable Purchasing Credits 4.1, 4.2, and 4.3, Green Guide for Healthcare. www.gghc.org/documents/ TechBriefs/GGHC_TechBrief_EPP.pdf

Additional resources

GEMI (2004) *Forging New Links: Enhancing Supply Chain Through Environmental Excellence*. Global Environmental Management Initiative.

Kaiser Permanante (2011) *Green Cleaners*, available online: http://practicegreenhealth.org/sites/default/files/upload-files/environmentalservices greencleanerssuccessstory11111.pdf (accessed 10/22/2012).

Practice Greenhealth, Greenin the OR Case Study (2011) *North Suburban Medical Centre: Fluid Management in the OR*, available online: http://practice greenhealth.org/sites/default/files/upload-files/casestudy_nsuburban_r5_web_ 0.pdf (accessed 10/22/2012).

Practice Greenhealth, Greenin the OR Case Study (2011) *The University of Maryland Medical Centre: Reusable Textiles in the OR*, available online: http://practicegreenhealth.org/sites/default/files/upload-files/casestudy_uofmd_ r6_web_0.pdf (accessed 10/22/2012).

Practice Greenhealth, Greening the Supply Chain, *Environmentally Preferable Purchasing*, available online: http://practicegreenhealth.org/sites/default/files/ upload-files/blc_statement_of_intent.pdf (accessed 10/22/2012).

10 Building brand, literally

Growth/brand + green building

Figure 10.1 Building green buildings

Executive summary

Leaders increasingly recognize the financial, environmental and social benefits of pursuing sustainable building retrofits and new construction. Among the drivers of sustainable decision-making is the potential for long-term reduction in life-cycle costs. Healthcare institutions are embracing commitments to environmentally friendly building design by pursuing Leadership in Energy and Environmental Design (LEED) standards and LEED for Healthcare, which incorporates the unique rules, regulations and operating conditions of sustainable healthcare environments. The impact of using LEED standards in healthcare facilities has important implications for the brand and brand elements that are communicated through facilities. Sustainability is a desirable brand element for employees and the various publics served by healthcare organizations. This chapter describes the sustainable facility design guidelines that align leadership priorities with environmental health practices in the planning, design and construction of facilities, as well as their impact on the institution's brand.

Storyline

Memorial Hospital conducted a market analysis to identify growth opportunities. It determined that building a cancer center will fulfill unmet community need. Fred discusses his vision for the cancer center with Melvin Monroe, Vice President of Design and Construction, and Fiona O'Malley, Director of Marketing and Communication. Their conversation quickly turns to the importance of making sustainability visible by intentionally integrating it into the building design and organizational brand.

MELVIN MONROE: Witnessing my father's recent cancer bout caused me to reflect on facility design through a whole new lens. I observed that the construction materials used in the cancer center include some materials that have been judged to be carcinogenic. Can you believe how ironic that is?

FIONA O'MALLEY: I'm so sorry to hear about your father.

MELVIN MONROE: Thank you, Fiona. There's nothing I can do about my father's situation now, but there is something we can do to improve the experience for other peoples' families. I think we need to be explicit about our commitment to sustainable design with this new cancer center project.

FRED: I'm not really sure what it would mean for us to commit to sustainable facility design, but however we incorporate it, sustainability needs to be visible if we want it to resonate with employees and patients. Sustainable design isn't helpful from a brand perspective unless we translate it into tangible features. Good intentions aren't good enough. We have to have concrete sustainability characteristics that we incorporate systematically into the facility design.

MELVIN MONROE: You want to design the facility out of concrete?

FIONA O'MALLEY: Oh, Melvin, that joke was awful.

FRED: What I was trying to say is that we should make our sustainability features obvious to even the casual observer. And then we have to point the sustainable features out to people so that they know what they're looking at. It can be educational.

MELVIN MONROE: This will be our first building designed to sustainable standards. I'm looking forward to this project.

FRED: How will people know if we invest in sustainability? For instance, how will the community know if we invest in sustainable transportation or waste management systems? Patients are unlikely to be poking around the dumpster exclaiming, "Oh, now this is a sustainable hospital!"

MELVIN MONROE: There are things we can do to indicate our sustainable commitments to the community, even for sustainable features that are less visible. For example, we could incorporate signage in the hospital facility to highlight energy conservation or on the side of shuttle bus, to highlight our reduced carbon footprint.

FRED: Some people might say that they don't need to care about the substance to care about the perception, but I find myself caring more as I think about my responsibility as CEO in an increasingly sustainable industry. I care a lot about how sustainable the building looks. I'd love to have a garden growing on the roof, with landscape design that recycles water. Solar panels would make our commitment visible. That's how we build a sustainable brand—by investing in and showcasing our sustainable features.

FRED: Feeling green today, Melvin?

MELVIN MONROE: Green with envy, sir.

Effects of the built environment

The US EPA created the chart in Table 10.1 to articulate the effects of the built environment on environmental and human health. This reality—that buildings impact public health—is not a typical leadership consideration, though it should be.

Table 10.1 The impact of buildings on health*

Aspect of built environment	Consumption	Environmental effects	Ultimate effects
Siting	Energy	Waste	Harm to human health
Design	Water	Air pollution	Environment degradation
Construction	Materials	Water pollution	Loss of resources
Operation	Natural resources	Indoor pollution	
Maintenance		Heat islands	
Renovation		Storm-water runoff	
Deconstruction		Noise	

*US EPA (2010) 'Green Building,' Washington, DC: Environmental Protection Agency. www.epa.gov/greenbuilding/pubs/about.htm

Brand new impact

Every organization has a *de facto* brand. Healthcare organizations are no exception. Hospitals tangibly articulate organizational brand when they invest in facilities and cutting-edge technologies because such assets are visible to the community.

What is brand?

Many of today's healthcare facilities are outdated, having been built during the Hill–Burton (1946) era.[201] Consider the facilities of. forward thinking, successful businesses: Think Google. Think Epic Think Starbucks. Think Whole Foods. Think Apple—"Think different." These companies are explicit in their sustainable design, ranging from facility design to product design. They purposely communicate that the company embraces sustainable values. For instance, Apple recycles used products; Whole Foods makes an effort to source local foods. Both companies streamline their services to provide a convenient, minimally wasteful customer experience. Companies that intentionally brand themselves attract clients, customers, suppliers and creative talent with shared values. Brand is one of several advantages accruing to hospitals that choose sustainable building design. Having a visibly sustainable building is, at a very practical level, one durable strategy for building sustainability into the hospital's brand.

What is a sustainable facility?

Sustainable design is the process of incorporating products and processes that meet the triple bottom line. Sustainable facilities are environmentally, socially and fiscally responsible in the long term. They are responsible stewards of community resources, including land, water and energy, while reducing waste and the use of chemicals.

One of the most prevalent sustainable building systems is the United States Green Building Council's (USGBC) Leadership in Energy and Environmental Design (LEED). There are roughly 9 billion square feet of LEED certified spaces with a growth rate of 1.6 million square feet a day.[202] LEED for Healthcare was designed to incorporate healthcare's unique challenges, such as 24/7 operations and air-quality management. The LEED for Healthcare rating system evolved from the Green Guide for Healthcare, a pilot rating developed by industry leaders.

Other third-party green building rating systems include:[203]

- Australia Greenhouse Building Rating (AGBR)
- BCA Green Mark (Singapore)
- Building Environment Assessment Method—Hong Kong (HK-BEAM)
- Building Research Environment Assessment Method Consultancy (BREEAM) (UK)
- Comprehensive Assessment System for Building Environment Efficiency (CASBEE) (Japan)
- Ecology, Energy Saving, Waste Reduction and Health (EEWH) (Taiwan)
- Energy Star (US EPA)
- European Environment Agency
- Green Building Council (Korea)
- Green Globe Rating System (United States)
- Green Star (Australia)
- India Green Building Council
- Leadership in Energy & Environmental Design — Canada (LEED-Canada)
- Leadership in Energy & Environmental Design (LEED-United States)
- Philippine Green Building Council

Build it, and they will come

Physicians as customers

Physicians are key hospital customers because most patients go to the hospital as directed by their physician. So while a hospital's direct-to-consumer (patient) brand is important, leaders cannot ignore the fact that only physicians admit patients, other than emergency room visits. Brand does, however, play a key role in elective procedures and for employee recruitment and retention.

How does a leader attract top talent in a tight market? The "sweet spot" in brand differentiation is linking product and service differentiation with talent recruitment. Physicians, patients and employees seek care at organizations that have visible, explicit commitment to shared values. A sustainable facility environment promotes the health of patients and employees, which is an attractive component of the organization's brand promise. Sustainable building design contributes to an organizational brand that attracts people who share sustainability values. While sustainable buildings are necessary, it is even more important to operationalize sustainable work processes and a culture of sustainability within the hospital walls. In other words, it is necessary but insufficient to incorporate sustainable facility elements that don't have an impact on work processes or culture.

Does LEEDing cost more?

Questions about cost implications of sustainable design typically arise once leaders recognize that sustainable facilities are a desirable option. Leaders typically ask, "Does building according to LEED standards cost more than building less sustainable solutions?" There are many gaps in most leaders' understanding of the somewhat complex answers to this question. First and foremost, there is considerable cost variation inherent in the planning and construction of sustainable buildings for a number of reasons. There are different levels of LEED standards that range from the most sustainable (platinum) to the least sustainable (certified) level of LEED. Sustainable features may, in aggregate, cost less or more to build to LEED standards, depending on which line items within the LEED rating system are incorporated. In general, the initial investment in high-level LEED standards is higher than the initial investment in low-level LEED standards.[204] Upfront construction costs for healthcare facilities average three per cent higher to build according to LEED standards than to not do so.[205] The question then emerges, is building sustainably "worth it" when the incremental building cost is spread over the useful life of the building, assuming the average useful life is thirty years?

Life-cycle cost analysis consistently demonstrates a healthy financial return on incremental capital investment because of energy and other operating cost savings.[206] In other words, the incremental difference in building cost for sustainable buildings is relatively small due to the long-term return on investment. But the question is not solely that of incremental building cost. Rather, what is the overall value equation that is determined by comparing incremental costs with the incremental benefits that result from the sustainable building in terms of patient, employee, physician and public perception? It is a question of value, not only expense, that should be considered.

Spending on healthcare construction over a one-year span in 2011 was estimated at over $527 billion.[207,208] With this significant portfolio of projected healthcare facility investment, leaders have a prime opportunity to incorporate sustainability into design concepts and work processes.

Buildings deliver on the brand promise

The life of Steve Jobs taught the world that exceptional design incorporates both functionality and the aesthetic features of products, services and companies.[209] Applied to healthcare, an architecturally striking cancer center communicates cutting-edge care. In other words, the facility design communicates an important element of the brand promise. Jobs made his mark by knitting together the left brain and right brain.[210] He captured the left brain's reliability, safety, consistence, quality and durability, and married that with the right brain's ability to capture the style and creative design for which Apple products are known.[211] Sustainability incorporates the evidence-based methodologies that yield predictable, proven results. And sustainability also requires the creative, right-brain innovation which is reflected in trying new methods to achieve a triple bottom line. High-performing leaders in healthcare have the ability to ambidextrously apply both left- and right-brain thinking. Leaders who embrace sustainability embrace that approach to accomplish their organization's mission—improving long-term health of their patients, their community and the planet.

Fred and Fiona are having a visioning section for a commercial being produced for the new building.

FRED: We can't just claim that Memorial Hospital is environmentally sustainable. If we promise A but deliver B, we're in trouble. It's essential that we practice sustainability or it will be readily apparent that our claim is insincere.

FIONA O'MALLEY: *(Director of Marketing and Communication)* I understand what you're saying, Fred, and as the person responsible for brand management, I fully agree with your point. Based on the dialogue I've been hearing, perhaps we should incorporate sustainability as an explicit part of our brand—from our workflow processes to our physical infrastructure. What do you think?

FRED: Are there any healthcare organizations that explicitly tie sustainability to their brand?

FIONA O'MALLEY: I can't find any that do. There are healthcare organizations that practice sustainability, but they don't explicitly link it to their brands.

(A pause of silence overtakes the room as Fred and Fiona consider brand options.)

FIONA O'MALLEY: I've been thinking, we can change what something costs and we can change how something looks. That's why leaders who are experts on cost-effectiveness will plug cost-effectiveness everywhere they touch. Similarly, sustainability-focused colleagues plug sustainability everywhere they touch. But the most influential leaders are those who protect the values nobody can change, the values that are fundamental to the hospital's culture. Once we build specific values into the culture, those values become the organization's brand. At that point, customers see our brand values as differentiators of Memorial Hospital. So, if you really believe that sustainability is a brand differentiator, we need the culture to demonstrate it.

(Fred stares out of the window, envisioning a brand defined by sustainability values.)

FRED: Healthcare organizations are increasingly associated with improving health, not just healing the sick. Inherently, then, sustainability is what our brand is moving toward. Our new brand is about looking upstream to prevent illness, helping patients to not show up at the hospital in the first place. At it's core, the principle of predict-and-prevent is the future paradigm of health.

FIONA O'MALLEY: I think sustainability is essential and implicit in the brand, but I think there is an element that needs to be more explicit. Our new brand is inherently about being more sustainable and sustaining oneself, but I don't know that a lot of people would connect the dots unless we make it obvious. Sustainable facilities would illustrate our commitment to sustainability.

FRED: I agree with you. There may be only two people in this hospital who reach that conclusion.

(Sustainability Director Amalie DuBois enters Fred's office, where she is greeted by Fred and Fiona.)

AMALIE DUBOIS: Good afternoon, Fred. Good afternoon Fiona.

FRED: Hello, Amalie. Fiona and I were just talking about how excellent it would be for our facilities to convey the sustainability brand we aim to build. If that was easy and obvious, everybody would be doing it. I think we probably have an answer for how we should do it, I just haven't thought of it yet.

AMALIE DUBOIS: Let me guess, you'd like for me to think about it.

FRED: That's right. You're good. You must be a mind-reader. What am I thinking now?

AMALIE DUBOIS: You're thinking you want to give me a raise.

(Laughter)

Green leases

Green leasing is new to healthcare, and relatively new to business at large. Green leases are precisely what the phrase implies—leasing space that incorporates sustainable practices into legal documentation.[212] The lease is explicit that the real estate management company responsible for managing the property uses vendors and processes committed to sustainability, such as waste management services that include recycling. Demand for green leasing is likely to increase as businesses focus on sustainability and integrate it into operational practices. For healthcare, this trend means that green leases will grow increasingly popular in outpatient clinics, physician offices, medical office buildings, corporate office space, data management centers and other leased healthcare spaces.

Healthcare facilities carry out meaningful roles besides brand building and their inherent functional purposes. They serve to educate and are agents of culture change within the community. One valuable aspect of LEED certification is signage that explicitly calls attention to sustainable features. Examples of educational signage include signs indicating that the cafeteria recycles, the toilet uses less water than traditional options, the carpet contains recycled content, the lights turn off automatically, and the healing garden water is gathered from rain barrels. Patients and employees are reminded that it is possible to incorporate all of these elements in a healthy home environment. Sustainable facilities, like those at Advocate Healthcare, clearly inform visitors, employees and patients about how to live more sustainable, healthful lifestyles.[213]

Core values

FRED: I think our employees ought to be our brand ambassadors, ambassadors of sustainability.

FIONA O'MALLEY: I think you're on to something. (*Fiona notates furiously on her iPad.*)

FRED: We need to first educate employees about why sustainability is important to the hospital and how we embrace sustainability. The problem is that we're talking about things Memorial Hospital could do, probably not things we currently do. I can think of a million messages...

FIONA O'MALLEY: Of all of the competing messages, let's pick one core message to focus on.

FRED: Okay, how about prevention? Come to Memorial Hospital and we'll help you prevent disease.

FIONA O'MALLEY: That's a possibility. Something like that would allow us to fold sustainability into the brand message, though perhaps not explicitly.

FRED: Gee, Fiona. I really hadn't thought about sustainability in this light until we started discussing it. I'm realizing that the environment we create speaks volumes about whether sustainability is perceived to be part of our core values.

FIONA O'MALLEY: That's right. We need to be very careful with the way we build brand into our permanent facilities. They'll articulate organizational values to the community long after you and I retire.

Figure 10.2 Watching growth

Green Building Guide Breakdown

Leadership Value Assessment

- Examines organization's values in relation to sustainability measures

Implementation Guide

- Provides a pathway to achieve sustainability measure

Consensus Based

Figure 10.3 Leadership value assessment

Internal guidelines

Let's assume that a leader decides to embrace the physical environment as a way to integrate organizational values around sustainability. LEED offers an array of guidelines, primarily for design, architecture, construction, engineering and related industries. Internal building guidelines may also be used by leaders to translate sustainability values into actual building projects. Kaiser Permanente is one example of an organization that relies on internal facility guidelines (Kaiser Permanente, 2011). Inova Health System has also developed internal guidelines for sustainable facility standards.

Brand building requires the promotion and communication of core themes or features. The features have to be designed so that they support delivery of the brand promise. In other words, it's not enough to know that you want sustainability features integrated throughout the building. The design team needs to understand what "sustainability features" mean and how to incorporate them. That includes a system of quantified goals and metrics to evaluate progress, as well as tools to measure the impact of sustainability practices and provide ongoing feedback about how to continuously improve.[214]

FRED: I think we ought to have sustainable building principles to articulate the character of our facilities. A logical place to start is the major renovation project coming next year. We need to focus on both substance and appearance for our sustainability principles, everything from vendor partnerships to signage.

MELVIN MONROE: Okay, I can't help you much on the vendor partnerships piece, but we can certainly develop sustainability principles for our construction projects. We just had a new young guy, Dwight, join the team, who's a recent college graduate and already passed the LEED exam. Apparently, learning and practicing sustainably is the way people are trained these days.

FRED: At this point, I think I'd be incompetent at practicing sustainability. I'd have to get Dwight to mentor me. If he can educate me about sustainability, anybody can be educated, right?

MELVIN MONROE: You said it, not me, sir.

99.1% of respondents answered that environmental sustainability ("Going Green") is important to them, but only 83% are satisfied with Inova's commitment to Going Green.

Available online: http://practicegreenhealth.org/webinars/green-operations-series-engaging-employees-marketing-sustainable-mission (accessed 10/22/2012).

It's who we are, not what we do

Sustainability is often a bolted-on external feature that goes something like this: "We got the budget down. We designed the building. We got the program ready. Did anyone apply for the LEED-certified thing? We get something if we do that." In healthcare, sustainability is still an "externality" that few organizations have fully integrated into how they think or, more importantly, who they are. Maturity will be evident in healthcare when sustainability comes from the inside out, and not the reverse.

FRED: Every time we have one of these conversations, I go back with a long list of things I need to do to help us think and behave more sustainably. Talking it through helps shed light on how relatively early we are on this sustainability journey. We are still in our infancy, still wearing diapers, as far as sophisticated sustainability organizations are concerned. There's something to be said for sustainability education.

FIONA O'MALLEY: Just imagine, Fred. Once we integrate sustainability into our core caretaking processes, we can begin to integrate sustainability into the community in more meaningful ways. Let's say we're going to send a new mother home with her baby. Today, we teach the mother about breast feeding; we teach her about how to put the baby in the crib safely. Part of our new parent training could also entail helping the parents to create a healthy, sustainable environment for their newborns. That includes how to maintain the home environment in a sustainable way. We need to build sustainability principles around the parent's obligation to optimize health for his or her child. Everything from the absence of lead paint in the home to the way diapers are disposed.

FRED: Enough diaper talk. Who's ready for lunch? In all seriousness, I do get what you're saying. We can organize our services around the concept of health, which is a friendly concept to parents, and a way to create sustainability ambassadors of our patients and families. I think it's a great way to get the nursing staff more involved, too.

Practical application: green buildings across the globe

The imperative

- Reducing employee, patient and visitor exposure to chemicals of concern.
- Improving patient outcomes.
- Improving employee performance and satisfaction.
- Reducing workplace injuries and employee health costs.

- Achieving long-term savings through energy and water efficiency, reduced waste, and lower operations and maintenance costs.
- Creating environments that promote healing.
- Minimizing long-term risk related to energy supply and prices.
- Promoting public health by reducing environmental impact.

The initiative

The world's first two LEED Platinum hospitals—Dell Children's Medical Center in Austin, Texas, USA and Kohinoor Hospital in Mumbai, India—showcase the universal benefits of green building, despite being located across the globe from each other (Dell Children's Medical Centre, 2008; Express Healthcare, 2011). Each building has capitalized on the unique features of its physical surroundings to create a healing environment that not only promotes environmental responsibility, but also yields significant financial savings, increased employee productivity and retention, and faster healing times, among other benefits.

LEED is an international certification program for green buildings, which rates buildings in five key areas. Dell Children's Medical Center and Kohinoor Hospital were designed to be top performers in each of these areas. Both hospitals undertook some of the same green building activities in each category—practices that tend to be universal throughout the global green building sector—while each organization also had unique ideas suited to their specific site.

- Both organizations used recycled and original site materials in the construction of their new buildings. Dell was located on the site of a former airport, and used the original runway materials in its parking lots and garages; Kohinoor used re-rolled steel and recycled frame wood in its exterior façade, flooring and walls.
- Both focused on increasing the amount of natural light in indoor areas, achieving it through different mechanisms—Dell through interior gardens and courtyard spaces; Kohinoor with large outward-facing windows and open skylights.
- Both committed to energy efficiency, approaching it in different ways. Dell used strategically placed air intakes, built a natural gas-fired power plant (75 per cent more efficient than coal), and installed an under-floor air-distribution system requiring less fan power than traditional ceiling systems. Kohinoor installed solar hot water heaters, procured green power from windmills, and focused on improving heating, ventilation and air conditioning performance by installing new, highly efficient systems.

The metrics

The design and construction team can help track building performance throughout the construction process, both on existing buildings and on new construction projects. Commonly tracked metrics include:

- quantity of construction and demolition waste reused or recycled
- amount of sustainable and/or recycled materials included in building
- total dollars spent on locally produced materials
- total cost and environmental savings related to improved energy and water efficiency (gallons of water reduced or pounds of CO_2 eliminated)
- quantity of chemicals avoided in building materials.

The lessons learned

- The most successful green building projects tailor common green building practices to the physical (site, climate) and social (regulatory environment, business culture) conditions of the region.
- Investing in green buildings takes only a small increase in initial cost over conventional buildings, but the benefits are long term and multi-fold. To successfully build a sustainable infrastructure that achieves long-term benefits, the appropriate expertise and planning must occur from the outset of the design and construction process.
- Creating "sustainable" buildings is a natural extension of healthcare's mission to "first, do no harm." Healthcare organizations that are pursuing this mission and have committed to being world-class providers simply cannot ignore the profound, measurable effects that sustainable hospital environments have on healing.
- Designing and building greener facilities is a popular way for healthcare organizations to distinguish themselves from competitors in an increasingly competitive market—especially since the physical healing environment has been so closely linked to patient outcomes. Pursuing commonly recognized ratings such as LEED certification helps validate and publicize green building efforts.
- That a hospital is "green" does not mean it functions less effectively than a conventional hospital, and also does not necessarily mean that it will cost more. Sustainable healthcare facilities look and function almost exactly the same as conventional healthcare facilities, but have the added benefits of conserving natural resources and showing concern for human comfort, indoor environment and employee productivity. Short-term increases in cost for building greener facilities are far outweighed by long-term savings from increased efficiency.

About the organizations

LEED is a Green Building Rating System developed by the US Green Building Council. LEED aims to recognize environmental leadership in the realty industry. Ratings are classified into four categories: LEED Certified, Silver, Gold and Platinum, with Platinum being the highest rating. In order to achieve LEED certification, buildings are rated in five key areas: sustainable site development, water savings, energy efficiency, materials selection and indoor environmental quality.

Kohinoor Hospital is the first hospital not only in India, but in Asia, to achieve Platinum rating. The 150-bed, multispecialty hospital is located in Mumbai. The Certifying Authority for Kohinoor Hospital is The Indian Green Building Council—(IGBC). The aim of IGBC is to assist in the creation of high-performance, healthful, durable, affordable and environmentally sound commercial and institutional buildings.

Dell Children's Medical Center of Central Texas, a member of the Seton Family of Hospitals was the first hospital in the world to receive the LEED Platinum designation, given by the US Green Building Council. The 470,000 square foot hospital opened in June 2007 on 32 acres that was once part of the former Mueller Municipal Airport, which has become one of the largest redevelopment efforts in the City of Austin's history.

Sources

'Kohinoor Hospital – Platinum LEED certified green hospital sets benchmarks,' www.hospitalinfrabiz.com/kohinoor-hospital-ndash-platinum-leed-certified-green-hospital-sets-benchmarks.html

'Kohinoor is a LEEDing light,' *Express Healthcare* July. www.expresshealthcare.in/201007/strategy02.shtml

'Dell Children's Medical Center is world's first Platinum hospital,' www.dellchildrens.net/about_us/news/2009/01/08/dell_childrens_medical_center_is_worlds_first_platinum_hospital_2

'Dell Children's Hospital gets LEED platinum,' www.bdcnetwork.com/dell-childrens-hospital-gets-leed-platinum

Leadership imperative

One of the principal strategies of leadership in sustainable healthcare organizations is helping colleagues understand why sustainability is core to health and how sustainability is translated into the organization. One effective way of branding the organization with sustainability values is by investing in facilities that communicate such values. The visible commitment to sustainability explicitly promotes the health of patients and employees. It is the leader's responsibility to challenge the design and construction team to collaborate with the brand team—an unlikely team in years past.

A leadership dialogue

1 How can leaders use the process of building design to communicate sustainability values and strengthen brand recognition?
2 Why is the LEED for Healthcare rating system considered a guide for leadership strategic planning?
3 What is the relationship between employee recruitment and sustainability values reflected within the hospital's built environment?
4 What are the components of leadership's business case for meeting LEED standards?
5 How can leaders make the case for considering green leasing?

Syllabus integration

Overview

Students will learn from a healthcare design professional guest lecturer, who will walk them through the LEED rating system, exploring how to balance healthcare capital improvement demands with environmental challenges. Students will be exposed to resource and code constraints, programmatic requirements and institutional cultural barriers.

Objectives

1 Make the business case for sustainable building design.
2 Measure, manage and communicate sustainable design value to the community.
3 Explain how leveraging sustainable design can help create value by enhancing brand, reputation, innovation and leadership.
4 Visit a sustainably designed healthcare organization to assess sustainable design.

Topics

1 Perkins+Will transparency tool
   (a) Pharos rating system
2 LEED
   (a) LEED exercise with architect/design professional
3 ASHRAE 90.1
4 The Living Building Challenge

Homework

Houghton, A., Vittori, G. and Guenther, R. (2009) 'Demystifying first-cost green building premiums in healthcare,' *Health Environments Research & Design Journal* 2(4): 10–45.

Kresge Foundation (n.d.) 'How do I build green?' Troy, MI: The Kresge Foundation, Green Building Initiative.

Practice Greenhealth (2009) 'Design & construction series: Sustainable healthcare architecture: where are we now? webinar January 9. www.practicegreenhealth. org

Additional resources

Practice Greenhealth and the Institute for Innovation in Large Organizations (2008) 'The business case for greening the healthcare sector.'

Practice Greenhealth (2009) 'Design & construction series: Metro Health Hospital's transition to a LEED hospital: design, construction and operations,' webinar August 14. www.practicegreenhealth.org

11 Water changes everything

Community benefit +water management

Figure 11.1 Growing community

Executive summary

Hospitals are reaching for a new definition of their role in community health that goes beyond traditional measures. Hospitals are one of the few types of institution that have the mission, intellectual resources and a reach into centers of influence. Hospitals have the ability to command attention and leadership potential to help guide the community toward improved sustainability. That is the full implication of sustainability for hospitals and the basis of their new social compact. This new social compact includes a responsibility to ensure potable water remains potable. One of the basic public health imperatives is access to clean water for drinking, bathing, food preparation and agriculture, among other daily activities.[215] Yet less than one per cent of the Earth's water is potable.[216] Healthcare leaders have a role to play in ensuring their organizations are not contributing to water contamination and is, instead, supporting efforts to protect the public's natural health resources.

A told story

DR JENNY BEA: *(Pediatrician)* Welcome to the Memorial Hospital medical staff meeting, Dr Goldberg. I had multiple patients come in last week complaining of the drizzlies and skin infections. The common thread between them is that they all swam in the river on Mellen Street for summer camp and said they may have swallowed water. I contacted the Health Department and found out that the river water is contaminated.

DR MORDECHAI GOLDBERG: *(Mature family physician)* Contaminated water? Where is it coming from? Not us, I hope.

DR JENNY BEA: It's interesting you ask, because I asked the same question. I'm not sure where the water contamination is coming from, but I'm in the process of following up with the Health Department and will be sure to share with you what I learn.

DR JENNY BEA: What I know is that I'm regularly visited by parents who come in dragging their kids along—they just want their kid's earaches fixed. They don't care about overuse of antibiotics so long as the earache goes away. I tend to give each patient a little extra dose, just to make sure they have enough. I spend a fair amount of time giving instructions about how to take the antibiotics, but no time on how to properly dispose of the excess drugs. Before now, that step of the process simply hasn't crossed my mind. I just focus on curing the child's pain.

DR MORDECHAI GOLDBERG: I can't say I've given water contamination much thought either, until this point. For all I know, my patients could be dumping unused drugs down the toilet, contaminating the water supply and not realizing they are contributing to the problem. Sounds like we need to be thinking about clean water as an end in itself, rather than a means to an end.

DR JENNY BEA: I agree.

> *(Dr Grisha Vladimir, the curmudgeonly orthopedic surgeon, joins the conversation along with Dr Shmuel Cohen, the young hospitalist who is new to Memorial Hospital.)*

DR GRISHA VLADIMIR: All I know is that they closed my favorite trout stream due to the water contamination. Now I can't take my grandkids fishing.

DR SHMUEL COHEN: Here we are talking about water supply out in the community, while we can't even get it right in our own facility. *(He lifts a plastic water bottle from the table and places it next to his reusable bottle*.) We keep serving water in plastic bottles. Don't people realize that the water from the faucet is safe to drink, free and produces far less waste? We're privileged to have that luxury, compared with other places in the world, and yet we still go out and buy bottled water! It's so wasteful.

"Healthcare systems are among a community's largest consumers of water. Consumption, however, varies greatly: Water use per capita ranges from 40 gallons per day to 350 gallons per day, depending on such factors as geographical location; services provided; size, age, and type of buildings; and water-use equipment and practices. A study of seven Massachusetts facilities found the potential for a reduction of almost 20 percent. Limiting water consumption provides hospitals with savings related to water supply and sewer costs. Some measures also can save energy costs, such as those that reduce the need for hot water. Water conservation also reduces the energy needed off-site to transport and process water and enables hospitals to be proactive stewards of their community's natural resources." (US Department of Energy, 2011).

Stop dumping in the river

Hospitals have a unique opportunity to provide community leadership. It is a complicated process to convert that commitment into clear and achievable health objectives for a specific community. The process requires informed, thoughtful and committed leaders to focus institutional attention on the consequences of unsustainable systems.

Not-for-profit healthcare organizations have a community charter. The hospital receives tax benefits in exchange for promoting the community's health. In exchange for tax exemption, not-for-profit hospitals provide charitable care and other community benefits. For-profit hospitals are not tax exempt, but still typically provide some quantity of charitable care.[217]

Not-for-profit

"The vast majority of hospitals in North America are organized as private, not-for-profit institutions. In Canada, 95 per cent of all hospitals are so owned. In the United States, around 10 per cent of all hospitals are for-profit institutions, whereas 70 per cent are not-for-profit hospitals and the balance is public institutions (generally run by counties or municipalities)".[218]

It is the healthcare leader's professional obligation to practice sustainable behavior as a benefit to the community, regardless of the hospital's for-profit or not-for-profit tax status. When leadership's business decisions benefit the operators and the people inside the system at the expense of innocent third parties—i.e. community members—leadership is not fulfilling its professional obligation. Said differently, when the hospital pollutes potable water sources, it is at the expense of the community and contradicts the healthcare leader's professional imperative.

Pharmaceutical waste dumping in potable water sources is a real concern. (Conley, 2011; WHO, 1999) The Joint Commission has guidelines on pharmaceutical waste, as does the EPA through the Resource Conversation and Recovery Act (RCRA) since 1976. RCRA regulations were written for the commercial industry and did not consider the potential impact of hospital-based pharmaceuticals. The US EPA recently began auditing hospitals with fines of up to $32,500 a day; hospitals audited have received fines between $40,000 and $250,000.[219] "Recent concerns regarding the documentation of drugs in drinking, ground, and surface waters have led to a rapid rise in public awareness and calls for action at the federal, state, and local levels."[220]

Are the implications of healthcare sustainability reflected in community benefit calculations? Many healthcare organizations are content with their traditional roles, equating community benefit activities with being responsive to tax exemption requirements around indigent care. It is an immensely important contribution, but at a level of engagement that often falls short of the organization's broader potential contribution. By the very definition of the healthcare mission, it can be argued that the achievement of sustainability requires a broader engagement by hospitals. Accountability is a timely topic because of not-for-profit healthcare's focus on the Internal Revenue Service (IRS) 990 form. Could sustainability be included as part of the IRS 990 forms? Yes, hospitals have the opportunity to enhance community benefit through sustainability. The question is not, how is sustainability related to reporting? The question is, to what extent is sustainability a fundamental dimension of the value of community benefit and accountability to the community?

Water facts

Over 70 per cent of the Earth's surface is covered with water. Approximately 97 per cent of the Earth's water can be found in oceans.[221]

Where is the water on a hospital campus?

- Cooling towers
- Faucets
- Flow controls
- Ice machines
- Irrigation
- Kitchens
- Laundry
- Showers and tubs
- Sterilizers
- Toilets
- Vacuum systems
- Washers
- Water treatment

Alternative sources of water

- Air conditioner condensate
- Cooling tower
- Foundation drain water
- Gray water
- On-site treated wastewater systems
- Rainwater harvesting
- Stormwater harvesting

Figure 11.2 Water, water everywhere

Water is a zero sum game

Potable water is a finite resource, of which healthcare organizations are major consumers. To put it explicitly, the more water the hospital uses, the fewer resources the hospital affords the rest of the community. It is natural for healthcare leaders to be concerned about the community's water supply when considering the 24 hours per day, 7-days-a-week, 365-days-a-year nature of healthcare operations.

There are many visible, if sometimes subtle, cues that patients and fellow clinicians identify regarding water management practices. For instance, the patient may see the nurse leave the water running after she washes her hands, or the physician may drink bottled water from the vending machine rather than carry a reusable water bottle. A patient who cares about sustainability may conclude that neither her clinical team nor the hospital cares about water stewardship.

Cost of water

Water is one of the most precious resources, not only for its importance as a vital human necessity, but also because of the associated financial value. According to the Earth Policy Institute, water prices have increased over the past five years:[222]

- 27 per cent in the United States
- 32 per cent in the United Kingdom
- 45 per cent in Australia
- 50 per cent in South Africa
- 58 per cent in Canada.
- In Tunisia, the price of irrigation water increased fourfold over a decade.

For the average usage of water for a resident of Washington, DC, 127,400 gallons at the price of $380, a vendor in the slums of Guatemala would charge more than $1700.[223]

The cost of water per gallon is more than the cost of gas per gallon

The cost of water exceeds the price of gasoline. "That 9-ounce bottle of Evian spring water at $1.49? That'll cost you about $21 a gallon."[224]

FRED: What if we eliminated bottled water to support our sustainability effort?

(Fred realizes he is drinking from a plastic water bottle he purchased in the vending machine earlier that day.)

FRED: Don't look at my bottled water, please. I forgot my reusable bottle at home today.

AMALIE DUBOIS: *(Sustainability Director)* I like the idea of eliminating plastic bottles, though we need to be cognizant that bottled water sales generate revenue. Eliminating bottled water would certainly mean taking a stance that is unlikely to be fully appreciated, though it's the right thing to do.

FRED: What if we simply ban plastic water bottles? We don't provide, don't stock and don't process purchase orders for bottled water? I'm talking about putting a ban on bottled water for meetings. We'd just serve out of pitchers, right?

AMALIE DUBOIS: Right.

FRED: This decision will be a politically charged issue. It's important not to eliminate bottled water, only to turn around and spend a million dollars installing water purifiers on ever tap water outlet. Just in case we're questioned, how does the quality and safety of our tap water measure up?

AMALIE DUBOIS: Our region is one of the top ten purified waters in the country. The water coming out of the sink faucet is tested 300–400 times a day in this area.[225] There's nobody regulating the quality of bottled water, other than studies that show there's more bacteria leaching from plastic water bottles than exist in the tap water.[226]

FRED: Really?

AMALIE DUBOIS: Yes. I know Dr Goldberg and Dr Bea expressed interest in the topic of water management as it relates to the public's health because they both have recently had ill patients as the result of contaminated water. Maybe they'll help us champion water management amongst the physician community. We could give Memorial Hospital reusable water bottles as a gift during Doctor's Day. Carrying a reusable water bottle is a visible way of demonstrating commitment to sustainability.

(Dr Hedge, Chief Medical Officer, enters the room.)

DR HEDGE: Good afternoon, Amalie. I've been thinking about our hand-washing policy and reflecting on this morning's medical staff meeting. I'm sure you heard that there was dialogue about our responsibilities with regard to water stewardship. From a sustainability perspective, do you recommend that we build our policy around hand washing or around foam-in-foam-out? I'm guessing that foam-in-foam-out might conserve more water. Clinically, there's no proven difference in safety outcomes.[227]

AMALIE DUBOIS: Using water for hand washing has less of an environmental impact than using foam.[228]

DR HEDGE: It does? That's counterintuitive.

AMALIE DUBOIS: I was surprised to learn that fact too. But think about all the containers that the foam is packaged in, all of the transportation that is involved—none of that reflects sustainable values. Besides, there are usually chemicals in the foam that aren't healthy when used over an extended time. In fact, the FDA [US Food and Drug Administration] has raised concerns about some of the chemicals used in the product.[229]

FRED: Sounds like our water management policy is starting to take form. Amalie, it'll be your responsibility to coordinate with Dr Hedge to ensure all our physicians receive a reusable Memorial Hospital water bottle for Doctor's Day. Also, please coordinate with Dr Hedge for our hand-washing policy. Let's underscore our unrelenting commitment to clinical quality and safety with an appreciation for sustainability implications.

Making cents in WaterSense

WaterSense is a US EPA program that labels water conserving-related consumer goods such as bathroom sinks, toilets, flushing urinals and showerheads. According to the EPA, if one in every six houses in America installed a WaterSense-labeled faucet, six billion gallons of water would be saved. This water savings would also equate to over $50 million in energy savings.[230]

Water = Energy

Both water and energy are fundamental natural resources that are intertwined on many healthcare campuses. Energy is required to store, treat, transport as well as heat and cool water. Conversely, a significant amount of water is used in cooling and heating towers to produce energy, such as the hospital cooling tower.[231]

Leadership imperative

Most not-for-profit healthcare organizations are content with their traditional roles, equating community benefit activities as defined by the IRS through which they have obtained their tax exemption. It is an immensely important contribution, but at a level of engagement that often falls short of the organization's potential contribution. To what extent is sustainability a fundamental dimension of the value of community benefit and accountability to the community? Should the value of sustainability net cost contributions be included on IRS form 990? It is likely that future regulators will, in some fashion, recognize the value of creating clean air, clean water, reduced waste disposal and improving community health as much as indigent care and medical education. This is the future of health that may well reach even the IRS.

The unintended consequences of well intended actions can have sustainability implications, such as in the case of using foam for hand washing. Sustainability practices may indirectly impact patient care. Though the relationship between water management and community benefit can be challenging, the reality is that hospital leaders have significant opportunities to positively impact the community by managing water processes according to sustainability principles. The most direct opportunities are through organizational operations, such as disposing pharmaceutical waste according to Joint Commission and EPA standards, and by reinforcing the actions that individuals can take to be effective water stewards, such as drinking from a reusable water bottle and hand washing.

FRED: Community benefit is why we exist. Everything we do is a community benefit, regardless of whether or not we get credit from the IRS for it.

CHAIRMAN OF THE BOARD: Very true. Very true.

FRED: It's interesting, up until this point I really hadn't thought about how we might incorporate sustainability into our community benefit framework.

CHAIRMAN OF THE BOARD: You know, Fred, I think it's about time we rethink our views on community benefit. Sure, we're a nonprofit organization and community benefit is the mission we were founded on. But what are the full implications of our community benefit, and how does sustainability weigh in?

Leadership dialogue

1   How can healthcare leaders lead by example in response to the increasingly important and visible community issue of water management?
2   What is the validity of the perception that a leader using a reusable water bottle is a display of "political correctness"?
3   Realizing that the elimination of bottled water from the hospital may be unpopular with some staff members, what are the pros and cons of using it to signal the institution's commitment to improved water management?

4 Water is used to create energy, and energy is used to process water. Why does—or why does not—linking water and energy management engage leadership in sustainability strategies?
5 How can administrative leadership engage physicians to help lead sustainability improvements?

Practical application: the important role of water

The imperative

- Reducing risk from long-term water scarcity and rising water prices.
- Protecting health by increasing access to clean drinking water.
- Reducing impacts of healthcare on water pollution levels.
- Achieving financial savings through water and energy efficiency.
- Engaging employees in a sustainability program.
- Acting as a responsible community member.

The initiative

Water fills different social and environmental roles throughout the world. The approach of healthcare organizations to water management in developed regions is often one of conservation and preservation—reducing water use and eliminating pollutants when possible. Such measures often target operations and equipment, sanitary and laundry fixtures, building maintenance, food service practices and outdoor water use, and include actions such as:

- installing low-flow fixtures and irrigation systems
- retrofitting or repairing inefficient machinery
- promoting closed-loop heating, ventilation and air conditioning systems that eliminate once-through water use
- collecting rainwater and gray water from other sources for non-potable use
- managing water pollution through use of technologies such as permeable pavers, bioswales and rain gardens.

The concept of water management takes on a different meaning in less-developed locations that face issues such as lack of reliable water infrastructure, lack of access to clean drinking water, and overall water scarcity. Hospitals in such regions have developed a variety of innovative solutions to manage common water-related issues within both their organizations and their local communities. Examples of such solutions include:

- Gaviotas Hospital in Colombia using a deep-soil water pump and simple solar energy distillation technology to provide purified water to the hospital and local community members
- Kisii Hospital in Kenya partners with international organizations to install new water pumps within a local community. Water for the hospital is stored and delivered overnight, leaving the pump free for community access throughout the day
- Sambhavna Clinic in India captures rainwater for washing laundry and irrigating its on-site garden of medicinal plants with naturally treated wastewater from its facilities.

The metrics

Regardless of the external water availability context, healthcare organizations throughout the world measure water in the same way:

- quantity, cost and types of water used
- savings from water conservation and efficiency projects.

The lessons learned

- Making employees part of the process—whether asking them to report leaks, audit water fixtures or suggest ideas for water conservation—brings additional perspectives to the table and contributes to the long-term success of a water management program.
- Water is not just a behind-the-scenes operational issue—it can also be a mechanism to engage the community and employees through community classes and demonstrations on conservation measures, such as water-efficient landscaping, making a rain barrel or building a rain garden.
- Despite the differences between hospitals around the world, all have similar basic water uses in equipment, operations and procedures—uses such as hand washing, laundry, sterilization and water-using medical equipment. Globally, the vast range in water usage between facilities of similar size and scope indicates that most hospitals are using much more water than is actually necessary. Hospitals in regions where the water supply is abundant can learn conservation tactics from those where water is less easily accessible.

About the organizations

Gaviotas Hospital is located in a small, self-sustaining town of 200 people in the remote plains of Colombia. The sixteen-bed rural hospital facility was self-sufficient, running entirely on natural processes and renewable energy sources until the building was closed in the early 1990s and converted into a bottling plant that now provides free drinking water to local residents.

Kisii Hospital is a Level 5 regional referral hospital that covers the South Nyanza, South Rift and entire Gusii Regions of Kenya. The 450-bed hospital offers basic services in curative, promotive, preventive and rehabilitative care.

The Sambhavna Clinic in Bhopal, India offers free medical care and rehabilitation through allopathy, ayurveda and yoga to individuals affected by the 1984 Bhopal gas disaster. It is located on about one acre of medicinal herb garden in the heart of the gas-affected area of Bhopal.

Sources

North Carolina Department of Environment and Natural Resources (2002) *Water Conservation Checklist*, http://infohouse.p2ric.org/ref/23/22006.pdf

Ellis, J. (2006) 'Gaviotas,' *WorldChanging* September 10, www.worldchanging.com/archives/004910.html

Anon (2007) 'Las Gaviotas: sustainability in the tropics,' *World Watch Magazine* 20(3), www.worldwatch.org/node/5020

Fay, A. (n.d.) 'Kenya – Kisii Hospital Project Report,' *Blue Planet Network*, http://blueplanetnetwork.org/projects/kenya

Somnath Baidya Roy (2006) 'Making life possible,' *Yes! Magazine* August 31, www.yesmagazine.org/issues/health-care-for-all/making-life-possible

The Bhopal Medical Appeal (n.d.) 'The clinics,' www.bhopal.org/the-clinics

Official Web-portal for Kisii Level5 Hospital, http://kisiihospital.org

Syllabus integration

Overview

This lesson provides an overview of approaches that may be used to protect the quality of water that is filtered through healthcare systems.

Objectives

1   Describe the environmental significance of water quality data.
2   Identify opportunities to efficiently manage water resources.
3   Assess why and how the community benefits from water management.

Topics

1   Factors that influence water operations.
2   Risk categories of water management.

3   Gray water analysis case study for promoting resource management, stewardship and conservation.
4   Social factors that influence the adaptability of sustainable water programs.

Homework

GEMI (2007) *Collecting the Drops: A Water Sustainability Planner*. Global Environmental Management Initiative, Water Sustainability Work Group.

GGHC (2007) *Reducing Potable Water Use Technical Brief*, available online: www.gghc.org/documents/TechBriefs/GGHC_TechBrief_Reducing-Potable-Water.pdf (accessed 10/22/2012).

GGHC (2007) *Sustainable Site Design: Stormwater Mitigation Technical Brief*, available online: www.gghc.org/documents/TechBriefs/GGHC_TechBrief_SiteDesign-Stormwater.pdf (accessed 10/22/2012).

Additional resources

GGHC (2007) *Reducing Potable Water Use Technical Brief*. Green Guide for Healthcare version 2.2. www.gghc.org/documents/TechBriefs/GGHC_TechBrief_Reducing-Potable-Water.pdf

Practice Greenhealth (2008) 'Design and construction series: Low flow water fixture selection for healthcare facilities,' webinar July 11. www.practicegreenhealth.org

Practice Greenhealth (2008) 'Operations series: Water use in facilities: laundry, stormwater and green roof case studies,' webinar July 25. www.practicegreenhealth.org

12 Environmental ethics in healthcare management

Figure 12.1 Planting sustainability

Executive summary

The purpose of this chapter is to help leaders understand the ethics surrounding sustainability in healthcare. The emphasis is on the "why" more than the "how". This chapter describes what is at stake if leaders operate according to the traditional, unsustainable healthcare paradigm.

The mission of healthcare organizations argues for sustainable management to improve the triple bottom line goals of community health. It is the ethical imperative of leadership to serve the health of the community, which includes the health of the environment that influences human health.

A told story

FRED: As it turns out, the Chairman of the Board's nudge to become a sustainable organization wasn't such a bad idea after all. Sure, it was painful to admit that I didn't have all the answers. I remember the Chairman wanted me to focus on "going green" while I was doing all I could just to survive. As for corporate responsibility, I now realize that sustainability is a foundational element of every institution's missional commitment to its community, and that is especially true for hospitals, which are fundamentally institutions of health and healing.

Mission alignment

There is more to sustainability than environmentalism and the threat to human health if we maintain *status quo*.[232] Sustainability leadership provides the platform for the emergence of an emphasis on improving health, not just healthcare. The concept of sustainability is at once philosophical and operational, ethical and practical. Truly sustainable organizations invest in products and services that are fiscally, socially and environmentally responsible, regardless of the industry within which they operate.[233] At its core, sustainability is a natural component of improving public health and well-being.[234] Given the growing body of research that demonstrates the direct impact of the environment on human health,[235] it is vital to recognize sustainability as a distinct social good.

Sustainability is a shared value across a variety of human endeavors and industries. However, healthcare's stake in sustainability is unique. Sustainability has a special relationship with healthcare ethics, with the health of the community, and with the many roles of healthcare organizations within the communities they serve. Sustainability aligns with the mission of healthcare organizations. The common mission of healthcare organizations is primarily related to improving the health of individuals and the health of the community. Is the goal of sustainability part of this mission itself, or is it a strategy for achieving this mission? For healthcare in particular, it would be inconsistent from an ethical leadership perspective to be excellent at quality and ignorant of sustainability.[236] Values associated with sustainability are part of the healthcare leader's commitment to professionalism.

Healthcare as an industry cannot independently solve the problems facing our environment, but it can be a model of response, a source of expertise and a catalyst of action. Embracing sustainability presents an opportunity to redefine the field of healthcare, both internally, within the hospital itself, and in the eyes of external stakeholders. Public commitment to sustainability provides a meaningful platform from which to make contributions to the health of the community. Through sustainability, hospitals face opportunities to explicitly exercise their commitments to prevention and wellness, thereby strengthening the compact between hospitals and the communities they serve.

The next frontier of leadership

Imagine a new leader phoning her healthcare administration professor after being assigned a sustainability task at work. The new leader phones her professor and says, "Professor, I'm in my first job and you neglected to teach me about sustainability. Why didn't you ever address sustainability during all the time I was in school?"

Our young leader chose a career in healthcare administration believing that such a career would not only challenge and reward her, but would also allow her to make a positive contribution to the health and well-being of others. As she advances in her career, our healthcare leader is exposed to ethical questions that make her uneasy. For instance, she worries that hazardous pharmaceutical waste could be inadvertently discarded alongside normal trash. She wishes more attention would be devoted to how the hospital can discard its trash with confidence that it will be handled properly. She wonders whether there are mechanisms within the hospital capable of resolving these potential conflicts in ways that benefit patient and community well-being.

Sustainability resources and solutions exist in increasing numbers of healthcare organizations. Yet, hospitals throughout the country do not sort their waste sustainably, adding unnecessarily to landfills while increasing hospital costs for disposing otherwise recyclable content.[237] This is just one common example of how sustainability plays into healthcare leadership thinking. What, if anything, can healthcare leaders do to resolve this conflict for their organizations? Why should healthcare leaders care about sustainability in the first place? Exploring these questions requires informed, thoughtful and committed leaders to focus institutional attention and its impacts on the health of the community.

CHAIRMAN OF THE BOARD: Fred, your ethical commitment is to improve the health of your patients and the community that Memorial Hospital serves. That commitment must be reflected in our organizational actions.

FRED: I understand your point. I also worry about employee engagement, which is, at its core, an exchange of values; it's a promise between the healthcare leader and my employees. The promise is that the leader will optimize involvement, engagement and employee opportunities to make meaningful contributions in the workplace. If I promise employees that they will be engaged in improving health, but operate in a way that degrades environmental health, then I've misled my employees. Ethics are as much about actions as they are about moral intent.

Community benefit

Community benefit is especially important to not-for-profit healthcare organizations because it is perhaps the most visible measure of organizational commitment to mission. Healthcare organizations have a community charter, in effect. The hospital receives tax benefits in exchange for promoting the community's health. In exchange for its tax exemption, not-for-profit hospitals provide charitable care. For-profit hospitals are not tax exempt, but still often provide some quantity of incidental charitable care.[238] [239] The point is that, regardless of tax status, it is the healthcare leader's professional mission to practice ethical behavior. When leadership's business decisions benefit the operators and the people inside the system at the expense of innocent third parties such as patients, leadership is not fulfilling its ethical promise to the community. That is the definition of unethical behavior: taking advantage of someone who is not a party to the basic business exchange, but who is harmed by the unauthorized taking of their interest. Certainly, many healthcare leaders do not consider sustainability as part of their ethical decision-making framework.

Why is sustainability an ethical issue?

FRED: You know, the reason I got into healthcare in the first place was because I wanted to make a difference in the lives of others. I was, and still am, committed to the belief that being a healthcare leader provides a unique opportunity to impact the world in a meaningful way.

CHAIRMAN OF THE BOARD: That's good to hear.

FRED: As we develop our new leadership strategies, I'm starting to get some of my old idealism back. It's been a great learning experience to see how we can achieve business results with a holistic strategy based on driving out waste, saving resources, moving upstream to prevent problems, and looking downstream for true life-cycle costs and benefits. It's led to a much more effective mindset focused on prevention long term. Our new organizational strategy is dedicated to both improving health and avoiding unintended harm. That's why I got into this business in the first place.

First and foremost, sustainability is central to the concept and definition of healthcare, and therefore it is the business of healthcare. Sustainability is about identifying root causes and fully analyzing the downstream effects, improving processes to reduce waste, and improving the health of the community. One cannot define the health of an individual or community holistically without considering the environment. Second, holistic leadership incorporates an ethic of sustainability that is central to the direction social and public policy is headed. Worldwide, capitated and bundled payments are an emerging strategy for reducing healthcare costs by reimbursing providers for clinically defined episodes of care.[240] [241] [242] Moving away from fee-for-service reimbursement will provide incentives to improve the health status of the population, reduce utilization and control costs. One could call it holistic leadership for a sustainable triple bottom line of healthcare.

The narrow value framework

If the value of the organization is restricted to curative care and serving as a doctors' workshop, then it has what can be defined as a narrow value framework. The weakness in the narrow value framework is that it does not align with the broad scope of the community's health needs. Restoring clinical health is certainly one dimension of an individual's health needs, but only one dimension.

Take obesity as an example. The hospital that embodies the narrow value framework may treat the obese patient through surgery and solve the weight problem in the short term. It is a wonderful outcome for the patient, who has struggled and receives an improved quality of life because of the restorative services of the hospital and surgical team. This value has been so substantial, in fact, that hospitals are well loved for their ability to restore health, even as they have not been particularly effective or incentivized to move upstream and prevent many of the root causes of the illnesses they treat.

The broad value framework

Most hospitals take a narrow view of where their resources can be deployed and which of the community's needs can be addressed. This choice is in part an ethical issue. The community has a broad set of health-related needs, and the hospital boasts an aggregation of skills and technology at considerable expense to the community's resources.

FRED: We've done some great things for our patients over the years. But I'm beginning to believe that we may have underperformed some of our potential as well. As we work to accelerate our improvement in quality, service and finances via our sustainability engagement approach, it seems we could think more broadly about our community service equation. There may well be a broader value equation we should be pursuing. We might win over the entire City Council, not just the Mayor, if we took on a broader community commitment that includes sustainability. I've always thought that it's leadership's business to address the community's health needs...

CHAIRMAN OF THE BOARD: I would hope so...

FRED: But now, in addition, I believe that, just as leadership should make it our business to raise awareness and educate the community about obesity, so too should leadership raise understanding of the consequences that impact our community's health and the planet's health. I guess we are back to that triple bottom line again; anything else seems incomplete in terms of our mission.

Current state

Sustainability is a form of accountability that translates into maximizing the productive life cycle of investments in the healthcare system.[243] Increasingly, communities across the country and the world believe that healthcare leaders should be accountable for business decisions, including decisions that impact the environment.[244] Healthcare leaders may be held to an even higher standard of accountability than commercial industry leaders because of their commitment to the Hippocratic oath: first, do no harm.[245] Given these expectations, future healthcare leaders are an ideal audience for sustainability education.[246] Leaders who shy away from their sustainability responsibilities are effectively shunning evidence-based management best practices that demonstrate short- and long-term cost savings as well as improved environmental and population health management.

Future state

The World Health Organization and the American Public Health Association are examples of leading health entities that cite the health of one's environment as a major indicator of human health.[247] The National Institute for Occupational Safety and Health and the Occupational Safety and Health Association focus on the impact of human-made built environments on inhabitant health and workplace productivity.[248] Practice Greenhealth, the Healthier Hospitals Initiative and the American Hospital Association are among the first organizations to partner with leaders in the healthcare delivery setting to identify environmental sustainability as a key component of the healthcare agenda.[249]

A paradigm shift is underway in which the future of healthcare could look noticeably different from the systems in place today. From the United States to Colombia, from China to Australia, national healthcare reform is in process.[250] In each instance, the national healthcare model highlights concerns for both population health management and individual health accountability. Part of this transformational change acknowledges environmental health influences on human health and well-being.

Successful organizations outside of the healthcare industry are already embracing and practicing sustainable business methods.[251] Now that successful business leaders in other industries are realizing the benefits of sustainability as a leadership value, the time has arrived for healthcare leaders to embrace a holistic leadership ethic. This new leadership ethic integrates sustainability values into an empowering and broad engagement of the total community to create a future of health.

Leadership imperative

It is unlikely that many leaders would argue that sustainability trumps all other goals. The principles of sustainability, fundamentally, are about doing more good and less harm with less waste. For most healthcare leaders today, sustainability means improving health, creating as little harm in the process as possible, and continuing to provide quality services with what is likely to be a shrinking supply of resources. This mindset is likely to be at the heart of priorities healthcare leaders will address in the future. For example, whether the objective concern is a better patient experience, less waste cost, less energy cost, community goodwill, brand equity, employee engagement, physician engagement, the process of managing each objective will likely be about creating more health as an organizational outcome with as few negative side effects as possible. Achieving business results while creating a sustainable organization is an international business trend with infinite applications to healthcare sustainability.[252]

Leadership dialogue

1   What is the place of sustainability in a healthcare leader's professional ethics?
2   Sustainability constitutes a new domain for many healthcare leaders, particularly the underlying issues like policy questions, implications for public health and the technical aspects of sustainability. How do leaders acknowledge the limits of their expertise while providing direction for change?
3   How can the ethics of sustainability be framed pragmatically to align with healthcare leaders' interests and priorities?

4 How can healthcare leadership manage the competition for resources between sustainability goals and other mission-related goals?
5 How can the healthcare leader remain true to her professional commitments while maintaining important relationships with business leaders who may not share her enthusiasm for tradeoffs to achieve sustainability goals?

Syllabus integration

Overview

This lecture is based on the concept that decision-makers who are responsible for preserving the value of our healthcare investments should take steps to mitigate environmental risks posed by the healthcare industry. Responsible behavior regarding healthcare sustainability supports community benefit; conversely, failure to address sustainability issues leads to profound questions about the exercise of governance and leadership responsibilities. This class is structured to start a conversation about leadership's role in taking measurable, evidence based approaches to healthcare sustainability.

Objectives

1 Explore corporate transparency as related to healthcare sustainability business practice.
2 Describe the critical linkage between leadership training and ethics.
   (a) Present elements of a leadership approach for managing healthcare ethics training needs.

Topics

1 Ethics of leadership.
2 Ethics of healthcare.
3 Employee and community training.

Homework

American College of Healthcare Executives Code of Ethics (amended 2011), available online: www.ache.org/abt_ache/code.cfm (accessed 10/22/2012).
Prepare for a final oral presentation and written content submission.

Additional resources

Bridgestar (2009) *How to Develop Yourself as a Nonprofit Leader*, Boston, MA: Bridgespan Group, available online: www.bridgespan.org/Publications-and-

Tools/Career-Professional-Development/DevelopMyself/How-to-Develop-Yourself-Nonprofit-Leader.aspx#.UHJPspiCmsg (accessed 10/22/2012).

US EPA (2009) *Green Team Checklist*. Energy Star, US Environmental Protection Agency.

Forward: evolution as epilogue

There is an inherent tension within any collaboration that exists on three different axes: the relationship between the collaborators, the evolution of the authors as they do the work, and the evolution of the ideas about which they are writing. It is fair to say that writing this book has brought about substantial change in each of these dimensions as the process progressed to a conclusion. The authors believe that the changes in each of these dimensions are instructive to other leaders who seek to grow professionally and bring about the kind of transformation of the healthcare system that only passionate, committed leaders can affect. In this epilogue, we seek to share our experience and to offer ourselves as a case study in how we grew through the process of collective thinking about leadership and the very human dimension of coming to be both better leaders and better persons.

It is hard to imagine three more different collaborators by background than a Canadian civil engineer, a healthcare leader just beginning her healthcare administration career, and a health system CEO with considerable tenure in that role. The organizing concept that galvanized this unlikely partnership was the idea that leaders in the healthcare sector do not understand enough about the current practice of sustainability to integrate it effectively into their leadership practices and priorities. The notion was that providing information about sustainability tools and change principles would empower leaders to enhance their personal competencies and create both more effective leaders and better strategic priority lists. This reorientation would improve the healthcare sector and enable leaders to achieve their mission, goals and individual career visions.

As the project progressed, the authors realized that their initial goals were substantially less powerful than the model of leadership that began to emerge. This new model was a compelling integration of sustainability principles and leadership imperatives that were meeting with great success in various locales in healthcare. In fact, it became apparent that sustainability ideas were capable of leveraging the existing agendas of healthcare leaders around quality, safety, cost, service, people, growth and community that provided an exciting vision of the future. A leadership approach that incorporated a holistic concept of organizational success, driven by a focus on a triple bottom line of organizational success, community success and sustainability success, was the vision that could energize the entire healthcare community. This new theory of leadership based on the core principles of sustainability and serving our patients, our community and environmental survivability was the only concept that could survive as a long-term model of success.

The authors did not begin their journey with this outcome in mind. In fact, they thought that three core principles would be apparent in this work.

- each individual author would bring knowledge and perspective which was a unique and a useful ingredient in creating a guide for leaders
- the principal problem was a lack of knowledge on the part of healthcare leaders
- the work of writing the book would represent a useful contribution to the field of healthcare management, but would have little impact on the authors themselves.

All three of these principles ended up being both incorrect and incomplete. After completing this book, the authors have become convinced of the following conclusions.

- The authors came to see change in their collective efforts, much as ingredients of flour, salt, yeast and water do not define bread—the product is uniquely different and more than the sum of its parts. It was, in fact, the learning that came from the authors' interactions that created value, rather than the contributions of the individual contributors. Much as yeast cannot bring about great wine without transforming itself, the basic character of the authors had to meld with the grapes and juice of other collaborators to understand the discoveries that came from their collaboration.
- The missing ingredient that leads to suboptimal leadership performance in healthcare is not a lack of knowledge, but rather the lack of a holistic view of leadership based upon the central mission of healthcare, which is to improve health. Knowledge is the essential grist which leaders bring to their craft. But it is much more important that the context for leadership be informed by the fundamental goals and motivations of the constituents and the owners of most community hospitals.
- The authors found that they both grew and evolved as leaders through the process of articulating this new leadership concept. While there may well be authors who begin a book with a well developed thesis that simply is recorded for the benefit of others, in this case the central concept evolved substantially as the authors themselves grew to understand the implications of the holistic view of leadership that emerged.

The authors celebrate the development of this new theory of holistic sustainability leadership as different people with different theories of leadership. We believe that the future of health must be joined by those leaders who believe that a triple bottom line of patient-centric, community-centric and environment-centric will provide the foundation for a sustainable healthcare system. Our new-found calling is to be the architects and advocates of this new concept of holistic leadership, which we believe will improve the health of the citizens and communities we serve.

It will also contribute to sustaining life on our planet and those who depend upon it. We invite all who agree with this goal to join the future of sustainable healthcare leadership.

Carrie Rich
Knox Singleton
Seema Wadhwa

Appendix

Sample Letter to Hospital Group Purchasing Organization Requesting Less-Toxic Products

Minnesota Technical Assistance Program ■ RESOURCE

Dear <insert name>:

As a health care provider deeply committed to public health, <insert your hospital's name> is re-examining the ways in which our operations affect our community. In particular, given the link between environmental quality and health, we are seeking to reduce the size of <insert your hospital's name>'s "environmental footprint."

<insert your hospital's name> is interested in procuring safe and cost-effective medical products whose manufacture does not produce mercury—a heavy metal—or persistent, bioaccumulative toxin (PBTs) emissions; which do not contain such materials; and which do not produce them when disposed or treated.

In June 1998, the American Hospital Association and the U.S. Environmental Protection Agency signed a Memorandum of Understanding with the goal of reducing the volume and toxicity of the medical waste stream. The partnership is now Hospitals for a Healthy Environment. Specific goals include reducing total volume of waste by 33 percent by 2005 and 50 percent by 2010; virtually eliminating mercury-containing waste by 2005; and minimizing other PBTs produced by the medical sector.

These goals are to be achieved through pollution prevention measures, such as the purchase of non-toxic medical products. Accordingly, we are asking <insert your GPO name> to inform us how you can help us and other members who wish to comply with the Memorandum of Understanding. Specifically, given the serious health risks posed by mercury and dioxins—highly potent persistent bioaccumulative toxins produced when polyvinyl chloride (PVC) is manufactured and incinerated—we are seeking <insert your GPO name>'s responses to the following questions:

- Which products that <insert your hospital's name> purchases from <insert your GPO name> contain mercury or PVC?

- Does <insert your GPO name> offer versions of these products that do not contain these materials, and if so, what are they?

- If <insert your GPO name> does not currently offer non-toxic versions of these products, does it plan to do so in the future?

- Is <insert your GPO name> willing to allow members to purchase non-toxic products off-contract without incurring financial penalties in doing so?

We appreciate your response to this inquiry. All sectors of the health care industry must cooperate with one another if the significant benefits to public health envisioned by Memorandum of Understanding are to be realized. The environmental consequences of medical product purchasing can no longer be ignored. We look forward to working with you to achieve these worthwhile goals.

Sincerely,

Developed by the Minnesota Center for Environmental Advocacy's Polyvinyl Chloride (PVC) Task Force and provided by MnTAP.

MnTAP is funded by a grant from the Minnesota Office of Environmental Assistance to the University of Minnesota, School of Public Health. © 2002 MnTAP. Reprint only with permission from MnTAP. Available in alternative formats upon request. Printed on recycled paper containing a minimum of 10% postconsumer waste.

MnTAP • University of Minnesota • 200 Oak Street SE, Suite 350 • Minneapolis • Minnesota 55455-2008
612/624-1300 • 800/247-0015 (Minnesota only) • FAX 612/624-3370 • www.mntap.umn.edu

Notes

1 Centers for Medicare and Medicaid Services (2009) *National Health Expenditures Fact Sheet.* Office of the Actuary/National Health Statistics Group, Department of Health & Human Services. https://www.cms.gov/NationalHealthExpendData/25_NHE_Fact_Sheet.asp

2 WHO (2011) 'Public Health and Environment (PHE), health through a better environment,' www.who.int/phe/en

3 Anon. (2010) 'Green lantern: how much trash does a hospital produce?,' *The Washington Post* October 18. www.washingtonpost.com/wp-yn/content/article/2010/10/18/AR2010101804465.html

4 Energy Information Administration (2008) 'Energy Star for healthcare,' www.energystar.gov/index.cfm?c=healthcare.bus_healthcare

5 Anon. (2007) 'Exposure to substances in the workplace and new-onset asthma: an international prospective population-based study (ECRHS-II),' *The Lancet* 370: 336–41. www.creal.cat/pdf/dossier_lancet_def_eng.pdf

6 Brundtland Commission (1987) *Report of the World Commission on Environment and Development: Our Common Future*, p. 43. www.un-documents.net/wced-ocf.htm

7 Inova is a not-for-profit health system based in Northern Virginia. Governed by a voluntary board of community members, Inova's vision is to optimize the health and well-being of each individual. Inova is reinventing itself around predicting and preventing disease, individualizing therapy and wellness, and transforming patient care through genomic research.

8 Studer, Q. (2003) *Hardwiring Excellence: Purpose, Worthwhile Work, Making a Difference*, Gulf Breeze, FL: Fire Star Publishing.

9 *ibid.*

10 Practice Greenhealth (2012) 'Sample job description: Healthcare Sustainability Director,' Reston, VA: Practice Greenhealth. http://practicegreenhealth.org/pubs/toolkit/greenteam/SampleJDSustainabilityDirector.pdf. Rich, C., Singleton, J. and Wadhwa, S. (2011) 'Teaching sustainability as part of healthcare management studies: challenges, best practices and case studies,' CleanMed 2011, Phoenix, Arizona, April 5–8, 2011.

11 Department of Transportation (2011) Electronic Code of Federal Regulations, July 7. Pipeline and Hazardous Materials Safety Administration. http://ecfr.gpoaccess.gov/cgi/t/text/text-idx?c=ecfr&tpl=/ecfrbrowse/Title49/49cfrv2_02.tpl

12 US EPA (2004) *Code of Federal Regulations Title 40 Protection of Environment, Section 311*, revised July 1. Washington, DC: Environmental Protection Agency. http://edocket.access.gpo.gov/cfr_2004/julqtr/40cfr311.1.htm

13 Anon. (2008) 'Fairfax County Board of Supervisors adopts green building policy,' Fairfax County Board of Supervisors, February 11. www.fairfaxcounty.gov/news/2008/030.htm

14 OSHA (2011) 'Hazardous waste,' Washington, DC: Occupational Health & Safety Administration, US Department of Labor. www.osha.gov/SLTC/hazardouswaste/index.html

15 Mufson, S. and Yang, J. L. (2011) 'A quarter of US nuclear plants not reporting equipment defects, report finds,' *The Washington Post* March 24. www.washingtonpost.com/business/economy/a-quarter-of-us-nuclear-plants-not-reporting-equipment-defects-report-finds/2011/03/24/ABHYa2RB_story.html

16 Derksen, D. and Whelan, E.-M. (2009) *Closing the Health Care Workforce Gap: Reforming Federal Health Care Workforce Policies to Meet the Needs of the 21st Century*. Washington, DC: Center for American Progress. www.americanprogress.org/issues/2010/01/pdf/health_care_workforce.pdf

17 Block, R. (n.d.) 'Boomers: you need to rethink seeking full time jobs with Gen Xers,' *Workforce50.com*. www.workforce50.com/Content/Articles/Art0025-Boomers-Rethink.cfm

18 Lewis, A. (2011) 'How my company hires for culture first, skills second,' *Harvard Business Review* January 26. http://blogs.hbr.org/cs/2011/01/how_my_company_hires_for_cultu.html

19 'The economic benefits of sustainable design,' www1.eere.energy.gov/femp/pdfs/buscase_section2.pdf

20 http://planning.ucsc.edu/pac/MtgNotes/gstf/attach/UC_sustainability_in_complete.pdf

21 Buchbinder, S.H. and Shanks, N.C. (2012) *Introduction to Health Care Management*. Burlington, MA: Jones and Bartlett Learning.

22 Anon. (2011) 'At long last...pay for outcomes starts to replace pay for performance,' *Managed Care Magazine* September. www.managedcaremag.com/archives/1109/1109.payforoutcomes.html

23 Mathur, Y. (2009) 'Health care reform explained,' *Business Today*. www.businesstoday.org/magazine/its-always-christmas-washington/health-care-reform-explained

24 Davis, K., Schoen, C. and Stremikis, K. (2010) *Mirror, Mirror on the Wall. How the Performance of the US Health Care System Compares Internationally*. Washington, DC: Commonwealth Fund. www.commonwealthfund.org/~/media/Files/Publications/Fund%20Report/2010/Jun/1400_Davis_Mirror_Mirror_on_the_wall_2010.pdf

25 The Health Care Marketplace Project (2011) 'Health care spending in the United States and selected OECD countries,' Kaiser Family Foundation. www.kff.org/insurance/snapshot/oecd042111.cfm

26 CMS (2012) *NHE Fact Sheet*. Centers for Medicare & Medicaid Services. www.cms.gov/Research-Statistics-Data-and-Systems/Statistics-Trends-and-Reports/NationalHealthExpendData/NHE-Fact-Sheet.html

27 Health Care Without Harm (n.d.) 'The campaign for environmentally responsible health care.' http://hcwh-newsletter.ecn.cz/about.shtml

28 Elkington, J. (n.d.) 'From the triple bottom line to zero,' www.johnelkington.com/activities/ideas.asp

29 http://practicegreenhealth.org

30 www.hcwh.org/all_regions/about

31 http://healthierhospitals.org

32 http://greenhospitals.net

33 www.epa.gov
34 www.energystar.gov/index.cfm?c=about.ab_index
35 EERE Information Center (2011) *Building Technologies Program: Join the Hospital Energy Alliance*. US Department of Energy, Energy Efficiency & Renewable Energy, Commercial Building Initiative. http://apps1.eere.energy. gov/buildings/publications/pdfs/alliances/hospital_energy_alliance_fact_ sheet.pdf
36 www.usgbc.org
37 Cram, P., Bayman, L., Popescu, L., Vaughan-Sarrazin, M., Cai, X. and Rosenthal, G. (2010) 'Uncompensated care provided by for-profit, not-for-profit, and government owned hospitals,' *BMC Health Services Research* 10(90): 1–13. www.biomedcentral.com/content/pdf/1472-6963-10-90.pdf
38 Berchicci, L. and Bodewes, W. (2005) 'Bridging environmental issues with new product development,' *Business Strategy and the Environment* 14: 272–85.
39 Bansal, P. and Roth, K. (2000) 'Why companies go green: a model of ecological responsiveness,' *Academy of Management Journal* 43(4): 717–48.
40 McKinsey & Company (2008) 'How companies think about climate change: a McKinsey global survey', *McKinsey Quarterly* February. www. mckinseyquarterly.com/How_companies_think_about_climate_change_A_ McKinsey_Global_Survey_2099
41 *ibid.*
42 Colburn, M. (2011) 'Overcoming cynicism: Lord Hastings' call to action at Net Impact,' *GreenBiz* November 2. www.greenbiz.com/blog/2011/11/02/ overcoming-cynicism-lord-hastings-call-action-net-impact
43 McKinsey & Company: 2008, 'How Companies Think About Climate Change: A McKinsey Global Survey', *The McKinsey Quarterly* February.
44 Makower, J. (2012) *State of Green Business Report 2011*. Oakland, CA: GreenBiz   Group.   www.greenbiz.com/research/report/2011/02/01/ state-green-business-report-2011?ms=41569
45 Ferracone, R. (2011) 'The role of environmental sustainability in executive compensation,'   *Forbes*   April   26.   www.forbes.com/sites/ robinferracone/2011/04/26/ the-role-of-environmental-sustainability-in-executive-compensation
46 Buechner, S. and Ellis, M. (2011) '3 ways to improve green business rankings,' *GreenBiz* November 3. www.greenbiz.com/blog/2011/11/03/3 -ways-improve-green-business-rankings
47 US News & World Report (2011) 'National University Rankings. Education Colleges.'   http://colleges.usnews.rankingsandreviews.com/best-colleges/ rankings/national-universities
48 Lacy, P. (2010) 'On the verge of a sustainability "tipping point",' *GreenBiz* June 24. www.greenbiz.com/blog/2010/06/24/verge-new-era-sustainability
49 Baier, P. (2011) 'How leading firms make their sustainability reports stand out,' *GreenBiz*, May 3. www.greenbiz.com/blog/2011/05/03/how-leading-firms-make-their-sustainability-reports-stand-out
50 Ernst & Young (2011) *Climate Change and Responsibility: Shareholders Press Boards on Social and Environmental Risks*. Ernst & Young. www. ey.com/Publication/vwLUAssets/CCaSS_social_environmental_risks/$FILE/ CCaSS_social_environmental_risks.pdf
51 AASHE (2010) *Higher Education Sustainability Staffing Survey*. Denver: Association for the Advancement of Sustainability in Higher Education. www.aashe.org/files/2010_staffing_survey_final.pdf

52 *ibid.*
53 *ibid.*
54 Covey, S.R. (1989) *The Seven Habits of Highly Effective People.* New York: Simon & Schuster.
55 *ibid.*
56 US Bureau of Labor Statistics (2010) 'The 2010 President's Budget for the Bureau of Labor Statistics.' Bureau of Labor Statistics. www.bls.gov/bls/budget2010.htm
57 Galbraith, K. (2009) 'Study cites strong green job growth,' *The New York Times* June 10. http://green.blogs.nytimes.com/2009/06/10/study-cites-strong-green-job-growth
58 Muro, M., Rothwell, J. and Saha, D. (2011) 'Sizing the clean economy: a national and regional green jobs assessment,' *Brookings Report* July 13. www.brookings.edu/reports/2011/0713_clean_economy.aspx
59 US Bureau of Labor Statistics (2010) *op. cit.* (note 56)
60 Inova Health System (n.d.) 'Our environmental commitment.' www.inova.org/about-inova/sustainability/index.jsp
61 Anon. (n.d.) 'Gundersen Lutheran teams with brewery on unique "green" endeavor,' Gundersen Lutheran. www.gundluth.org/?id=3069&sid=1
62 Brown, J. (2010) *Benchmarking Sustainability in Health Care Awards Benchmark Report.* Reston, VA: Practice Greenhealth. www.cleanmed.org/2010/downloads/presentations/C4/Brown.pdf
63 Griffith, J.R. and White, K.R. (2007) *The Well-Managed Healthcare Organization,* 6th edn. Chicago, IL: Health Administration Press.
64 Brown, J. (2010) *Benchmarking Sustainability op. cit.* (note 62)
65 *ibid.*
66 *ibid.*
67 Gidlason, D.S. (n.d.) 'Public health vs. the doctor's office,' Nutramed. www.nutramed.com/medicalcare/public_health.htm
68 Epstein, R. (1995) 'Communication between primary care physicians and consultants,' *Archives of Family Medicine* 4(5): 403–9. www.ncbi.nlm.nih.gov/pubmed/7742962
69 Pho, K. (2011) 'Primary care doctors and specialists need to better communicate,' KevinMD.com. www.kevinmd.com/blog/2011/01/primary-care-doctors-specialists-communicate.html
70 Beeson, S. (2006) *Practicing Excellence: Five Reasons Medical Groups and Hospitals Striving for Culture Change Must Get Physicians on Board.* Gulf Breeze: Five Starter Publishing
71 Collins, A. (2011) 'Food, health and the environment: the role of the clinician,' FoodMed.org. www.foodmed.org/2011/presentations/E2-Collins.pdf
72 Caper, P. (2009) 'Health care should be driven by mission, not money,' Physicians for a National Health Program, December 7. www.pnhp.org/news/2009/december/health-care-should-be-driven-by-mission-not-money
73 Terry, K. (2009) 'Hospital EHRs don't make paper go away,' *CBS News* July 29. www.cbsnews.com/8301-505123_162-43840588/hospital-ehrs-dont-make-paper-go-away/
74 *ibid.*
75 Turley, M., Porter, C., Garrido, T., Gerwig, K., Young, S., Radler, L. and Shaber, R. (2011) 'Use of electronic health records can improve the health care industry's environmental footprint,' *Health Affairs* 30(5): 938–46. http://content.healthaffairs.org/content/30/5/938.abstract

76 *ibid.*
77 Partners HealthCare System, Massachusetts, 2009 (interview).
78 Turley *et al.* (2011) *op. cit.* (note 75).
79 Brown, J. (2010) *Benchmarking Sustainability op. cit.* (note 62)
80 Lean Enterprise Institute (2009) 'What is Lean?,' Cambridge, MA: Lean Enterprise Institute. www.Lean.org/whatsLean
81 *ibid.*
82 Doman, J.L. (2007) 'Leveraging lean process improvement methodology to promote economic and environmental sustainability: obstacles and opportunities,' MSc thesis, Department of Civil Engineering, Technology Environmental Management & Safety, Rochester Institute of Technology, Rochester, NY, USA.
83 Lean Enterprise Institute (2009) *op cit.* (note 80).
84 Anon. (n.d.) 'A brief history of Lean,' *Strategos Lean Briefing.* www. strategosinc.com/just_in_time.htm
85 HealthCare Value Network (n.d.) HealthCare Value Leaders. www. healthcarevalueleaders.org
86 AHA   (n.d.)   'Waste,'   American   Hospital   Association.   www. sustainabilityroadmap.org/topics/waste.shtml
87 Doman (2007) *op. cit.* (note 82).
88 Lantz, P., Lichtenstein, R. and Pollack, H. (2007) 'Health policy approaches to population health: the limits of medicalization,' *Health Affairs* 26(5): 1253–57. http://content.healthaffairs.org/content/26/5/1253.full
89 Lisha Lo (2011) *Teamwork and Communication in Healthcare.* Edmonton: Canadian Patient Safety Institute. www.patientsafetyinstitute.ca/English/ toolsResources/teamworkCommunication/Documents/Canadian%20 Framework%20for%20Teamwork%20and%20Communications%20 Lit%20Review.pdf
90 Association of Bay Area Governments (2003) 'Why are hospitals rethinking regulated medical waste management?,' www.abag.ca.gov/bayarea/dioxin/ pilot_projs/MW_Background.pdf
91 *ibid.*
92 *ibid.*
93 *ibid.*
94 *ibid.*
95 Gordon, E. (2012) 'Fast food's slow exit from hospitals,' *Kaiser Health News* April 12. http://capsules.kaiserhealthnews.org/index.php/2012/04/ fast-foods-slow-exit-from-hospitals
96 Watters, C., Sorensen, J., Fiala, A. and Wismer, W. (2003) 'Exploring patient satisfaction with foodservice through focus groups and meal rounds,' *Journal of the American Dietetic Association* 103(10): 1347–49. www.journals.elsevierhealth.com/periodicals/yjada/article/S0002-8223(03) 01077-0/abstract
97 Paris, L. (2011) 'Pew finds serious gaps in oversight of US drug safety,' *Pew Health Group Safety* July 12. www.pewhealth.org/news-room/press-releases/ pew-finds-serious-gaps-in-oversight-of-us-drug-safety-85899367931
98 Anon. (2011) 'Outsourcing sees stimulus effect,' *Modern Healthcare* August 11.   www.modernhealthcare.com/article/20100920/MAGAZINE/100919 948
99 US EPA (2012) 'Medical waste frequent questions,' US Environment Protection Agency. www.epa.gov/osw/nonhaz/industrial/medical/mwfaqs. htm#1

100 Association of Bay Area Governments (2003) *op. cit.* (note 90).
101 Department of Health and Children (2005) *Waste Management in Hospitals.* Government of Ireland. http://audgen.gov.ie/documents/vfmreports/49_ Waste_Management_in_Hospitals.pdf
102 Brown, J. (2010) *Benchmarking Sustainability op. cit.* (note 62)
103 *ibid.*
104 Towers Watson and National Business Group on Health (2010) *Raising the Bar on Health Care.* www.towerswatson.com/assets/pdf/1345/TW_15565_ NBGH.pdf
105 Practice Greenhealth (2012) 'Practice Greenhealth 2012 Environmental Excellence Awards.' http://practicegreenhealth.org/awards/award-winners
106 Brown, J. (2010) *Benchmarking Sustainability op. cit.* (note 62)
107 *ibid.*
108 *ibid.*
109 *ibid.*
110 *ibid.*
111 Association of Bay Area Governments (2003) *op. cit.* (note 90).
112 e-Stewards (2010) 'The e-waste crisis introduction,' http://e-stewards.org/ the-e-waste-crisis
113 *ibid.*
114 Brown, J. (2010) *Benchmarking Sustainability op. cit.* (note 62)
115 *ibid.*
116 *ibid.*
117 Cal Recycle (2006) Medical waste posters and stickers. www.calrecycle. ca.gov/ReduceWaste/Business/posters/redbag.htm
118 Elkington, J. (n.d.) 'From the triple bottom line to zero,' www.johnelkington. com/activities/ideas.asp
119 Manos, D. (2010) 'Experts name 9 ways to fix healthcare workforce shortage,' *Health Care Finance News* January 15. www. healthcarefinancenews.com/news/ experts-name-9-ways-fix-healthcare-workforce-shortage
120 McCain, M. (2011) *Ambulatory Care of the Future: Optimizing Health, Service, and Cost by Transforming the Care Delivery Model.* The Chartis Group. www.chartis.com/files/pdfs/Ambulatory_Care_of_the_Future.pdf
121 Gershon, R.R.M., Pogorzelska, M., Qureshi, K.A., Stone, P.W., Canton, A.N., Samar, S.M., Westra, L.J., Damsky, M.R. and Sherman M. (2008) 'Home health care patients and safety hazards in the home: preliminary findings,' Agency for Healthcare Research and Quality. www.ahrq.gov/ downloads/pub/advances2/vol1/Advances-Gershon_88.pdf
122 PACE (n.d.) 'State resources,' National PACE Association. www.npaonline. org/website/article.asp?id=203
123 Gershon et al. (2008) *op. cit.* (note 121)
124 News Medical (2010) 'Sg2: Demand for outpatient services to increase by nearly 22% over the next decade,' *News Medical* January 6. www.news-medical.net/news/20100106/Sg2-Demand-for-outpatient-services-to-increase-by-nearly-2225-over-the-next-decade.aspx
125 PACE (n.d.) 'Program of All-Inclusive Care for the Elderly,' Medicaid. www. medicaid.gov/Medicaid-CHIP-Program-Information/By-Topics/Long-Term-Services-and-Support/Integrating-Care/Program-of-All-Inclusive-Care-for-the-Elderly-PACE/Program-of-All-Inclusive-Care-for-the-Elderly-PACE. html

126 APHA (n.d.) *At the Intersection of Public Health and Transportation: Promoting Healthy Transportation Policy.* American Public Health Association. www.apha.org/NR/rdonlyres/43F10382-FB68-4112-8C75-49 DCB10F8ECF/0/TransportationBrief.pdf

127 Gallup (n.d.) 'Employee engagement.' www.gallup.com/consulting/52/Employee-Engagement.aspx

128 US DOT (2010) 'Transportation is a public health issue; DOT doing its part to keep kids moving,' United States Department of Transportation July 16. http://fastlane.dot.gov/2010/07/dot-doing-its-part-to-keep-kids-moving. html

129 Policy Link (n.d.) 'The food trust.' www.policylink.org/atf/cf/%7B97c6d565-bb43-406d-a6d5-eca3bbf35af0%7D/GROCERYGAP_EXECSUMMARY. PDF

130 Ross, A. (2010) 'Planning, transport, and health inequalities – a recent history and future progress,' Local Government Improvement and Development. www.idea.gov.uk/idk/core/page.do?pageId=23454074

131 NICE (2008) 'Physical activity and the environment,' National Institute for Health and Clinical Excellence. http://publications.nice.org.uk/ physical-activity-and-the-environment-ph8

132 NICE (2008) 'Guidance on the promotion and creation of physical environments that support increased levels of physical activity,' London: National Institute for Health and Clinical Excellence. http://guidance.nice. org.uk/PH8

133 US DOT (2010) *op. cit.* (note 128).

134 Minnesota Life and Securian (2008) 'The new buzz in health: wellness programs offer savings for employers, a new revenue source for producers,' Minnesota Life. www.lifebenefits.com/lb/pdfs/F62382-20%20Get%20 More%2012.pdf

135 US DHHS (2003) 'Prevention makes common "cents",' Washington, DC: US Department of Health and Human Services. http://aspe.hhs.gov/health/ prevention

136 Berry, L., Mirabito, A. and Baun, W. (2010) 'What's the hard return on employee wellness programs?,' *Harvard Business Review.* http://hbr. org/2010/12/whats-the-hard-return-on-employee-wellness-programs/ar/1

137 Denning, E. (2011) 'Exercise in the workplace: part of Surgeon General's vision for healthy and fit nation,' *Corporate Fitness Works* February 18. www.corporatefitnessworks.com/2011/02/ exercise-in-the-workplace-part-of-surgeon-generals-vision-for-healthy-fit-nation/

138 Walsh, D. (2012) 'Taking sustainability seriously,' *Green at Work* January 27. http://greenatwork.com/blog/2012/01/27/taking-sustainability-seriously/

139 Nutramed (2011) 'Cars, trucks, air pollution and health,' Alpha Online. www.nutramed.com/environment/cars.htm

140 *ibid.*

141 US EPA (n.d.) 'Clean Air Act,' Washington, DC: US Environmental Protection Agency. www.epa.gov/air/caa/

142 'bryandamis' (2011) 'A holistic approach to environmental public health,' *National Environmental Health Promotion Network* September 29. http:// nehpnblog.com/?p=73

143 National Prevention Council (2011) *National Prevention Strategy: America's Plan for Better Health and Wellness.* Rockville: National Prevention, Health

Promotion and Public Health Council. www.healthcare.gov/prevention/nphpphc/strategy/report.pdf

144 Oglethorpe, D. (2008) 'Local food – miles better?,' *World Watch* 22(3): 12–15. www.europeansupplychainmanagement.co.uk/article-page.php?contentid=4203&issueid=174

145 WebMD (2009) 'Food & recipes: healthy eating,' *WebMD* October 12. www.webmd.com/food-recipes/tc/healthy-eating-overview

146 Hyde, L. (2011) 'Confessions of a formal education enabler,' *Museum Commons* August 8. http://museumcommons.blogspot.com/2011_08_01_archive.html

147 Hand, L. (2009) 'Employer health incentives,' *Harvard School of Public Health*. www.hsph.harvard.edu/news/hphr/winter-2009/winter09healthincentives.html

148 *ibid*.

149 Ornish, D. (2009) 'Mostly plants,' *American Journal of Cardiology* 104(7): 957–58. http://engine2diet.com/wp/wp-content/uploads/Dean-Ornish-Mostly-Plants.pdf

150 Whitlock, J.L. (2003) 'Strategic thinking, planning, and doing: how to reunite leadership and management to connect vision with action,' Washington, DC: George Washington University Center for Excellence in Municipal Management, mimeo.

151 'Why local?,' *Get Local Foods*. http://getlocalfoods.com/Why-go-Local/The-Issue.aspx

152 Krebs, A. (n.d.) 'Corporate agribusiness: monopolising subsistence,' *Converge*. www.converge.org.nz/pirm/corpag.htm

153 Wickel, R. (2012) 'From class to farm: students grow understanding of food production,' *The Pendulum: Elon University's Student News Organization*, May 1. http://elonpendulum.com/2012/05/from-class-to-farm-students-grow-understanding-of-food-production

154 Brown, D., Berko, P., Dedrick, P., Hilliard, B. and Pfleeger, J. (2010) *Burgerville: Sustainability and Sourcing in a QSR Supply Chain*. Portland, OR: Center for Global Leadership in Sustainability, School of Business Administration, Portland State University. www.sba.pdx.edu/cgls/media/Burgerville%20Supply%20Chain%20-%20Case%20Study%20CGLS-RR-11-01.pdf

155 Campbell II, T. and Campbell, C.T. (2008) 'The benefits of integrating nutrition into clinical medicine,' *Israel Medical Association Journal* 10: 730–32.

156 Sustainable Table (2009) 'Why buy local?,' *Sustainable Table*. www.sustainabletable.org/issues/whybuylocal/#fn8

157 Frith, K. (2007) '"Is local more nutritious?" It depends,' Center for Health and the Global Environment, Harvard Medical School. http://chge.med.harvard.edu/sites/default/files/resources/local_nutrition.pdf

158 CDC (2012) 'Overweight and obesity,' Centers for Disease Control and Prevention. www.cdc.gov/obesity/data/facts.html

159 Sabrina, A. (2010) 'America's obesity epidemic to cost $550 billion by 2030: study. *International Business Times*, May 8. www.ibtimes.com/articles/338553/20120508/america-s-obesity-epidemic-hangs-550-billion.htm

160 Parker-Pope, T. (2008) 'Boosting health with local food,' *New York Times WellBlogs*, June 6. http://well.blogs.nytimes.com/2008/06/06/boosting-health-with-local-food/

161   Drewnowski, A. and Darmon, N. (2005) 'Food choices and diet costs: an economic analysis,' *Journal of Nutrition* 135(4): 900–4. www.ncbi.nlm.nih.gov/pubmed/15795456

162   Ornish, D. (2012) 'Holy Cow! What's good for you is good for our planet,' *Archives of Internal Medicine* (online first) E9–E10. www.natap.org/2012/newsUpdates/archinternmed.2012.174v1.pdf

163   Martinez, S., Hand, M., Pollack, S. *et al.* (2010) *Local Food Systems Concepts, Impacts, and Issues.* Washington, DC: US Department of Agriculture. www.ers.usda.gov/Publications/ERR97/ERR97.pdf

164   Sustainable Table (2009) *op. cit.* (note 156).

165   'Buy fresh buy local,' *Food Routes.* www.foodroutes.org/buy-fresh-buy-local.jsp

166   Flower, J. (1993) 'Getting paid to keep people healthy: two ways of integrating a healthcare system,' *Healthcare Forum Journal* 36(2): 51–6.

167   Ornish, D. (2009) *op. cit.* (note 149).

168   Lipson, D.J. and Simon, S. (2010) 'Quality's new frontier: reducing hospitalizations and improving transitions in long-term care,' *Mathematica Issue Brief* 7. www.mathematica-mpr.com/publications/pdfs/health/LTQA_brief.pdf

169   Mikkonen, J. and Raphael, D. (2010) *Social Determinants of Health: The Canadian Facts.* Toronto: York University School of Health Policy and Management. www.unnaturalcauses.org/assets/uploads/file/The_Canadian_Facts.pdf

170   'Balanced menus challenge,' *Health Care Without Harm.* www.noharm.org/lib/downloads/food/Balanced_Menus_Challenge.pdf

171   Fauntleroy, G. (2007) 'Obesity leads to more hospital admissions, longer stays,' *Health Behavior News Service* December 11. www.cfah.org/hbns/archives/getDocument.cfm?documentID=1631

172   Practice Greenhealth (n.d.) 'Energy, water, & climate.' http://practicegreenhealth.org/topics/energy-water-climate

173   Newby-Clark, I. (2009) 'Creatures of habit,' *Psychology Today*, July 17. www.psychologytoday.com/blog/creatures-habit/200907/we-are-creatures-habit

174   US EPA (2004) 'Leaders in healthcare tap the power of superior energy management,' Washington, DC: Environmental Protection Agency. www.energystar.gov/ia/business/healthcare/factsheet_0804.pdf?9b81-81ae

175   WHO and Health Care Without Harm (2009) 'Healthy hospitals – healthy planet – healthy people,' Geneva: World Health Organization. www.who.int/globalchange/publications/climatefootprint_report.pdf

176   Energy Star (n.d.) 'About Energy Star,' US Environmental Protection Agency and US Department of Energy. www.energystar.gov/index.cfm?c=about.ab_index

177   Hospitals and Healthcare Networks (n.d.) 'Containing energy expenses,' www.hhnmag.com/hhnmag_app/jsp/articledisplay.jsp?dcrpath=HHNMAG/Article/data/01JAN2012/0112HHN_Feature_Gatefold 2&domain=HHN MAG

178   Energy Star (n.d.) 'Building contest.' www.energystar.gov/index.cfm?fuseaction=buildingcontest.eui

179   Odell, A.M. (2007) 'Working for the Earth: green companies and green jobs attract employees,' *GreenBiz* October 16. www.greenbiz.com/news/2007/10/16/working-earth-green-companies-and-green-jobs-attract-employees

180 Anon. (2010) 'Kaiser Permanente unveils sustainability scorecard for medical products,' Environmental Leader: *Environmental and Energy Management News* May 4. www.environmentalleader.com/2010/05/04/kaiser-permanente-launches-sustainability-scorecard-for-medical-products/

181 Dresser, T. (2012) 'Hazardous waste generation & management,' US Environmental Protection Agency, May 22. www.epa.gov/region7/education_resources/teachers/ehsstudy/ehs9.htm

182 National Cancer Institute (n.d.) President's cancer panel – annual reports. National Cancer Institute. http://deainfo.nci.nih.gov/ADVISORY/pcp/annualReports/index.htm

183 Highfield, R. (2006) 'The reality is that everything is made of chemicals,' *The Telegraph*, November 8. www.telegraph.co.uk/news/uknews/1533519/The-reality-is-that-everything-is-made-of-chemicals.html

184 Breast Cancer Fund (n.d.) 'Chemicals glossary: bisphenol A (BPA),' Breast Cancer Fund. www.breastcancerfund.org/clear-science/chemicals-glossary/bisphenol-a.html

185 EWG (n.d.) '232 toxic chemicals in 10 minority babies,' Environmental Working Group. www.ewg.org/minoritycordblood/home

186 Physicians For Social Responsibility (n.d.) 'Hazardous chemicals in health care.' www.psr.org/resources/hazardous-chemicals-in-health.html

187 *ibid.*

188 Poladian, C. (2012) 'Asthma rates continue to soar in the US,' *Medical Daily* May 17. www.medicaldaily.com/news/20120517/9921/asthma-prevalance-increase-usa.htm

189 US EPA (2010) 'Essential principles for reform of chemicals management legislation,' US Environmental Protection Agency. www.epa.gov/oppt/existingchemicals/pubs/principles.html

190 *ibid.*

191 AMA (n.d.) 'AMA's Code of Medical Ethics,' American Medical Association. www.ama-assn.org/ama/pub/physician-resources/medical-ethics/code-medical-ethics.page

192 Kanter, R.M. (2008) 'A financial turnaround requires culture change,' *Harvard Business Review* October 29. http://blogs.hbr.org/kanter/2008/10/a-financial-turnaround-require.html

193 US EPA (2010) 'Essential principles for reform of chemicals management legislation,' *op. cit.* (note 189).

194 NPHPPHC (2011) *National Prevention Strategy: America's Plan for Better Health and Wellness.* Rockville: National Prevention, Health Promotion and Public Health Council. www.healthcare.gov/prevention/nphpphc/strategy/report.pdf

195 Hughes, R. (n.d.) 'Tools and strategies for quality improvement and patient safety,' Agency for Healthcare Research and Quality. www.ahrq.gov/qual/nurseshdbk/docs/HughesR_QMBMP.pdf

196 Casey, J. (2007) *A Lean Enterprise Approach to Process Improvement in a Health Care Organization.* Massachusetts Institute of Technology. http://dspace.mit.edu/bitstream/handle/1721.1/42345/233976521.pdf

197 O'Brien-Pallas, L., Griffin, P., Shamian, J. *et al.* (2006) 'The impact of nurse turnover on patient, nurse, and system outcomes: a pilot study and focus for a multicenter international study,' *Policy Politics Nursing Practice* 7(3): 169–79.

198 Health Forum LLC (n.d.) 'Fast facts on US hospitals,' American Hospital Association. www.aha.org/research/rc/stat-studies/fast-facts.shtml

199   Klein, E. (2012) 'Why an MRI costs $1,080 in America and $280 in France,' *The Washington Post* March 3. www.washingtonpost.com/blogs/ezra-klein/ post/why-an-mri-costs-1080-in-america-and-280-in-france/2011/08/25/ gIQAVHztoR_blog.html

200   Practice Greenhealth (2011) 'Greening the OR: fluid management systems in theOR.'http://practicegreenhealth.org/webinars/greening-or-fluid-management-systems-or

201   Health Resources and Services Administration (n.d.) 'Hill–Burton free and reduced-cost health care,' US Department of Health and Human Services. www.hrsa.gov/gethealthcare/affordable/hillburton/

202   US Green Building Council (n.d.) 'About LEED.' https://www.usgbc.org/ ShowFile.aspx?DocumentID=18694

203   Anon. (n.d.) 'A comparison of the world's various green rating systems,' *FM Link*. www.fmlink.com/article.cgi?type=Magazine&title=A%20comparison %20of%20the%20world%27s%20various%20green%20rating%20 systems&pub=RFP%20Office%20Space&id=31124&mode=source

204   Northbridge Environmental Management Consultants (2003) *Analyzing the Cost of Obtaining LEED Cetification*. Westford, MA: Northbridge for The American Chemistry Council. www.cLeanair-coolplanet.org/for_communi ties/LEED_links/AnalyzingtheCostofLEED.pdf

205   *ibid.*

206   *ibid.*

207   Y Charts (2012) 'US total health care construction spending: 41.29 B for March 2012.' http://ycharts.com/indicators/us_total_health_care_construc tion_spending

208   Clancy, C.M. (2008) 'Designing for safety: evidence-based design and hospitals,' *American Journal of Medical Quality* 23(1): 66–9.

209   Gow, P. (2012) 'An experience of "yes": independent schools begin to explore and exploit the power of design thinking,' Washington, DC: National Association of Independent Schools. www.nais.org/publications/ ismagazinearticle.cfm?Itemnumber=156249&sn.ItemNumber=145956

210   Shontell, A. (2011) '11 Unusual ways Steve Jobs made Apple the world's most admired tech company,' *Business Insider* October 6. www. businessinsider.com/steve-jobs-apple

211   *ibid.*

212   White, G. (2009) 'Introduction to green leasing,' *Green Real Estate Law Journal* February 6. www.greenrealestatelaw.com/2009/02/introduction-to-green-leasing

213   Healthier Hospitals Initiative (n.d.) 'Advocate health care.' http:// healthierhospitals.org/get-inspired/leadership-spotlight/advocate-health-care

214   Fiksel, J., McDaniel, J. and Mendenhall, C. (1999) 'Measuring progress towards sustainability principles, process, and best practices,' Columbus, OH: Batelle   Memorial   Institute.   www.eco-nomics.com/images/ Sustainability%20Measurement%20GIN.pdf

215   Linn, A. (2007) 'Corporations find business case for going green,' MSNBC April   18.   www.msnbc.msn.com/id/17969124/ns/business-going_green/t/ corporations-find-business-case-going-green/#.T8RMcNVPujN

216   AWWA (n.d.) 'How much of the Earth is covered with water?,' Fairfax County Water Authority, American Water Works Association. www.fcwa. org/story_of_water/html/earth.htm

217   Federation of American Hospitals (2003) 'FTC/DOJ Hearings on Health Care and Competitive Law and Policy Statement of the Federation of

American Hospitals—Hospital's Non-Profit Status,' Federal Trade Commission. www.ftc.gov/ogc/healthcarehearings/docs/030410fay.pdf

218 Taylor, D. (2002) 'What price for-profit hospitals?,' *Canadian Medical Association Journal* 166(11): 1418–19. www.cmaj.ca/content/166/11/1418. full.pdf+html

219 Smith, C. (2007) *Managing Pharmaceutical Waste: A 10-Step Blueprint for Healthcare Facilities.* Houston: PharmEcology Associates, LLC. www. ohanet.org/SiteObjects/6F006F9A10C2D431388243EE89AF9377/waste_ ppt.pdf

220 *ibid.*

221 USGS (1984) 'How much water is there on, in, and above the Earth?,' US Geological Survey. http://ga.water.usgs.gov/edu/earthhowmuch.html

222 Clark, E.H. (2007) 'Water prices rising worldwide,' Earth Policy Institute, Plan B Updates March 7. www.earth-policy.org/index.php?/plan_b_ updates/2007/update64

223 *ibid.*

224 Carpenter, M. (2006) 'The pumped-up price of water,' *Pittsburgh Post-Gazette* March 17. www.post-gazette.com/stories/sectionfront/life/ the-pumped-up-price-of-water-432952/

225 City of Toronto (n.d.) 'Living In Toronto: frequently asked questions.' www.toronto.ca/water/faq.htm

226 Anon. (2010) 'Bottled water contains more bacteria than tap water,' *The Telegraph* May 25. www.telegraph.co.uk/health/healthnews/7763038/ Bottled-water-contains-more-bacteria-than-tap-water.html

227 Roylance, F. (2007) 'Manufacturers may be the only ones cleaning up,' *Los Angeles Times* February 11. http://articles.latimes.com/2007/feb/11/news/ adna-germs11/2

228 Anon. (2008) 'Fate of personal care products linked to environmental pollution and human health concerns,' *Science Daily.* www.sciencedaily. com/releases/2008/05/080516100942.htm

229 US FDA (2010) 'Triclosan: What consumers should know,' US Food and Drug Administration. www.fda.gov/forconsumers/consumerupdates/ ucm205999.htm

230 US EPA (n.d.) 'What is WaterSense?,' Washington, DC: Environmental Protection Agency. www.epa.gov/watersense/about_us/what_is_ws.html

231 NNEC (n.d.) 'The energy–water nexus,' New York: Network For New Energy Choices. www.newenergychoices.org/index.php?page=ew_intro&sd =ew

232 Dentzer, S. (2011) 'Embarking on a new course: environmental health coverage,' *Health Affairs* 30(5): 810.

233 IFC Sustainability (2012) 'Leadership in sustainability and corporate governance,' International Finance Corporation. www.ifc.org/sustainability.

234 MPHI View on Sustainable Society (2012) 'Sustainability,' Medicine and Public Health Initiative. www.mphi.net/?p=303&lang=en-us

235 Boone, T. (2012) *Creating a Culture of Sustainability.* Chicago: UIC Medical Center.

236 Singleton, J. (1992) 'Preserving the environment can bring hospitals savings, improved stature,' presented at Modern Healthcare Weekly Business News: Our Environment: A Healthcare Commitment, Hyatt Regency, Crystal City, Arlington, VA, March 8–9.

237 WWF (2011) 'Hospital waste factsheet,' World Wildlife Fund. www. wwfpak.org/factsheets_hwf.php

238 Day, K. (2006) 'Hospital charity care is probed,' *The Washington Post* September 13. www.washingtonpost.com/wp-dyn/content/article/2006/09/12/AR2006091201409.html

239 Federation of American Hospitals (2005) 'Future of hospital care: how will we pay the bill?,' A hospital payment symposium, Washington, DC, 15 July 2005. www.fah.org/fahCMS/Documents/Future%20of%20Hospital%20Care/Future%20Hospital%20Payment%20conference%20transcript%2007.15.05.pdf

240 CMS (2012) 'HCAHPS: Patients' Perspectives of Care Survey,' US Department of Health and Human Services, Centers for Medicare & Medicaid Services. https://www.cms.gov/HospitalQualityInits/30_HospitalHCAHPS.asp

241 Cromwell, J., Dayhoff, D. and Thoumaian, A. (1997) 'Cost savings and physician responses to global bundled payments for Medicare heart bypass surgery – innovations in fee-for-service financing and delivery,' *Healthcare Financing Review* 9(1): 41–57.

242 Satin, D. and Miles, J. (2009) 'Performance-based bundled payments: benefits and burdens of this pay-for-performance strategy,' *Minnesota Medicine* October. www.minnesotamedicine.com/PastIssues/October2009/SpecialReportOct2009/tabid/3209/Default.aspx

243 Freund, F. (2009) *Business Model Concepts in Corporate Sustainability Contexts*. Lüneburg, Germany: Leuphana Centre for Sustainability Management.

244 GEMI (2004) 'Environment: value to the investor,' Global Environmental Management Initiative. www.gemi.org/resources/GEMI%20Clear%20Advantage.pdf

245 NIH (2010) 'Greek medicine,' US National Library of Medicine, National Institutes of Health, Department of Health & Human Services. www.nlm.nih.gov/hmd/greek/greek_oath.html

246 Rich, C., Wadhwa, S. and Singleton, J. (2012) 'How to teach environmental sustainability in healthcare management education,' in *Teaching Sustainability*. Allendale, MI: Grand Valley State University, in press.

247 Tsai, T. (2010) 'Second chance for health reform in Columbia,' *The Lancet* 375(9709): 109–10. www.thelancet.com/journals/lancet/article/PIIS0140-6736(10)60033-5/fulltext

248 Johnson, J. (2008) 'Rapporteur's Report: Services sector,' *Journal of Safety Research* 39: 191–94. www.cdc.gov/niosh/topics/PtD/pdfs/Johnson.pdf

249 Umbdenstock, R. (2011) 'Hospital environmental sustainability: video intro,' American Hospital Association. www.hospitalsustainability.org

250 Thomas (2011) 'China's Health Reforms Progress,' *International Insurance News* 11 March. www.globalsurance.com/blog/chinas-healthcare-reforms-progress-324520.html

251 Warde, A. (n.d.) 'Going green to stay in the black,' University of California. www.uci.edu/features/2011/02/feature_marriott_110214.php

252 Colburn, M. (2011) 'Overcoming cynicism,' op. cit. (note 42).

References

AASHE (2010) *Higher Education Sustainability Staffing Survey.* Denver: Association for the Advancement of Sustainability in Higher Education. www.aashe.org/files/2010_staffing_survey_final.pdf

Abe, L. (2012) 'Kaiser Permanente Hawaii launches new app and mobile-optimized kp.org,' *Kaiser Permanente News Center* January 25. http://xnet.kp.org/newscenter/pressreleases/hi/2012/012512kporgmobileoptimized.html

AHA (n.d.) 'Waste,' American Hospital Association. www.sustainabilityroadmap.org/topics/waste.shtml

AHRQ (n.d.) 'Guide to health care quality,' Rockville, MD: Agency for Healthcare Research and Quality. www.ahrq.gov/consumer/guidetoq

Anon. (2008) 'Fairfax County Board of Supervisors adopts green building policy,' Fairfax County Board of Supervisors, February 11. www.fairfaxcounty.gov/news/2008/030.htm

Anon. (n.d.) 'A brief history of Lean,' *Strategos Lean Briefing.* www.strategosinc.com/just_in_time.htm

Anon. (n.d.) 'A comparison of the world's various green rating systems,' *FM Link.* www.fmlink.com/article.cgi?type=Magazine&title=A%20comparison%20of%20the%20world%27s%20various%20green%20rating%20systems&pub=RFP%20Office%20Space&id=31124&mode=source

Anon. (n.d.) 'Buy Fresh Buy Local,' Millheim PA: Food Routes. www.foodroots.org/buy-fresh-buy-local.jsp

Anon. (n.d.) 'Gundersen Lutheran teams with brewery on unique "green" endeavor,' Gundersen Lutheran webiste. www.gundluth.org/?id=3069&sid=1

Association of Bay Area Governments (2003) 'Why are hospitals rethinking regulated medical waste management?,' www.abag.ca.gov/bayarea/dioxin/pilot_projs/MW_Background.pdf

AWWA (n.d.) 'How much of the Earth is covered with water?,' Fairfax County Water Authority, American Water Works Association. www.fcwa.org/story_of_water/html/earth.htm

Baier, P. (2011) 'How leading firms make their sustainability reports stand out,' *GreenBiz,* May 3. www.greenbiz.com/blog/2011/05/03/how-leading-firms-make-their-sustainability-reports-stand-out

Bansal, P. and Roth, K. (2000) 'Why companies go green: a model of ecological responsiveness,' *Academy of Management Journal* 43(4): 717–48.

Bartels, K.A. and Parker, K.A. (2011) *Teaching Sustainability/Teaching Sustainably*, Sterling, VA: Stylus Publishing.

Bartlett, A. (1997–98) 'Reflections on sustainability, population growth, and the environment – revisited,' *Renewable Resources Journal* 15(4): 6–23. http://dieoff.org/page146.htm

Berchicci, L. and Bodewes, W. (2005) 'Bridging environmental issues with new product development,' *Business Strategy and the Environment* 14: 272–85.

Brown, D., Berko, P., Dedrick, P., Hilliard, B. and Pfleeger, J. (2010) *Burgerville: Sustainability and Sourcing in a QSR Supply Chain*. Portland, OR: Center for Global Leadership in Sustainability, School of Business Administration, Portland State University. www.sba.pdx.edu/cgls/media/Burgerville%20Supply%20Chain%20-%20Case%20Study%20CGLS-RR-11-01.pdf

Brown, J. (2010) *Benchmarking Sustainability in Health Care Awards Benchmark Report*. Reston, VA: Practice Greenhealth. www.cleanmed.org/2010/downloads/presentations/C4/Brown.pdf

BSR/GlobeScan (2011) *BSR/GlobeScan State of Sustainable Business Poll 2011: Fact Sheet*. www.bsr.org/files/BSR_GlobeScan_State_of_Sustainable_Business_Poll_2011_Fact_Sheet.pdf

Buchbinder, S.H. and Shanks, N.C. (2012) *Introduction to Health Care Management*. Burlington, MA: Jones and Bartlett Learning.

Buechner, S. and Ellis, M. (2011) '3 ways to improve green business rankings,' *GreenBiz* November 3. www.greenbiz.com/blog/2011/11/03/3-ways-improve-green-business-rankings.

Burdick, D. (2011) 'Instead of more care, better care: when patients' needs are put first, the system can save money and improve outcomes,' *The Baltimore Sun* December 21.

Bureau of Labor Statistics (2010) *The 2010 President's Budget for the Bureau of Labor Statistics*. Washington, DC: US Department of Labor. www.bls.gov/bls/budget2010.htm

Cal Recycle (2006) Medical waste posters and stickers. www.calrecycle.ca.gov/ReduceWaste/Business/posters/redbag.htm

Campbell II, T. and Campbell, C.T. (2008) 'The benefits of integrating nutrition into clinical medicine,' *Israel Medical Association Journal* 10: 730–32.

Carpenter, M. (2006) 'The pumped-up price of water,' *Pittsburgh Post-Gazette* March 17. www.post-gazette.com/stories/sectionfront/life/the-pumped-up-price-of-water-432952/

CDC (2012) 'Chronic Disease Prevention and Health Promotion: Health and Sustainability Guidelines for Federal Concessions and Vending Operations,' Atlanta, GA: Centers for Disease Control and Prevention. www.cdc.gov/chronicdisease/resources/guidelines/food-service-guidelines.htm

Chen, Y., Lai, S. and Wen, C. (2006) 'The influence of green innovation performance on corporate advantage in Taiwan,' *Journal of Business Ethics* 67(4): 331–39.

Chopra, S. and Meindl, P. *Supply Chain Management*, (2nd ed) Upper Saddle River: Pearson Prentice Hall.

Clark, E.H. (2007) 'Water prices rising worldwide,' Earth Policy Institute, Plan B Updates March 7. www.earth-policy.org/index.php?/plan_b_updates/2007/update64

CMS (2012) 'Bundled payments for care improvement,' US Department of Health and Human Services, Centers for Medicare & Medicaid Innovation. http://innovations.cms.gov/initiatives/bundled-payments/index.html

CMS (2012) 'HCAHPS: Patients' Perspectives of Care Survey,' US Department of Health and Human Services, Centers for Medicare & Medicaid Services. https://www.cms.gov/HospitalQualityInits/30_HospitalHCAHPS.asp

CMS (2012) 'NHE Fact Sheet,' US Department of Health and Human Services, Centers for Medicare & Medicaid Services. www.cms.gov/Research-Statistics-Data-and-Systems/Statistics-Trends-and-Reports/NationalHealthExpendData/NHE-Fact-Sheet.html

Colburn, M. (2011) 'Overcoming cynicism: Lord Hastings' call to action at Net Impact,' *GreenBiz* November 2. www.greenbiz.com/blog/2011/11/02/overcoming-cynicism-lord-hastings-call-action-net-impact

Conley, M. (2011) *Household Pharmaceutical Waste Disposal*, Portland, OR: State of Oregon Department of Environmental Quality, available online: www.deq.state.or.us/lq/pubs/factsheets/sw/HouseholdPharmaceuticalWaste Disposal.pdf (accessed 10/22/2012).

Covey, S.R. (1989) *The Seven Habits of Highly Effective People*. New York: Simon & Schuster.

Cromwell, J., Dayhoff, D. and Thoumaian, A. (1997) 'Cost savings and physician responses to global bundled payments for Medicare heart bypass surgery – innovations in fee-for-service financing and delivery,' *Healthcare Financing Review* 9(1): 41–57.

Currie, J.M. (2007) *The Fourth Factor: A Historical Perspective on Architecture and Medicine*. Washington, DC: American Institute of Architects.

Day, K. (2006) 'Hospital charity care is probed,' *The Washington Post* September 13. www.washingtonpost.com/wp-dyn/content/article/2006/09/12/AR200609 1201409.html

Dell Children's Medical Centre (2008) *Dell Children's Medical Centre is World's First Platinum Hospital*, available online: www.dellchildrens.net/about_us/news/2009/01/08/dell_childrens_medical_center_is_worlds_first_platinum_hospital_2 (accessed 10/22/2012).

Dentzer, S. (2011) 'Embarking on a new course: environmental health coverage,' *Health Affairs* 30(5): 810.

Department of Transportation (2011) Electronic Code of Federal Regulations, July 7. Pipeline and Hazardous Materials Safety Administration. http://ecfr.gpoaccess.gov/cgi/t/text/text-idx?c=ecfr&tpl=/ecfrbrowse/Title49/49cfrv2_02.tpl

Derksen, D. and Whelan, E.-M. (2009) *Closing the Health Care Workforce Gap: Reforming Federal Health Care Workforce Policies to Meet the Needs of the 21st Century*. Washington, DC: Center for American Progress. www.americanprogress.org/issues/2010/01/pdf/health_care_workforce.pdf

Doman, J.L. (2007) 'Leveraging lean process improvement methodology to promote economic and environmental sustainability: obstacles and opportunities,' MSc thesis, Department of Civil Engineering, Technology Environmental Management & Safety, Rochester Institute of Technology, Rochester, NY, USA.

Drewnowski, A. and Darmon, N. (2005) 'Food choices and diet costs: an economic analysis,' *Journal of Nutrition* 135(4): 900–4. www.ncbi.nlm.nih.gov/pubmed/15795456

Dyllick, T. and Hockerts, K. (2002) 'Beyond the business case for corporate sustainability,' *Business Strategy and the Environment* 11: 130–41.

EERE Information Center (2011) *Building Technologies Program: Join the Hospital Energy Alliance*. US Department of Energy, Energy Efficiency & Renewable Energy, Commercial Building Initiative. http://apps1.eere.energy.gov/buildings/publications/pdfs/alliances/hospital_energy_alliance_fact_sheet.pdf

Energy Star (n.d.) 'About Energy Star,' US Environmental Protection Agency and US Department of Energy. www.energystar.gov/index.cfm?c=about.ab_index

Epstein, M. (2009) *Making Sustainability Work: Best Practices in Managing and Measuring Corporate Social, Environmental, and Economic Impacts*. San Francisco, CA: Berrett-Koehler. www.bkconnection.com/static/Making_Sustainability_Work_EXCERPT.pdf

Ernst & Young (2011) *Climate Change and Responsibility: Shareholders Press Boards on Social and Environmental Risks*. Ernst & Young. www.ey.com/Publication/vwLUAssets/CCaSS_social_environmental_risks/$FILE/CCaSS_social_environmental_risks.pdf

Ernst & Young (2011) *Climate Change and Sustainability*, available online: http://www.ey.com/Publication/vwLUAssets/CCaSS_social_environmental_risks/$FILE/CCaSS_social_environmental_risks.pdf (accessed 22/10/2012).

EU Commission – DG Environment (2008) *Promoting Innovative Business Models with Environmental Benefits*. Kongens Lyngby, Denmark: COWI. http://ec.europa.eu/environment/enveco/innovation_technology/pdf/nbm_report.pdf

EWG (n.d.) '232 toxic chemicals in 10 minority babies,' Environmental Working Group. www.ewg.org/minoritycordblood/home

Express Healthcare (2011) *Creating a Healthy Living Continuum*, available online: www.expresshealthcare.in/201108/market01.shtml (accessed 22/10/2012).

Fauntleroy, G. (2007) 'Obesity leads to more hospital admissions, longer stays,' *Health Behavior News Service* December 11. www.cfah.org/hbns/archives/getDocument.cfm?documentID=1631

Federation of American Hospitals (2005) 'Future of hospital care: how will we pay the bill?,' A hospital payment symposium, Washington, DC, 15 July 2005. www.fah.org/fahCMS/Documents/Future%20of%20Hospital%20Care/Future%20Hospital%20Payment%20conference%20transcript%2007.15.05.pdf

Ferracone, R. (2011) 'The role of environmental sustainability in executive compensation,' *Forbes* April 26. www.forbes.com/sites/robinferracone/2011/04/26/the-role-of-environmental-sustainability-in-executive-compensation

Fiksel, J., McDaniel, J. and Mendenhall, C. (1999) 'Measuring progress towards sustainability principles, process, and best practices,' Columbus, OH: Batelle Memorial Institute. www.eco-nomics.com/images/Sustainability%20Measurement%20GIN.pdf

Flower, J. (1993) 'Getting paid to keep people healthy: two ways of integrating a healthcare system,' *Healthcare Forum Journal* 36(2): 51–6.

Fraj-Andres, E., Martinez-Salinas, E. and Matute-Vallejo, J. (2008) 'A multidimensional approach to the influence of environmental marketing and orientation on the firm's organizational performance,' *Journal of Business Ethics* 263–86.

Freeman, D. (2011) 'Will electronic health records save the planet?,' *CBS News: HealthPop* May 4. www.cbsnews.com/8301-504763_162-20059811-10391704.html

Freemantle, T. (2011) 'China's health reforms progress,' *International Insurance News* March 11. www.globalsurance.com/blog/chinas-healthcare-reforms-progress-324520.html

Freund, F. (2009) *Business Model Concepts in Corporate Sustainability Contexts.* Lüneburg, Germany: Leuphana Centre for Sustainability Management.

Galbraith, K. (2009) 'Study cites strong green job growth,' *The New York Times* June 10. http://green.blogs.nytimes.com/2009/06/10/study-cites-strong-green-job-growth

Gallup (n.d.) 'Employee engagement.' www.gallup.com/consulting/52/Employee-Engagement.aspx

GEMI (2004) *Clear Advantage: Building Shareholder Value.* Washington, DC: Global Environmental Management Initiative. www.gemi.org/resources/GEMI%20Clear%20Advantage.pdf

Gershon, R.R.M., Pogorzelska, M., Qureshi, K.A., Stone, P.W., Canton, A.N., Samar, S.M., Westra, L.J., Damsky, M.R. and Sherman M. (2008) 'Home health care patients and safety hazards in the home: preliminary findings,' Agency for Healthcare Research and Quality. www.ahrq.gov/downloads/pub/advances2/vol1/Advances-Gershon_88.pdf

Gladwell, M. (2002) *The Tipping Point: How Little Things Can Make a Big Difference*, New York, NY: Back Bay Books.

Gow, P. (2012) 'An experience of "yes": independent schools begin to explore and exploit the power of design thinking,' Washington, DC: National Association of Independent Schools. www.nais.org/publications/ismagazinearticle.cfm?Itemnumber=156249&sn.ItemNumber=145956

Griffith, J.R. and White, K.R. (2007) *The Well-Managed Healthcare Organization*, 6th edn. Chicago, IL: Health Administration Press.

Hand, L. (2009) 'Employer Health Incentives,' *Harvard Public Health* winter issue. Boston, MA: Harvard School of Public Health. www.hsph.harvard.edu/news/hphr/winter-2009/winter09healthincentives.html

Harter, J.K., Schmidt, J.S., Asplund, J.W., Killham, E.A. and Agrawal, S. (2010) "Casual Impact of Employee Work Perceptions on the Bottom Line of Organizations", *Perspectives on Psychological Science*, 5: 4, pp.378-89.

HCWC (n.d.) 'About us.' Reston, VA: Health Care Without Harm. www.hcwh.org/all_regions/about

Health Forum LLC (2012) 'Fast Facts on US Hospitals,' Washington, DC: American Hospital Association. www.aha.org/research/rc/stat-studies/fast-facts.shtml

HealthCare Value Network (n.d.) HealthCare Value Leaders. www.healthcarevalueleaders.org

HER Center (2012) *Guide to JCAHO Environment of Care Standard 3.10.1.* Healthcare Environmental Resource Center. www.hercenter.org/regsandstandards/jcaho3.10.1.cfm

IFC (2012) 'IFC sustainability.' Washington, DC: International Finance Corporation, World Bank Group. www.ifc.org/sustainability

Jacobson, J.A. and Gully, G.E. (1996) 'Dialogue to action: including public expectations in healthcare ethics,' *HEC Forum* 8(1): 29–43.

Johnson & Johnson (2010) *2010 Sustainability Report.* New Brunswick, NJ: Johnson & Johnson. www.jnj.com/connect/caring/environment-protection

Johnson, J. (2008) 'Rapporteur's Report: Services sector,' *Journal of Safety Research* 39: 191–94. www.cdc.gov/niosh/topics/PtD/pdfs/Johnson.pdf

Kaiser Permanente (2011) *Kaiser Permanente Design Standards & Guidelines Symposium 2011*, available online: www.signup4.net/UPLOAD/KAIS11A/NFSX24E/Seminar%20Descriptions%202010%20for%20web.pdf (accessed 10/22/2012).

Kell, G. and Lacy, P. (2010) 'Study: sustainability a priority for CEOs,'. *BloombergBusinessweek* June 25. www.businessweek.com/managing/content/jun2010/ca20100624_678038.htm

Klein, E. (2012) 'Why an MRI costs $1,080 in America and $280 in France,' *The Washington Post* March 3. www.washingtonpost.com/blogs/ezra-klein/post/why-an-mri-costs-1080-in-america-and-280-in-france/2011/08/25/gIQAVHztoR_blog.html

Lacy, P. (2010) 'On the verge of a sustainability "tipping point",' *GreenBiz* June 24. www.greenbiz.com/blog/2010/06/24/verge-new-era-sustainability

Lean Enterprise Institute (2009) 'What is Lean?,' Cambridge, MA: Lean Enterprise Institute. www.Lean.org/whatsLean

Lipson, D.J. and Simon, S. (2010) 'Quality's new frontier: reducing hospitalizations and improving transitions in long-term care,' *Mathematica Issue Brief* 7. www.mathematica-mpr.com/publications/pdfs/health/LTQA_brief.pdf

Makower, J. (2012) *State of Green Business Report 2011.* Oakland, CA: GreenBiz Group. www.greenbiz.com/research/report/2011/02/01/state-green-business-report-2011?ms=41569

McCain, M. (2011) *Ambulatory Care of the Future: Optimizing Health, Service, and Cost by Transforming the Care Delivery Model.* The Chartis Group. www.chartis.com/files/pdfs/Ambulatory_Care_of_the_Future.pdf

McKinsey & Company (2008) 'How companies think about climate change: a McKinsey global survey', *McKinsey Quarterly* February. www.mckinseyquarterly.com/How_companies_think_about_climate_change_A_McKinsey_Global_Survey_2099

Mikkonen, J. and Raphael, D. (2010) *Social Determinants of Health: The Canadian Facts.* Toronto: York University School of Health Policy and Management. www.unnaturalcauses.org/assets/uploads/file/The_Canadian_Facts.pdf

MPHI (2012) 'View on sustainable society.' Medicine and Public Health Initiative. www.mphi.net/?p=303&lang=en-us

Mufson, S. and Yang, J. L. (2011) 'A quarter of US nuclear plants not reporting equipment defects, report finds,' *The Washington Post* March 24. www.

washingtonpost.com/business/economy/a-quarter-of-us-nuclear-plants-not-reporting-equipment-defects-report-finds/2011/03/24/ABHYa2RB_story.html

Murlis, H. and Schubert, P. (2001) *Engage Employees and Boost Performance*, Hay Group Working Paper, Philadelphia, PA: Hay Group.

Muro, M., Rothwell, J. and Saha, D. (2011) 'Sizing the clean economy: a national and regional green jobs assessment,' *Brookings Report* July 13. www.brookings.edu/reports/2011/0713_cLean_economy.aspx

Naylor, C. and Appleby, J. (2012) *Sustainable Health and Social Care*, London: The King's Fund.

NICE (2008) 'Guidance on the promotion and creation of physical environments that support increased levels of physical activity,' London: National Institute for Health and Clinical Excellence. http://guidance.nice.org.uk/PH8

NIH (2010) 'Greek medicine,' US National Library of Medicine, National Institutes of Health, Department of Health & Human Services. www.nlm.nih.gov/hmd/greek/greek_oath.html

NNEC (n.d.) 'The energy–water nexus,' New York: Network For New Energy Choices. www.newenergychoices.org/index.php?page=ew_intro&sd=ew

Northbridge Environmental Management Consultants (2003) *Analyzing the Cost of Obtaining LEED Cetification*. Westford, MA: Northbridge for The American Chemistry Council. www.cLeanair-coolplanet.org/for_communities/LEED_links/AnalyzingtheCostofLEED.pdf

NPHPPHC (2011) *National Prevention Strategy: America's Plan for Better Health and Wellness*. Rockville: National Prevention, Health Promotion and Public Health Council. www.healthcare.gov/prevention/nphpphc/strategy/report.pdf

Nutramed (2011) 'Cars, trucks, air pollution and health,' Alpha Online. www.nutramed.com/environment/cars.htm

Oglethorpe, D. (2008) 'Local food – miles better?,' *World Watch* 22(3): 12–15. www.europeansupplychainmanagement.co.uk/article-page.php?contentid=4203&issueid=174

Olshansky, S., Passaro, D., Hershow, R., Layden, J., Carnes, B., Brody, J., Hayflick, L., Butler, R., Allison, D. and Ludwig, D. (2005) 'A potential decline in life expectancy in the United States in the 21st century,' *New England Journal of Medicine* 352: 1138–45.

Ornish, D. (2009) 'Mostly plants,' *American Journal of Cardiology* 104(7): 957–58. http://engine2diet.com/wp/wp-content/uploads/Dean-Ornish-Mostly-Plants.pdf

Ornish, D. (2012) 'Holy Cow! What's good for you is good for our planet,' *Archives of Internal Medicine* (online first) E9–E10. www.natap.org/2012/newsUpdates/archinternmed.2012.174v1.pdf

OSHA (2011) 'Hazardous waste,' Washington, DC: Occupational Health & Safety Administration, US Department of Labor. www.osha.gov/SLTC/hazardouswaste/index.html

PACE (n.d.) 'Program of all-inclusive care for the elderly,' Baltimore, MD: Medicaid. www.medicaid.gov/Medicaid-CHIP-Program-Information/By-Topics/Long-Term-Services-and-Support/Integrating-Care/Program-of-All-Inclusive-Care-for-the-Elderly-PACE/Program-of-All-Inclusive-Care-for-the-Elderly-PACE.html

Paton, S. (n.d.) 'Four days with W. Edwards Deming,' Palos Verdes Estates, CA: The W. Edwards Deming Institute. http://deming.org/index.cfm?content=653

Patton, S., Poorsina, R. and Kahn, R. (2011) 'Health information technology can create significant environmental benefits,' *Kaiser Permanente News Center* May 4. http://xnet.kp.org/newscenter/pressreleases/nat/2011/050411greenhit.html

Paulus, R., Davis, K. and Steele, G. (2008) 'Continuous innovation in health care: implications of the Geisinger experience,' *Health Affairs* 27(5): 1235–45. http://content.healthaffairs.org/content/27/5/1235.short

Practice Greenhealth (2012) 'Sample job description: Healthcare Sustainability Director,' Reston, VA: Practice Greenhealth. http://practicegreenhealth.org/pubs/toolkit/greenteam/SampleJDSustainabilityDirector.pdf

Reindhardt, U. (2011) 'Healthcare crisis: who's at risk?,' Public Broadcasting Service. www.pbs.org/healthcarecrisis/Exprts_intrvw/u_reinhardt.htm

Rhea, S. (2010) 'Food for thought,' *Modern Healthcare* March 8. www.modernhealthcare.com/article/20100308/magazine/100309982#

Rich, C., Singleton, J. and Wadhwa, S. (2011) 'Teaching sustainability as part of healthcare management studies: challenges, best practices and case studies,' CleanMed 2011, Phoenix, Arizona, April 5–8, 2011.

Rich, C., Wadhwa, S. and Singleton, J. (2012) 'How to teach environmental sustainability in healthcare management education,' in *Teaching Sustainability*. Allendale, MI: Grand Valley State University, in press.

Roberts, G. (2011) 'Shades of green: the evolution of hospital sustainable design standards,' *Health Facilities Management* November. www.hfmmagazine.com/hfmmagazine_app/jsp/articledisplay.jsp?dcrpath=HFMMAGAZINE/Article/data/11NOV2011/1111HFM_FEA_Archdes&domain=HFMMAGAZINE

Ross, A. (2010) 'Planning, transport, and health inequalities – a recent history and future progress,' London: Local Government Association. www.idea.gov.uk/idk/core/page.do?pageId=23454074

Rymer, C. and Futterman, M. (2008) 'Sustainability must start with the obvious,' *The Cornell Daily Sun* February 28. http://cornellsun.com/node/28296

Satin, D. and Miles, J. (2009) 'Performance-based bundled payments: benefits and burdens of this pay-for-performance strategy,' *Minnesota Medicine* October. www.minnesotamedicine.com/PastIssues/October2009/SpecialReportOct2009/tabid/3209/Default.aspx

Scottish Government (2011) 'Summary of the Draft Health and Environmental Sustainability Framework,' Edinburgh: The Scottish Government. www.scotland.gov.uk/Publications/2011/12/1188

Shontell, A. (2011) '11 Unusual ways Steve Jobs made Apple the world's most admired tech company,' *Business Insider* October 6. www.businessinsider.com/steve-jobs-apple

Singleton, J. (1992) 'Preserving the environment can bring hospitals savings, improved stature,' presented at Modern Healthcare Weekly Business News: Our Environment: A Healthcare Commitment, Hyatt Regency, Crystal City, Arlington, VA, March 8–9.

Skinner, J. and Brownlee, S. (2009) 'Is more care better? The evidence suggests no,' *Health Affairs Blog* December 10. http://healthaffairs.org/blog/2009/12/10/is-more-care-better-the-evidence-suggests-no

Studer, Q. (2003) *Hardwiring Excellence: Purpose, Worthwhile Work, Making a Difference*, Gulf Breeze, FL: Fire Star Publishing.

Studer, Q. (2004) *Hardwiring Excellence: Purpose, Worthwhile Work, Making a Difference*, Gulf Breeze, FL: Fire Starter Publishing.

Taylor, D. (2002) 'What price for-profit hospitals?,' *Canadian Medical Association Journal* 166(11): 1418–19. www.cmaj.ca/content/166/11/1418.full.pdf+html

Tice, L. (2011) 'Hospitals require employee, volunteer flu shots,' *Lewiston–Auburn Sun Journal* October 21. www.sunjournal.com/news/city/2011/10/21/hospitals-require-employee-volunteer-flu-shots/1104210

Tregaskis, S. (n.d.) 'Green health care: hospitals are becoming healthier places due to new efforts to protect the environment,' *Organic Gardening*. www.organicgardening.com/living/green-health-care?page=0,0

Tsai, T. (2010) 'Second chance for health reform in Columbia,' *The Lancet* 375(9709): 109–10. www.thelancet.com/journals/lancet/article/PIIS0140-6736(10)60033-5/fulltext

Turley, M., Porter, C., Garrido, T., Gerwig, K., Young, S., Radler, L. and Shaber, R. (2011) 'Use of electronic health records can improve the health care industry's environmental footprint,' *Health Affairs* 30(5): 938–46. http://content.healthaffairs.org/content/30/5/938.abstract

UIC (n.d.) 'The history of health informatics,' University of Illinois at Chicago. http://healthinformatics.uic.edu/history-of-health-informatics

Umbdenstock, R. (2011) 'Hospital environmental sustainability: video intro,' American Hospital Association. www.hospitalsustainability.org

University of Maryland (2012) University of Maryland Medical Center Sustainability Principles. www.umm.edu/green/pdf/sus_principles_final.pdf

US Bureau of Labor Statistics (2010) 'The 2010 President's Budget for the Bureau of Labor Statistics.' Bureau of Labor Statistics. www.bls.gov/bls/budget2010.htm

US Census Bureau (2010) 'Industry by occupation for the civilian employed population 16 years and over: 2010 American community survey 1-year estimates,' US Census Bureau. http://factfinder2.census.gov/faces/tableservices/jsf/pages/productview.xhtml?pid=ACS_10_1YR_S2405&prodType=table

US Census Bureau (2012) '1940–2010: How has America changed?,' Washington, DC: US Census Bureau. www.census.gov/1940census/then_and_now/index.html

US Department of Transportation (2010) 'Transportation is a public health issue; DOT doing its part to keep kids moving,' *Fast Lane* July 16. http://fastlane.dot.gov/2010/07/dot-doing-its-part-to-keep-kids-moving.html

US EPA (2004) *Code of Federal Regulations Title 40 Protection of Environment, Section 311*, revised July 1. Washington, DC: Environmental Protection Agency. http://edocket.access.gpo.gov/cfr_2004/julqtr/40cfr311.1.htm

US EPA (2004) 'Leaders in healthcare tap the power of superior energy management,' Washington, DC: Environmental Protection Agency. www.energystar.gov/ia/business/healthcare/factsheet_0804.pdf?9b81-81ae

US EPA (2009) *The Environmental Professional's Guide to LEAN & Six Sigma*. Washington, DC: Environmental Protection Agency. www.epa.gov/lean/environment/toolkits/professional/resources/Enviro-Prof-Guide-Six-Sigma.pdf

US EPA (2010) 'Green Building,' Washington, DC: Environmental Protection Agency. www.epa.gov/greenbuilding/pubs/about.htm

US EPA (2011) 'Benefits and Costs of the Clean Air Act: Second Prospective Study – 1990 to 2020,' Washington, DC: Environmental Protection Agency. www.epa.gov/air/sect812/prospective2.html

US EPA (2012) 'Clean Air Act,' February 17. Washington, DC: Environmental Protection Agency. www.epa.gov/air/caa

US EPA (n.d.) 'What is WaterSense?,' Washington, DC: Environmental Protection Agency. www.epa.gov/watersense/about_us/what_is_ws.html

USGS (1984) 'How much water is there on, in, and above the Earth?,' US Geological Survey. http://ga.water.usgs.gov/edu/earthhowmuch.html

USGBC (2011) 'What LEED is,' US Green Building Council. www.usgbc.org/DisplayPage.aspx?CMSPageID=1988

US National Library of Medicine (2010) Greek Medicine, National Institutes of Health, Department of Health & Human Services. www.nlm.nih.gov/hmd/greek/greek_oath.html

US News & World Report (2011) 'National University Rankings. Education Colleges.' http://colleges.usnews.rankingsandreviews.com/best-colleges/rankings/national-universities

Waterprint (n.d.) 'How much does it take?,' *Waterprint*. http://waterprint.net/app_index.html

Waterprint (n.d.) 'Wine,' *Waterprint*. http://waterprint.net/wine.html

White, G. (2009) 'Introduction to green leasing,' *Green Real Estate Law Journal* February 6. www.greenrealestatelaw.com/2009/02/introduction-to-green-leasing

Whitlock, J.L. (2003) 'Strategic thinking, planning, and doing: how to reunite leadership and management to connect vision with action,' Washington, DC: George Washington University Center for Excellence in Municipal Management, mimeo.

WHO (1999) *Guidelines for Safe Disposal of Unwanted Pharmaceuticals in and after Emergencies*, available online: www.who.int/water_sanitation_health/medicalwaste/unwantpharm.pdf (accessed 10/22/2012).

WHO and Health Care Without Harm (2009) 'Healthy hospitals – healthy planet – healthy people,' Geneva: World Health Organization. www.who.int/globalchange/publications/climatefootprint_report.pdf

WHO (2011) *Modern Health Care Delivery Systems, Care Coordination and the Role of Hospitals*, WHO: Copenhagen, available online: www.euro.who.int/__data/assets/pdf_file/0008/158885/BRU-report-Modern-health-care-delivery-systems.pdf (accessed 10/22/2012).

WWF (2011) 'Hospital waste factsheet,' World Wildlife Fund. www.wwfpak.org/factsheets_hwf.php

Index

References in **bold** indicate tables and in *italics* indicate figures.